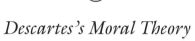

Descartes's Moral Theory

Descartes's Moral Theory

DESCARTES'S
MORAL THEORY

John Marshall

Cornell University Press

ITHACA AND LONDON

First published 1998 by Cornell University Press

Printed in the United States of America

LIBRARY OF CONGRESS CATALOGING-IN-PUBLICATION DATA

Marshall, John, b. 1933

    Descartes's moral theory / John Marshall.

       p. cm.

    Includes bibliographical references and index.

    ISBN 0-8014-3567-6 (alk. paper)

      1. Descartes, René, 1596–1650—Ethics. 2. Ethics, Modern—17th century. I. Title.

    B1878.E7M37 1998

    170′.92—dc21   98-28008

Cornell University Press strives to use environmentally responsible suppliers and materials to the fullest extent possible in the publishing of its books. Such materials include vegetable-based, low-VOC inks and acid-free papers that are recycled, totally chlorine-free, or partly composed of nonwood fibers.

Cloth printing 10 9 8 7 6 5 4 3 2 1

For Gail

For Gail

Contents

Acknowledgments

WHEN in the early 1980s I first read Geneviève Rodis-Lewis's splendid book *La Morale de Descartes*, it occurred to me that there should be a similar work in English designed to introduce Descartes's moral thought to an anglophone audience, an audience—like myself at the time—not inclined to think of Descartes as a moral theorist. It was only years later, however, with the good wishes of the Dean of the Faculty at the University of Virginia, Raymond Nelson, who generously granted me leave from teaching duties, and with the considerable encouragement of my wife, Gail, that I came to think seriously that I might be the author of such a book. So it was with this goal in mind that I applied to the Camargo Foundation in Cassis for a residential grant, and it was later as a guest of the Foundation in the spring of 1991 that I spent many happy hours working on the first draft of the present study. I am very grateful to the Foundation and to its executive director, Michael Pretina, who did much to make my stay agreeable as well as profitable, and much as well to keep my wife in touch with her law practice and to guide my eleven-year-old daughter, Starling, in the ways of the local culture. I am grateful also to three others who very early on gave me encouragement: Martha Bolton, Jude Dougherty, and B. J. Diggs.

At a later stage Daniel Devereux, the chairman of my department, arranged for the two of us to offer a graduate seminar on Stoic and Cartesian ethics; we were joined by our colleagues Jorge Secada and James Cargile and, much to the delight and profit of everyone, by Lawrence Becker of the College of William and Mary, who was at the time writing a book on Stoic ethics. I owe a considerable debt of gratitude to them all and to three students who attended: Michael Marshall, John Anderson, and Jay Morris. A few months later Becker invited me to present my work to his discussion group at William and Mary. So I am doubly indebted to him and owe special thanks to his wife, Charlotte, who produced on that occasion—which was also Descartes's birthday—a celebratory and suitably decorated cake.

I also express my thanks to Veronique McNelly for helping me with my translations, to Clark Thompson for sharing with me his considerable knowledge about the period, to Marjorie Greene for her encouragement at a late stage of the project, and finally to Cambridge University Press for granting me permission to quote so extensively from their recent three-volume edition of Descartes's writings.

JOHN MARSHALL

Rapidan, Virginia

Note on Sources

CITATIONS of Descartes's works are, first, to the volume and page number of the new French edition, *Oeuvres de Descartes*, ed. Ch. Adam and P. Tannery, rev. ed. (Paris: J. Vrin/C.N.R.S., 1964–76), and, second, to the volume and page number of *The Philosophical Writings of Descartes*, trans. J. Cottingham, R. Stoothoff, and D. Murdoch, 3 vols. (Cambridge: Cambridge University Press, 1985–91). Except where I indicate otherwise, I adhere to these translations.

Descartes's Moral Theory

Introduction

To teach how to live without certainty, and yet without being paralyzed by hesitation, is perhaps the chief thing that philosophy, in our age, can still do for those who study it.

BERTRAND RUSSELL,
A History of Western Philosophy

1. WHEN Leibniz was asked about Descartes's contribution to philosophy, he wrote to a correspondent that Descartes's ethics was largely derivative from Seneca and amounted to no more than a morality of patience without hope. "We need only inspect the incomparable manual of Epictetus and the Epicurean of Laercia," Leibniz wrote, "to admit that Descartes has not much advanced the practice of morality."[1] The true morality, he claimed, must give us hope and must therefore depend on our knowing that we are immortal and will be rewarded or punished in the hereafter by a just God. Neither Descartes's God nor his immortality, he went on, is of the right sort, his God being little different from Spinoza's and his immortality lacking continuity of memory.

This is not a generous assessment, even if it is in one respect more accurate than Henry Sidgwick's, expressed nearly two centuries later and shared by many anglophone philosophers today, that Descartes did not touch on ethics proper. Descartes did write on ethics and with much of what Descartes wrote Leibniz was evidently familiar. His misgivings about Descartes on God and immortality, however, are, if not misplaced, in any event premature, for in contrast to Leibniz Descartes held that neither a conception

---

1. Leibniz 1989, 241. I am grateful to Larry Becker for this reference.

of how to live well nor the motivation to live morally should depend on assumptions concerning the hereafter. What Leibniz saw as a weakness, therefore, Descartes claimed as a strength. As for Leibniz's claim about Descartes's originality, I think a careful look at the theory to be set out here will
be answer enough, although in passing we could note that Descartes's theory of morality, conceived as it was within the larger framework of Cartesian metaphysics and an emerging scientific conception of nature, surely
must contain some originality and move beyond ancient Stoicism.

2. One place Descartes touched on morality is the letter-preface to the
French edition of his *Principles of Philosophy*. Since this passage, though not
very helpful, is quite well known, it deserves some comment at the start:
"The whole of philosophy," he wrote, "is like a tree. The roots are metaphysics, the trunk is physics, and the branches emerging from the trunk are
all the other sciences, which may be reduced to three principal ones, namely
medicine, mechanics and morals. By 'morals' I understand the highest and
most perfect moral system, which presupposes a complete knowledge of
the other sciences and is the ultimate level of wisdom" (9B:14; 1:186). In
his *Principles*, Descartes systematically set out his metaphysics and the general principles of his physics—the root and trunk of philosophy. There he
claimed to know beyond reasonable doubt "the principal attributes of
God, the nonmaterial nature of our souls . . . [and] the true principles of
material things" (9B:14; 1:186). This confidence, however, has not been his
legacy; few would now claim certain knowledge on Cartesian grounds that
"there is a God on whom all things depend, whose perfections are infinite,"
or that our soul "subsists apart from the body, and is much nobler than the
body" (4:291–92; 3:265). Nor would many claim to know with Cartesian
certainty "the true principles of material things" or "the general composition of the entire universe." What, then, is to become of his ethics if his
metaphysics and physics are not available to provide the requisite nourish-
ment? To be sure, our knowledge of the two branches, mechanics and
medicine, not to mention the natural science of physics, vastly exceeds
Descartes's, and perhaps in ways congenial to his cast of mind, but would
this knowledge alone, unaccompanied by the proper metaphysics, bring us
close to a Cartesian perfect moral system?

On one interpretation of the tree image, it would. According to this
reading, the perfected Cartesian ethics was to be a system of Kantian hypothetical imperatives. Adhering to it would assure health, long life, and
control over nature, all combining to make us happy. This reading fits with
what Descartes had written earlier in part 6 of the *Discourse on the Method*,
where he admitted that he believed he could not keep his method and es-

says on scientific topics secret "without sinning gravely against the law which obliges us to do all in our power to secure the general welfare of mankind," since we could use scientific knowledge to "make ourselves, as it were, the lords and masters of nature. . . . This is desirable . . . for the invention of innumerable devices which would facilitate our enjoyment of the fruits of the earth and all the goods we find there" (6:62; 1:143). And concerning medicine specifically he added that we could apply the knowledge he hoped to secure by the careful use of his method "for the maintenance of health, which is undoubtedly the chief good and the foundation of all the other goods in this life. For even the mind depends so much on the temperament and disposition of the bodily organs that if it is possible to find some means of making men in general wiser and more skillful than they have been up till now, I believe we must look for it in medicine" (6:62; 1:143).

Although they are a bit overstated, the main points in these passages are both clear and noncontroversial: assuming we have the right ends, better science will give us more reliable knowledge about how to attain these ends, and this knowledge will therefore be a proper part of practical wisdom, that is, of knowledge how to act and to live well. On the other hand, these passages certainly do not imply that he conceived the whole of morality to be applied natural science.

Nor does what he writes elsewhere on moral topics. In his correspondence contemporaneous with the letter-preface to the *Principles* he emphasizes the critical role within morality of knowledge of metaphysics and of general physics, but here he clearly is not thinking of morality as applied natural science. If we are to live well and happily, he writes to Princess Elizabeth, we should know that there is a God, that all things are expressly sent by God, that the universe is vast, and that the earth enjoys no privileged status. And in a 1646 letter to Hector-Pierre Chanut, who had written that he was planning to undertake a study of moral philosophy, he wrote:

> I agree with you entirely that the safest way to find out how we should live is to discover first what we are, what kind of world we live in, and who is the creator of this world, or the master of the house we live in. But I cannot at all claim or promise that all I have written is true, and besides there is a very great distance between the general notion of heaven and earth, which I have tried to convey in my *Principles*, and a detailed knowledge of the nature of man, which I have not yet discussed. However, I do not want you to think I wish to divert you from your plan, and so I must say in confidence that what little knowledge of physics I have tried to acquire has been a great help to me in establishing sure

foundations in moral philosophy. Indeed I have found it easier to reach satisfactory conclusions on this topic than on many others concerning medicine, on which I have spent much more time. So instead of finding ways to preserve life, I have found another, much easier and surer way, which is not to fear death. But this does not depress me, as it commonly depresses those whose wisdom is drawn entirely from the teaching of others, and rests on foundations which depend only on human prudence and authority. (4:441–42; 3:289)

Descartes does not make it clear in this letter precisely how his knowledge of physics helped him to establish sure foundations in moral philosophy. Nor does he give a clear indication of what he took moral philosophy to be. At about the time of this letter, however, he was at work on a theory of the passions, of which one aim was to establish their physical causes; it may be to this work that he was alluding in the letter. In any event, Descartes did conceive moral wisdom to consist, in part, of knowledge of our own nature as psychophysical beings and, more particularly, knowledge of how to get control over our passions and to get the most from them. This is the part of moral wisdom that he offers in his *Passions of the Soul*.

There is, however, a further part of Cartesian moral wisdom, indeed, the principal part, that is not in the least suggested by the tree image. This part, concerned with values and norms and above all with moral virtue, is not applied science, nor does it depend on natural scientific knowledge. It is the part far better represented in Descartes's dedicatory letter to Elizabeth in the Latin edition of the *Principles* of 1644, where, revisiting the theme of his *morale par provision* of the *Discourse*, he wrote: "whoever possesses the firm and powerful resolve always to use his reasoning powers correctly, as far as he can, and to carry out whatever he knows to be best, is truly wise, so far as his nature permits" (8A:2; 1:191) .

It is true, nonetheless, that the moral wisdom Descartes himself had in mind does depend on his metaphysics. To this extent, then, his famous image is faithful to his conception of a perfect morality.

3. Although readers today find much of Cartesian metaphysics doubtful, the Cartesian *cogito* holds a truth that we cannot easily escape and that is at once central to Cartesian ethics and, I would argue, to any theoretical understanding of morality. This is the fact of our own agency and autonomy. What kind of fact this is, is controversial. Descartes believed that what was disclosed in the *cogito* could be interpreted as a substantial self—a soul—with the property of free will and the potential for immortality. But even if we doubt that what is disclosed to us in practical deliberation (or in theoretical reflection, for that matter) can bear such a rich metaphysical interpretation, we cannot but see ourselves as agents possessing

autonomy so long as we entertain the practical question, What should I do? This question is fundamentally normative; accordingly, when we pose it we assume not only our autonomy, since we are asking the question of ourselves, but our rationality, because when we deliberate we are presented with a variety of considerations—stemming from desires, impulses, felt habitual tendencies to act, and previously embraced principles of action—among which we choose, seeking of course to do so in a way that will withstand our own retrospective critical examination. And since what we (and Descartes) call reason is essentially our capacity for critical examination and reflection—whatever metaphysical sense we can make of our autonomy and rationality—this capacity seems inescapable from our perspective as agents. Much of Descartes's moral theory, though not all of it, can stand on this metaphysically thin interpretation of the *cogito*.

Yet Descartes was acutely aware that reasons that agents consider good may in fact not be good. From an outer perspective our putative reasons and practical judgments can be seen to be products of our culture or other causes of which we are not aware and over which we have no control; for when we look at ourselves as we might look at others—when we regard ourselves not as we do within practical deliberation but from outside—we are prey to the unsettling thought that what appear to us to be good reasons from within are just common prejudices when appraised from without. In the domain of theory, as distinct from practice, Descartes adopted a method of inquiry that was to be proof against mere prejudice, so that what looks compelling from the inside cannot be called into doubt from the outside. In this way the autonomy of the theorist, the subject of pure inquiry, is secure. But for a number of reasons, as Descartes himself was to insist, this method is not suitable for the deliberating agent who is obliged to act without certainty and for reasons that may not hold up under closer scrutiny. Indeed, it would not be far wrong to interpret Descartes's moral theoretical project to be that of working out a way for us to live well and happily in the face of uncertainty, an uncertainty that, owing to our finitude, is not fully eliminable.

4. The book falls into three main parts. The first deals with the *morale par provision* of the *Discourse*; the second treats what I call Descartes's final morality and focuses on his account of virtue, which is found in his correspondence and in the *Passions of the Soul*; the third, a rather more speculative part, sets out a Cartesian theory of value and a system of duties.

Descartes's conception of a *morale par provision* addresses an important practical problem of a general nature, not a problem peculiar to the Cartesian project of pure inquiry. A *morale par provision* has the following features. (*a*) It is a particular person's morality, made up of first-order moral precepts and ideals of good character and second-order views about what one is responsible for. Typically—and certainly in the case of Descartes—this morality is shared by a larger community, of which for this very reason one takes oneself to be a member. When I say that a morality is, say, Marcus's morality, I mean that it is embedded to a significant degree in his character. Marcus not only owns up to the beliefs in question but has affective and conative dispositions that support allegiance to the beliefs he professes. We might say that the *morale par provision* has a practical grip on Marcus; Marcus defers to it in his deliberations, in his self-criticism, and in his appraisal of the conduct and character of others (even those outside his community). *(b)* If Marcus's practical grip on his morality is reasonably firm, he may nonetheless be vulnerable to a number of doubts about it. He may have some doubts about the correctness or validity of the first- and second-order precepts. He may also have some doubts about the importance of morality in his life. His cognitive grip on his morality, then, may not be ideally secure. He has lively beliefs but admits that they are short of certain knowledge—or at least that some of them are. *(c)* Marcus has a general cognitive procedure and is somewhat hopeful that by following it he may be able to remove some of his doubts about his morality and perhaps, in some as yet unforeseen way, to alter or expand its content. It might be argued that the only morality any reflective person has in the current age is a *morale par provision* and that all of us are in a situation not unlike that of Descartes in the *Discourse*.

Descartes's final morality is, in fact, only a more fully elaborated form of the earlier morality of the *Discourse*. That this is so is a matter of controversy, one to be taken up in due course. This final morality is not the perfect morality referred to in the letter-preface of the *Principles*, a perfect morality of the distant future, one that would require a knowledge perhaps as unimaginable to us today as our own knowledge (skepticism aside) would have been to Descartes's contemporaries. On the other hand, this final morality contains a well-developed account of virtue and happiness, one not to be dismissed readily as a mere relic of seventeenth-century neo-Stoicism.

Descartes stands near the end of a great tradition of moral theory that began with the ancients, a tradition that took its point of departure from the question of how we should live, where "we" refers to each human being and the question is designed to take account of a full life, one's life as a whole. This is the tradition in which the *summum bonum* is a central organizing concept. The highest good is, of course, happiness, but the controversies among theorists in this tradition concern precisely how happiness—living well—is best understood. In the main, Descartes takes his stand with the Stoic argument that virtue is necessary and sufficient for happiness. On the other hand, he affirms what classic Stoics deny: for human well-being and happiness, passions are necessary. The heading of the final article of his *Passions of the Soul* reads, "*It is on the passions alone that all the good and evil of this life depends*" (II:488; I:404).

Descartes also stands at the beginning of modern moral theory, if we take this to have begun more or less with Hobbes—the Hobbes who famously said that he had no use whatever for the *summum bonum* as an organizing principle. Descartes evidently read some Hobbes and once wrote that Hobbes was a good moral philosopher, if not such a good metaphysician. What he learned from Hobbes is not clear. One thing he would not accept from Hobbes is his theory of obligation. Descartes does not work with a theory of obligation according to which to be obligated is to be under the threat of some sort of sanction. He mentions this common idea in his dedicatory letter preceding the *Meditations*, but it does not figure at all in his correspondence or in the *Passions*. Moreover, he does not tie being bound by a moral law to his own interest. Rather, he seems to commit himself to the view that the moral "ought" is a function of the objective value of ends.

Yet, like Hobbes, he is a modern moral philosopher in the sense that he works out a morality in the light of the evolving modern conception of science and nature (which conceptions he helped to initiate). He disassociates himself, in effect, from any natural law tradition that presupposes a teleological framework. And though he does introduce a teleological framework of his own with respect exclusively to human beings, this serves a limited and indeed largely epistemological purpose in his moral theory. He does not read off moral laws from this framework. What we discover in the *cogito* is our own freedom, the freedom of our own reason, which sets us apart from everything else in nature. We are rational, and insofar as we act under the guidance of our own reason, we seek the good. It is rarely within our cognitive power, however, to achieve certainty concerning what, specifically, is the best thing to do in particular circumstances; and even when we act with reasonable confidence, the good we seek often turns out to have been beyond our power. We are, in short, free to reason and to choose but also limited in our capacity to know and to control. In one respect, then, the good we aspire to achieve is elusive. In another respect, however, it is not—at least not according to the defining line of argument of Descartes's ethics. For according to this ethics, the highest good for us, virtue crowned with supreme contentment, is entirely in our power, so long as we have our reason.

For many readers, as I noted above, it may come as a surprise to hear mention of Descartes's moral theory. It is true, of course, that he did not write a single treatise on the subject, and it is also true that his discussions of moral philosophical topics over the years yielded no fully developed theory. On the other hand, we do find illuminating discussions of important issues in moral theory, which, though they may appear to be occasional pieces, show consistency and depth of thought and together make up a coherent version of neo-Stoicism of sufficient interest to deserve more attention that it has heretofore received in anglophone circles. This is the moral theory to be set out in the present book.

In closing I should add that I have not been much concerned with such methodological questions as whether I am writing as a historian of philosophy, as a historian of ideas, or simply as one philosopher interested in another. I aim to be fair to Descartes and to write sympathetically. As a philosopher, however, I am mainly interested in his arguments. While I have taken some pains to provide a general context for his reflections on moral topics, I have not done so in a manner that will satisfy the standards of a good historian of ideas. Whether what remains is a good history of moral philosophy, I must leave to readers to decide. Many of Descartes's assumptions and premises I do not accept, but for the most part I have left criticism to one side and have tried only to make lines of argument clear. I have, however, taken sides on several issues of interpretation. Finally, since the Cartesian texts dealing with ethics are not generally familiar, I have been very generous with quotation.

Part I

THE MORALITY
OF THE "DISCOURSE"

IT has long been customary to take what Descartes in the *Discourse* calls a *morale par provision* to be a provisional morality—a morality, that is to say, which Descartes felt obliged to adopt as a stopgap measure to carry him through the period of doubt and which he expected to replace with another and better morality at the end of inquiry. In line with this dismissive view, commentators have not taken the *morale par provision* as something to be examined seriously as a morality, or even as Descartes's morality. Some, encouraged by Descartes's remark to Frans Burman, have gone so far as to say that he included it only as an afterthought and then only to forestall the objection that his recommended method subverted not only traditional philosophy and science but morality as well.[1] Yet even if one grants that Descartes had good reason to be cautious about what he said and did not say in the *Discourse*, we should not take his comment to Burman to indicate that the commitments and attitudes expressed in his *morale par provision* were not his commitments or his attitudes. And in fact what he wrote later on ethics, to look no further, unequivocally bears this out. Moreover,

---

1. In his conversation with Burman, Descartes is reported to have said, "The author does not like writing on ethics, but he was compelled to include these rules [of the *morale par provision*] because of people like the Schoolmen; otherwise, they would have said that he was a man without any religion or faith and that he intended to use his method to subvert them" (Cottingham 1976, 49). Cottingham thinks that this remark provides "a fascinating insight into . . . Descartes's general attitude toward ethics" (118).

as I shall argue in Part One, once we take quite seriously Descartes's statement of his *morale* and his commentary on it, we find the beginnings of a powerful moral conception, for which he gives not a little supporting argument. There are many fine commentaries on this *morale*, but none, I believe, does Descartes's *morale par provision* full justice.

CHAPTER ONE

Descartes's Morale par Provision

I. ACCORDING to what I shall call the standard interpretation of the *morale par provision* as Descartes sets it out in the *Discourse*, Descartes adopted a so-called provisional morality simply as a prophylactic against the disorienting effect of methodic doubt on practice. This view of the matter is not wrong, so far as it goes, but it is superficial. Not only does it not do full justice to the text, it lacks sensitivity to the special situation Descartes found himself in during the period in question. We need a more illuminating and more realistic account.

The standard view is this. When Descartes was twenty-three he decided to take up as a lifelong project the search for certain knowledge in the sciences and, above all, in philosophy, on which he took the sciences to depend. He had been disappointed by the philosophy he had studied, complaining that he had found only controversy, preconception, and prejudice, but nothing absolutely certain (6:22; 1:122). What was lacking, he believed, was an effective method of inquiry—indeed, a method of the sort that was then beginning to take shape in his own mind as he reflected on his earlier progress in mathematics. So, preparing himself eventually to make progress in philosophy, he set about practicing and perfecting this method, which, by the time he composed the *Discourse*,[1] he had reduced to four rules: to break up complex problems into simpler ones until the simplest

---

1. He had made several earlier attempts to formulate this method, as we can see from the *Rules for the Direction of the Mind*. For a brief account of the evolution of Descartes's method in the *Discourse*, see Garber 1987.

elements are reached (the second rule); to recombine these simples in an orderly and perspicuous manner in order to make the original problem clear and intelligible (the third rule); and to make a careful review of these procedures to ensure that nothing has been overlooked (the fourth rule). The crux of the method was the first rule, the rule of *évidence*: "never to accept anything as true if I did not have evident knowledge of its truth: that is, carefully to avoid precipitate conclusions and preconceptions, and to include nothing more in my judgments than what presented itself to my mind so clearly and so distinctly that I had no occasion to doubt it" (6:18: 1:120).

Descartes states emphatically, however, that he intended to restrict the scope of his first rule to the pure search for truth, for he saw how foolish it would be to apply it to the practical problems of everyday life, where we rarely if ever have the luxury of waiting until we have certain knowledge before we act. For practice, as distinct from theory, he therefore suspended the rule of evidence and followed instead his *morale par provision*. This, in brief, is the standard account.

What is seldom noticed, however—and what this brief account so far does not make clear—is that Descartes embraced this *morale* long before he decided to apply rigorously the rule of evidence and to rid himself of his former opinions. Indeed, according to his own narrative, he adopted his *morale par provision* at the time he dedicated himself to the search for truth, which was in 1620. Yet he says quite explicitly that he did not at this time divest himself of all his previous opinions (6:15; 1:118). In his search for truth, he says, he resolved not to proceed precipitately at the beginning. "Nor," he continues, "would I begin rejecting completely any of the opinions which may have slipped into my mind without having been introduced there by reason, until I had first spent enough time in planning the work I was undertaking and in seeking the true method of attaining the knowledge of everything within my mental capabilities" (6:17; 1:119). So it is clear that he had his *morale par provision* in hand well before he was prepared to abandon all the opinions he had hitherto accepted. Just when this moment arrived is not clear from the *Discourse*, but we may suppose that it was in 1628, when he turned his attention to metaphysics. In any case, he relied on his *morale* not only before he rid himself of all his earlier opinions but also afterward, and did so for the special reason given above: the affairs of everyday life press us to decide what to do in the absence of certain knowledge.

We suppose, then, a Descartes sufficiently practiced in his method that he is prepared to implement the rule of *évidence*. He nonetheless restricts its scope specifically to pure inquiry, where the sole aim is absolutely certain knowledge; and he continues to rely on his *morale par provision* in the affairs of everyday life, where the aim, broadly speaking, is to live well and happily.[2] To illustrate the folly of not insulating practice from theory he gives the example of a traveler lost in the middle of a forest who turns this way and that or, worse, stays in one place because he does not know for certain which is the best way out and cannot settle on a plan of action. The decisive traveler, by contrast, although similarly uncertain, elects to walk in a single direction and keeps resolutely to his plan, just as if he knew for certain that his chosen path was the best way out.

I shall return to this helpful illustration below. Less helpfully, however, Descartes first introduces his *morale* using a different image:

> Now, before starting to rebuild your house, it is not enough simply to pull it down, to make provision for materials and architects (or else train yourself in architecture), and to have carefully drawn up the plans; you must also provide yourself with some other place where you can live comfortably while building is in progress. *Accordingly, lest I should remain indecisive in my actions while reason obliged me to be so in my judgements, and in order to live as happily as I could during this time, I formed for myself a provisional moral code* [une morale par provision] *consisting of just three or four maxims*, which I should like to tell you about. (6:22; 1:122; my italics)

The *Discourse* is not the only place Descartes refers to such a *morale*; he mentions it again in the letter-preface to the French edition of the *Principles*. If, he says there, one is to search methodically for certain knowledge of first causes and principles, beginning only with such ordinary wisdom as one gains from experience, conversation, and the best books, one "should try before anything else to devise for himself a code of morals [*une morale*] which is sufficient to regulate the actions of his life. For this is something which permits of no delay, since we should endeavour above all else to live well." Referring back to the *Discourse*, he adds, he has summarized there "the principal rules of logic and . . . an imperfect moral code [*une morale imparfaite*] which we may follow provisionally [*par provision*] while we do not yet know a better one" (9B:15; I 186–87).[3]

---

2. Descartes repeats this point several times, often referring back to his discussion in the *Discourse*. See "Second Set of Replies" (7:149; 2:106), "Fourth Set of Replies" (7:248; 2:172), and "Fifth Set of Replies" (7:350; 2:243)—not to mention the letter-preface to the *Principles of Philosophy*, to be discussed below. He writes in the First Meditation: "I know that no danger or error will result from my plan, and that I cannot possibly go too far in my distrustful attitude. This is because the task now in hand does not involve action but merely the acquisition of knowledge" (7:22; 2:15).

3. As he had earlier in the *Rules for the Direction of the Mind*, Descartes here says that everyone should purge himself of his old opinions, at least on philosophical and scientific matters,

2. In both the *Discourse* and the *Principles*, Descartes may appear to restrict the need for a *morale par provision* to those who take up pure inquiry. But the need is more general, since it arises from doubts antecedent to pure inquiry, as I will explain below. First, however, consider the question whether everyone who does take up inquiry must form the same *morale*. In his introductory remarks to the *Discourse* Descartes suggests as much, since he says that he derived (*tirée*) his *morale* from his method. Yet he does not spell out how or just why the *morale* he describes follows from the rules of method. Nor in the *Principles* does he point to a tight connection between the rules of method and the precepts of a *morale par provision*; indeed, if anything, he seems to allow that each pure inquirer might form a different *morale*. It is not surprising, then, that commentators by and large agree that Descartes had to form his *morale* only as a condition for getting on with pure inquiry and that he did not construct it by following the rules of his method.[4] But more needs to be said on both these points. In the first place, the need for a *morale par provision* does not arise initially from a com-

---

so that the need for a *morale par provision* would be universal. Moreover, the suggestion in this passage is that it would be the same *morale* that each one needs.

4. It is only in his note to the reader at the beginning of the *Discourse* that Descartes speaks of deriving the morality from the method. The reader will find, he writes, "some of the moral rules [the author] has derived from his method" (6:1; 1:111). Geneviève Rodis-Lewis, the principal recent French commentator, writes of the *morale* that "it is not 'derived from the method' as a consequence of the four precepts of the second part, but is rather called for by them, since it permits their rigorous application" (Rodis-Lewis 1970, 18.) Other commentators who support substantially the same view include Étienne Gilson and Pierre Mesnard. Gilson writes: "As M. L. Lévy-Bruhl has pointed out (*Descartes*, unpublished lectures), morality must come last in the order of the sciences to be constructed in accordance with the Cartesian method; this does not mean: 'A morality contructed by means of the rules of my method,' but simply, 'It is the method that requires that we give ourselves *une morale provisoire*, owing to its requirement that we place everything in doubt, while the demands of ordinary life admit of no delay'" (Gilson 1947, 81; also 231–34). And Mesnard concludes: "The provisional morality draws its existence from methodic doubt; its legitimacy has a two-part basis: it permits the mind to continue in peace the pursuit of truth and the conquest of the sciences; it responds immediately to the urgent character of the problems of everyday life" (Mesnard 1936, 53).

One who does not follow the prevailing view is Robert Cumming. Cumming's view is that the *morale par provision* is Descartes's first construction of the method, first because the rules of construction require that it be first. He distinguishes within the method the first rule, which is a rule of verification, and the other rules, which he calls rules of construction. Thus, according to the second rule, Descartes, as the first order of business, divides each of the difficulties he needs to examine to see how best to resolve them. His first difficulty, in view of his rule of verification, is to determine how best to deal with the fact that he must act while he suspends belief in everything that is not evident. Cumming's interpretation is highly ingenious, but not persuasive. Nonetheless, it is a move in the right direction, since it seems that some methodologically based account of the content and number of the rules of the *morale par provision* is in order. It is not enough to say that Descartes needs some morality or other; a commentator needs to explain, if possible, why we get the one we are given.

mitment to pure inquiry; it arises from more commonplace skeptical considerations. Moreover, the connection between Descartes's method and the precepts that make up his *morale* is tighter than his own remarks suggest.

3. Before we examine further what gives rise to this *morale* and how its precepts do (or do not) depend on the rules of method, we should have them before us. Descartes says that his *morale* is made up of "three or four" maxims, listing them in a way that leaves some doubt about the status of the fourth.

> The first was to obey the laws and customs of my country, holding constantly to the religion in which by God's grace I had been instructed from my childhood, and governing myself in all other matters according to the most moderate and least extreme opinions—the opinions commonly accepted in practice by the most sensible of those with whom I should have to live. (6:23; 1:122)

> My second maxim was to be as firm and decisive in my actions as I could, and to follow even the most doubtful opinions, once I had adopted them, with no less constancy than if they had been quite certain. (6:24; 1:123)

> My third maxim was to try always to master myself rather than fortune, and change my desires rather than the order of the world. (6:25; 1:123)

> Finally, to conclude this moral code [cette morale], I decided to review the various occupations which men have in this life, in order to try to choose the best. Without wishing to say anything about the occupations of others, I thought I could do no better than to continue with the very one I was engaged in, and devote my whole life to cultivating my reason and advancing as far as I could in the knowledge of the truth, following the method I had prescribed for myself.[5] Since beginning to use this method I had felt such extreme contentment that I did not think one could enjoy any sweeter or purer one in this life. Every day I discovered by its means truths which, it seemed to me, were quite important and were generally unknown by other men; and the satisfaction they gave me so filled my mind that nothing else mattered to me. Besides, the sole basis of the foregoing three maxims was the plan I had to continue my self-instruction. (6:27; 1:124)

5. In part 1, rather less generous about other callings, he makes the same point: "when I cast a philosophical eye upon the various activities and undertakings of mankind, there are almost none which I do not consider vain and useless. Nevertheless I have already reaped such fruits from this method that I cannot but feel extremely satisfied with the progress I think I have already made in the search for truth, and I cannot but entertain such hopes for the future as to venture the opinion that if any purely human occupation has solid worth and importance, it is the one I have chosen" (6:3; 1:112).

4. These are Descartes's precepts *par provision*. He compares them to a temporary dwelling that he will occupy while he constructs a more permanent one. Fixing on this image, perhaps, or for some other reason, commentators often refer to Descartes's *morale* as a *morale provisoire* (provisional morality), even if Descartes himself does not. However natural *morale provisoire* may seem as a gloss on Descartes's own *morale par provision*, it may be misleading,[6] even if Descartes's image plays into it.

The metaphor of occupancy itself does not pose much difficulty, since it expresses the idea that he lives within a set of rules, principles, and ideals that he has internalized and with which he is, so to speak, at home. But owing to what having moral beliefs entails, a difficulty arises from Descartes's suggestion that he could elect to occupy a morality on an interim basis and as a matter of convenience, a difficulty exacerbated by the attendant image of his moving out of his old morality and tearing it down. Of course, if one's idea of a provisional morality were that of a body of optional precepts that one chooses to adhere to for reasons of convenience, then Descartes's metaphor is apt. Choosing a set of precepts would be much like deciding which one among several clubs to join. But such a body of precepts could not properly be called one's morality, any more than could the rules of one's selected club.

To take the term fairly broadly at first, one's morality just is that constellation of beliefs, values, and ideals to which one defers at the most basic level, both in guiding one's choices—choices of individual actions, specific plans, policies, and even styles of life—and in justifying these choices,

6. From the last quarter of the nineteenth century French commentators have generally referred to Descartes's *morale* as a *morale provisoire*, according to Michèle Le Doeuff. Le Doeuff writes: "One can establish from a seventeenth-century dictionary that '*par provision*' does not mean 'provisional.' It is a juridical term meaning 'what a judgement awards in advance to a party'; thus one can award *par provision* a sum of a thousand *livres* damages to a plaintiff suing for assault. The *provision* is not liable to be put in question by the final judgement; it is first installment. . . . The expression 'provisional morality' is a devaluing one; it designates something which is destined to be replaced, something probably inadequate, to be invalidated once something better is found: something which awaits its own rejection. Whereas the word *provision* signifies the validity of this morality. There is in this term a positive notion of consumption. . . . *Provision* is that which is, at most, capable of completion, but not withdrawal. Thus there is here a difference of meaning regarding the value of this morality" (Le Doeuff 1989, 60–62). I am grateful to Jorge Secada for calling Le Doeuff's work to my attention.

English translations similarly skew interpretation. Among English translators we find "provisional code of morals" (Kemp Smith 1958), "provisional moral code" (Descartes 1985), and "code of morals for the time being" (Haldane and Ross 1911). To avoid prejudicing the issue by translation, I shall continue to use *morale par provision*, hoping to make clear just what Descartes's conception of this *morale* is.

both to oneself and, where called upon, to others.[7] Thus, if in some special context one were obliged to select a particular set of rules under the rubic "provisional morality," one would have to defer to one's basic morality to justify this choice. A provisional morality so understood could not, therefore, be bedrock. To choose a provisional morality in this way would presuppose one's already having a morality in the broad sense just defined.

The fact is that beyond a certain point Descartes's metaphor is inapt and does not fairly represent the situation in which he finds himself on the occasion of taking up pure inquiry. If we occupy a morality in the sense of having its values, goals, and precepts embedded in our character, we cannot tear down that very morality. Tearing down our morality, it is scarcely too much to say, would be tantamount to tearing ourselves down—losing our character and identity. Of course, we who occupy a particular morality can understand that others "occupy" other moralities. And we can understand how, through some voluntary efforts on our part, we might effect changes in our morality. And perhaps this is something we can and often should do.[8] But we can do so only a bit at a time and only under the direction either of the deeper values in the morality we have or through some compelling new insight. Thus, whereas we have no difficulty in understanding how and why one might move into a temporary home, we cannot similarly understand how anyone could move out of one's *morality* into a temporary one.[9] If, therefore, we are to make clear sense of the relevant texts in the *Discourse* as autobiographical narrative, we need some different account of the derivation, formation, and adoption of Descartes's *morale* than his occupancy metaphor suggests.

So, setting the image aside, we should take the qualifying *"par provision"* to signify, unproblematically, that this *morale* is the one Descartes provides for himself during his search for truth and that it is, as a *morale*, acknowl-

7. This remark may need qualifying. I suppose that if one never looked further than one's own subjective preferences to ground one's choices, one should not be credited with having a morality, even in this broad sense. One who considers values as going no deeper or having no basis other than this is one who has opted out of morality in this broad sense—and it may be in any sense. It is quite clear, however, that Descartes does not endorse such a subjectivist view of value.

8. It is one of Descartes's chief concerns in the *Passions of the Soul* to show how we can improve our character through modifying our emotional dispositions. But he also had to establish a normative standard of improvement.

9. Even if we take the *morale par provision* to be in some relevant sense imperfect, we shall require an intelligible narrative which builds either on the values this morality incorporates or on new value discoveries that lead from it to a comparatively more perfect morality. Here again, the latter cannot conceivably be embraced by a brute act of will or even on the strength of some reasonable doubts about its being perfect.

edged to be in some respects doubtful and imperfect. It is not doubtful, of course, that he needs this *morale* if he is to manage his everyday affairs well. This is true, however, whether one is a pure inquirer or not. So it would seem to follow that everyone needs a *morale*, although pure inquirers— peculiarly sensitive to the doubtful and imperfect status of the *morale* they have *par provision*—differ in this respect from less reflective members of society. Nonetheless, from the inquirer's perspective (before the end of inquiry), everyone's *morale* necessarily appears as *par provision*, even if those noninquirers whose *morale* is in view do not themselves see it this way. Now, there is nothing odd about the notion of a *morale par provision* if it is understood in this way. A *morale par provision* is just some person's de facto morality seen as in some respects doubtful and imperfect. The contrasting notion is that of a perfect morality, which is a de facto morality that is not, from this point of view, doubtful and imperfect.

5. Unlike the question, What is the meaning of "*par provision*"? the question, Is the *morale par provision* a morality? is seldom if ever asked. But it needs asking for at least three reasons. First, it is not clear that a set of precepts adopted simply because one needs *some* rules to live by, at least while one is ignorant of what the best rules might be, should count as a morality. Much will depend on how this choice of precepts is itself grounded. Second, it is not obvious that the precepts themselves are plausible candidates for the label "moral precepts." In fact, the precepts are a mixed lot. We might well wonder, to take the most dubious case, how the intention to take up science as one's life's work could be appropriately described as part of one's morality. Finally, it is not clear how precepts that have no claim to general—let alone universal—validity or applicability can constitute a morality. In the next several sections and in the following two chapters, I will clarify these matters and vindicate Descartes's description.

To begin with, it will be helpful to bear in mind a rough distinction, alluded to above, between a broad and a narrow sense of morality. Taking the term in the broadest sense, one's morality is a set of fundamental values expressed in one's character and, for the more reflective, in one's conception of the good life. To formulate a proper conception of the good life was the aim of philosophers within the tradition in which Descartes was himself working.[10] They were asking, What is the good for man? What is

---

10. In his *Commentary*, Gilson writes: "[Descartes] remains in moral theory the heir of the Greek ideal transmitted to the modern period by medieval scholasticism and the Christian Stoicism of the 16th century; the final end of morality is for him, therefore, the supreme good that alone can give us wisdom" (Gilson 1947, 230). For an illuminating account of the conception of morality among the ancients, see Annas 1993, 27–46 (a chapter entitled "Making Sense of My Life as a Whole").

our supreme good? or, assuming that happiness is the supreme good, What is happiness? What is involved in living the happy life? And they supposed that a single answer would apply to all. Descartes came near the end of this tradition, which some judge to have come to an abrupt end with Thomas Hobbes. We should have little difficulty in seeing how the maxims that make up his *morale par provision* constitute his reflective answer to such questions. To be sure, they are maxims formulated by someone who acknowledges that he lacks perfect wisdom and the knowledge required to assert with absolute confidence that these maxims define how to live as well and as happily as one possibly can, but they are nonetheless of the right sort to constitute a morality in the broad sense.

But within this morality, broadly conceived, we find a part that comes closer to matching our more modern conception of morality, a conception that is much narrower in scope, a conception in which the concept of duty, for example, has a central place. This rough distinction between a broad and narrow conception of morality was not, in fact, foreign to ancient ethics and was well marked in the writings popular in Descartes's period. Pierre Charron relied on it in organizing *De la sagesse*, and he probably took his lead from Cicero, who wrote near the beginning of *De officiis* that "every treatise on duty has two parts: one, dealing with the doctrine of the supreme good; the other, with the practical rules by which daily life in all its bearings may be regulated."[11] In any event, although Descartes's *morale par provision* is a morality in the broad sense, it contains within the first maxim a morality in the narrower sense—"the practical rules by which daily life in all its bearings may be regulated."

6. To vindicate Descartes's description of his four maxims as a morality, I propose to take them one by one, since what needs to be said differs in each case. I start with the fourth maxim—Descartes's resolve to spend his life cultivating his reason and searching for truth. When Descartes introduces his *morale* he says that it contains three or four maxims, which indicates that the fourth is in some general way different from the others. And it does appear to be distinctive. First, it lacks the generality of the others, which look like rules for living well that might be commended to all of us, whatever our particular vocation. Indeed, the fourth maxim seems little more than Descartes's resolution to continue to devote himself to scien-

11. Cicero 1990, 9. Charron's work is filled with quotations from Cicero, among many other ancient writers, so it is not in the least unlikely that he was influenced by the passage quoted here. In this passage, "duty" translates *officio*, which is Cicero's Latin for the Greek *kathékonta* and hardly has the meaning of "duty" in modern English. It means "appropriate action" and includes strict moral requirements (in our modern sense), what Kant called imperfect duties, and conduct that falls outside morality (again in our more modern sense).

tific and philosophical inquiry as his life's work. Second, this maxim is the "sole basis" of all the others.[12]

Descartes tells us that despite his studies and his travels, he still lacks a clear and distinct vision of how to live with assurance. He also says that it is just such knowledge that he most earnestly desires and that he has been encouraged by practicing his method to think that he might, with diligence, acquire it. He is referring specifically to his state of mind during the winter of 1619–20, but readers of the *Discourse* cannot but assume that this was also his state of mind at the time of its composition. On the other hand, he is evidently not without settled opinions about how to live and what is worthwhile—opinions, moreover, that he expresses with some warmth, as though he fully expected them to survive the critical scrutiny to which he planed to subject them. One of these opinions is that contentment is worth pursuing for its own sake. There are others. In justifying his choice of vocation, he refers to the value of the knowledge he expects to obtain as well as to the value of the further fruits of this knowledge. What brings him utmost contentment, he says, is advancing knowledge. But knowledge is not—or not just—a means to contentment. In the first place, he strongly suggests that knowledge has value for its own sake. And even if we discount this suggestion, he leaves no doubt later, in part 6 of the *Discourse*, about the instrumental value of knowledge and the value of the ends to which it is the means. Here he refers to the advances in knowledge he had made by 1637:

> they opened my eyes to the possibility of gaining knowledge which would
> be very useful in life, and of discovering a practical philosophy which

12. Now it might seem to follow, if we combine these two points, that only one who takes up methodic inquiry as a vocation would be bound by the three maxims. And if we assume that Descartes's choice to take up methodic inquiry is not one that we are in any way bound to imitate, then these maxims will not have the general validity I spoke of above. However, engagement with inquiry admits of degree. Descartes is an extreme case. So, assuming that Descartes is correct that engagement with inquiry is a sound basis for the three maxims, it remains to be seen what our level of engagement should be and therefore what normative force these maxims will have. One message of the *Discourse*, however, although disguised by Descartes's autobiographical presentation, is that so far as we ourselves lack a clear and distinct understanding of how best to conduct ourselves in this life, we are all in need of *une moral par provision*. This line of argument is explicit in the letter-preface to the French edition of the *Principles of Philosophy* and is foreshadowed in the *Rules*. In the passage from this preface quoted above Descartes describes the *morale* formulated in the *Discourse* as "an imperfect moral code which we may follow provisionally while we do not yet know a better one" [une morale imparfaite, qu'on peut suivre par provision pendant qu'on n'en sait point encore de meilleure]. And if this is so, then we may infer that we should form for ourselves the very one Descartes formed for himself. And the reason for this, in turn, is that it is our reason—the same in each of us—that governs this formation. What is recommended in the letter-preface is serious methodical philosophical reflection through (Cartesian) metaphysics, which will gain for us the most important truths we need to know in this life. See the letter to Elizabeth, September 15, 1645 (4:290–96; 3:265–67).

might replace the speculative philosophy taught in the schools. Through this philosophy we could know the power and action of fire, water, air, the stars, the heavens and all the other bodies in our environment, as distinctly as we know the various crafts of our artisans; and we could use this knowledge—as artisans use theirs—for all the purposes for which it is appropriate, and thus make ourselves, as it were, the lords and masters of nature. This is desirable not only for the invention of innumerable devices which would facilitate our enjoyment of the fruits of the earth and all the good we find there, but also, and most importantly, for the maintenance of health. (6:62; 1:142–43)

To be sure, in 1619, when Descartes chose his vocation, he had not yet made the discoveries he refers to here, so we should perhaps not see humanitarian considerations as playing a major role in his original choice. On the other hand, since he is still strongly committed to his vocation in 1637 and to his *morale par provision*, we should take these unequivocal expressions of humanitarian values very seriously. In explaining his decision to publish the *Discourse* (and the accompanying essays) he says that not to publish would be to sin "gravely against the law which obliges us to do all in our power to secure the general welfare of mankind" (6:61; 1:142).[13] The law that would require publishing the results of inquiry, however, would also warrant undertaking the inquiry in the first place.[14]

The main point is that Descartes's justifies his fourth maxim by referring us to a moral law that he warmly embraces. It is evidently a law that belongs to Descartes's own morality. Which morality? Certainly to his morality at the time of composing the *Discourse*. Is this morality his *morale par provision*? It would appear that the answer must be yes in one sense and no in another. On the one hand, since he represents his own morality at this time as *une morale par provision*, we must infer that this law is part of this moral-

13. A few pages later he writes: "Every man is indeed bound to do what he can to procure the good of others, and a man who is of no use to anyone else is strictly worthless" (6:66; 1:145).

14. Objecting to Gilson, who suggested that Descartes pursued philosophy basically for philanthropic reasons, Ferdinand Alquié writes: "Descartes seems less desirous of spreading truth than of acquiring it, less concerned to make it known than to make use of it himself, both to know better and to know himself better" (Alquié 1988, 1:565). Of course, Descartes may have had several motives both for doing research and publishing. To be sure, he had a great thirst for discovery and invention, both sources of his greatest contentment, as we have seen. But this takes nothing from Gilson's point. In the first place, Descartes is quite explicit about the law to secure the general welfare of mankind. And if, as he believed, by choosing his special vocation he would help to secure this worthy end, then he could not fail to see this as a further reason for this very choice. The point I am concerned to make in the present context, however, is that Descartes in no uncertain terms declares his allegiance to a specific moral law to secure the welfare of mankind.

ity. On the other hand, since his fourth maxim is the ground of the others and this law is in turn the ground of the fourth maxim, the law might appear at once to stand outside the *morale par provision* and to serve as its moral foundation, a foundation unqualified by "*par provision.*" But the correct way to view the matter is that the law is neither more nor less *par provision* than the other elements of Descartes's morality. "*Par provision*" qualifies the morality as a whole and signals that it is a morality yet to withstand critical inquiry.

To conclude, when we look to the reasons Descartes gives for his choice of vocation, we see that they are moral reasons. They are moral reasons in the sense that they refer us to values that are embedded in Descartes's own morality, taking morality in both the broad sense and the narrow. When I speak of Descartes's own morality, I mean his pre-doubt morality, the morality he had before he committed himself specifically to his scientific and philosophic vocation. If, therefore, the choice of vocation is, as he says, the sole basis for the three maxims of his *morale par provision*, it follows that this specific *morale* has a foundation in Descartes's pre-doubt *morale*. And if this is correct, then we have a good part of our solution to the first problem. We can see how the formation of his *morale par provision* is continuous with his own morality at the time of its formation. It is significant, moreover, that these values are not idiosyncratic. The rationale for his choice of vocation is not only intelligible but also sufficiently justified in terms of values he could count on his readers to share.

7. If, Descartes says, he needs some precepts to guide his practical deliberation while his method requires him to suspend belief in theoretical matters, it is not the case that his doubt about morality first arises from the hyperbolic doubt of the method. Nor is it this methodic doubt alone that calls for a *morale par provision*, for Descartes has ample reason, prior to methodic doubt, to question his moral opinions: a battery of skeptical arguments bequeathed to him by Sextus Empiricus and vivified by Montaigne. So although Descartes says that he required a *morale par provision* as a condition for his search for truth, we find by following his own narrative account that the need for such a *morale* actually antedates the methodological skepticism of his method. Methodic doubt is procedural and confined to the context of theory. The pure inquirer asks what, if anything, can be known beyond the possibility of doubting; he has doubts about matters that at the level of common sense are morally certain. But doubts about our own moral outlook arise for us whether we are pure inquirers or not. Indeed, the hope of the inquirer is, in the end, to put to rest those doubts that have their origin in skeptical reflections of a more traditional, less exotic kind. And it is in response to such skeptical arguments that the need

for a *morale par provision* initially arises, for in taking these arguments to heart, which Descartes claims to have done in the *Discourse*, he also had to take a critical distance from his moral convictions, no matter how well embedded they were in his affective and conative dispositions and no matter how warmly he endorsed them. To be sure, Descartes says he adopted his *morale* at the time he decided definitely to take up the methodical search for truth as his life's work.[15] This does not imply, however, that the need for this *morale* first arose from methodic doubt. After all, the Pyrrhonist considerations summarized in the *Discourse* are presented as shaking his confidence only in areas that lacked the perspicuity and *évidence* of mathematics. In his method he took the clarity of mathematical knowledge as his standard and sought to find this same standard satisfied elsewhere.[16]

This is the context in which he places himself as he rehearses the traditional skeptic's case. "The same man," he writes, "with the same mind, if brought up from infancy among the French or Germans, develops otherwise than he would if he had always lived among the Chinese or cannibals. . . . Thus it is custom and example that persuade us, rather than any certain knowledge" (6:16; 1:119).[17] Certain knowledge, for its part, is not the product of erudition, for, as Descartes writes—expressing a sentiment he might have found in Cicero, Montaigne, or Charron—"Nothing can be imagined which is too strange or incredible to have been said by some philosopher" (6:16; 1:118). And nothing, he continues, can be imagined which is too outrageous not to have been commended by some moralist. The ancients, he says, "extol the virtues, and make them appear more estimable than anything else in the world; but they do not adequately explain how to recognize a virtue, and often what they call by this fine name is nothing but a case of insensibility, or pride, or despair, or parricide" (6:8; 1:114).[18]

15. This would imply, we may note in passing, that he had by then formulated its precepts in something close to the form presented in 1637. Since the formulations of the maxims of his *morale* are very close to those to be found in writings available to Descartes in 1619—by Michel de Montaigne, Pierre Charron, and Guillaume Du Vair—this is a plausible conjecture.

16. The methodic doubt described in the *Discourse* is not the full, hyperbolic doubt of the later *Meditations*, where even the standard of *évidence* is called into question.

17. From studying the great book of the world with its great variety of customs and opinions, Descartes writes, "I learned not to believe too firmly anything of which I had been persuaded only by example and custom" (6:10; 1:116). Here Descartes is following the path of Montaigne in his "Apology for Raimond Sebond," Charron in the second book of *On Wisdom*, and, in general, the Pyrrhonian tradition of Sextus Empiricus, a point that could hardly have been lost on Descartes's early readers.

18. He is alluding to the Stoic rejection of the passions, to the pride connected with this rejection, to the Stoic acceptance of and even glorifying of suicide, and to L.-J. Brutus's condemning his own children to die, presiding at their execution, and to M.-J. Brutus's killing of Caesar (see Gilson 1947, 131–32). For a discussion of Descartes's own attitudes toward Stoic insensibility and pride, see D'Angers 1976.

Far from invoking methodological doubt in these passages, Descartes professes to be moved by the more common argument from relativity. We should, he concludes, take to heart that reasonable individuals and peoples differ about how to live well and happily, and we should concede that we ourselves are no more qualified to dismiss their opinions as absolutely false than they are ours.[19]

Yet if Descartes's uncertainty echoes that of Montaigne and others, his characteristic cognitive optimism does not; for, unlike the skeptics, he had in hand a standard of truth—namely, *évidence*—by which, at the end of methodic inquiry, he expected to discover a firm foundation for a true morality, a morality beyond the threat of skepticism. And it is in the light of this possibility that he characterizes the morality he has as *une moral par provision*. Thus, to the question raised above about the sense in which Descartes's morality is *par provision*, part of the answer is that a morality *par provision* is a morality that one keeps at a critical distance because of the force of skeptical arguments. To describe it as *par provision* is also, in part, to express optimism about eventually being able to answer these arguments.

---

19. The first modern edition of Sextus Empiricus's *Outlines of Pyrrhonism* was brought out by Henri Etienne in 1562; it soon became "the dominant philosophical text of the age," according to J. Annas and J. Barnes. Its literary influence is seen in Montaigne's "Apology," which contains many of Sextus's skeptical arguments, and is passed on through Charron's *On Wisdom*. Descartes complains in his reply to the Second Objections that skepticism still flourishes. His own aim was not only to defeat it but also to defeat distinctively epistemological skepticism (see Annas and Barnes 1985, 5–6).

Richard Tuck also notes that Descartes's moral skepticism does not derive from hyperbolic doubt: "Two problems remained about Descartes's reply to the sceptic. The first was that even if his argument against his own hyperbolical doubt was accepted, it was not clear how far it met the *ancient* sceptical case, which had after all not been based on the hyperbolical doubt. Moral relativism in particular seemed on the face of it to be untouched by Descartes's argument, for as we have seen, in ancient scepticism it was wholly independent of any epistemological doubt. That is why there is, as is well known, no developed moral theory in Descartes's *oeuvre*, though he did say that his programme might eventually, and in some unspecified way, issue in one. Because of the absence of any such theory, we find in general in his writings only the sceptical premises, and not the anti-sceptical conclusions drawn from them which we might have expected, and which Descartes intended to draw one day" (Tuck 1988, 247). Tuck goes on to suggest that Descartes remained a moral skeptic, since his resolution of hyperbolic doubt, which could give him physics and metaphysics, could not get him ethics. "There was nothing in our assured knowledge of the physical world which could tell us anything about the moral world, despite Descartes's hope that the link could be made. So he remained a pretty pure sceptic in these matters, a point underlined by the fact that the only political philosopher he was at all drawn to was Machiavelli, just as Charron and the others had been" (248). Although I agree with Tuck that Descartes's *morale par provision* is not motivated by hyperbolic doubt, I would reject his claim that Descartes remained a moral skeptic, as well as his claim that he was "drawn to" Machiavelli. The one moral philosopher he expresses some grudging respect for is Hobbes, although, as I will argue later, he does not seem to have learned much from him.

8. We turn now to the first maxim, according to which Descartes resolves *(a)* to obey the laws and customs of his country; *(b)* to continue to hold firmly to his Catholic faith; *(c)* in all other matters,[20] to govern himself "according to the most moderate and least extreme opinions—the opinions commonly accepted in practice by the most sensible of those with whom [he] should have to live." Of these, in the present context only the third part merits much discussion. The first part is plainly justified on prudential grounds and presumably on moral grounds as well.[21] More difficult to explain is the second part. If Descartes exempts articles of his faith from doubt, we may be inclined ask, does he not already have a morality sufficient to guide him in the conduct of everyday life?[22] The answer, of course, will depend on what range of activities he takes this morality to apply to. It will certainly control specifically religious practice. But beyond special duties of worship, confession, and penance, Christian moral doctrine commends other duties, as well as ideals of character. These make up the body of common morality, a morality that is not specifically religious, much less specifically Catholic. To simplify exposition, then, I shall distinguish between Descartes's strictly religious activity and the nonreligious activity of everyday life. I shall restrict the scope of part *b* of the first maxim to the former—for the following reasons. First, Descartes made a radical distinction between articles of faith and beliefs with other credentials. He held, implicitly in the *Discourse*, explicitly in the later *Principles of Philosophy*, that faith transcends methodic doubt and the kind of evidence it aspires to (8A:39; 1:221–22).[23] His method did not, therefore, require that

20. Where custom ends and other matters begin is not carefully defined, nor need it be for Descartes's purposes. Other matters will certainly include areas of conduct properly regulated by maxims of prudence and precepts of morality. Thus, in some sense, Descartes elected to take his moral instruction from the example of the more sensible of those with whom he had to live. One issue I examine is precisely what this sense is.

21. In fact the public practice of the Catholic faith was proscribed in Holland, where Descartes was living during much of the time between 1620 and 1637, but he continued to practice it nonetheless. See Rodis-Lewis 1970, 19 n. 1.

22. As one commentator, Alfred Espinas, writes, "He sets aside religion purely and simply with all its consequences. It is therefore useless to look for a morality; he has one." Espinas is among those commentators who believe that all talk of a provisional morality as required by the method is pretense. "The provisional, nearly fictional character of these rules," he continues, "is not without some irony that Descartes presents to his reader this morality that lacks any duty worthy of the name; as he says in his private notes, *personam induit*, he wears a mask" (Espinas 1925, 18).

23. For a thorough examination of Descartes's religious thought, see Gouhier 1924. Speaking of the young Descartes, Gouhier endorses Gaston Milhaud's view: "Apropos of the Descartes of 1619, Milhaud reached a conclusion full of good sense; he had 'a naively religious cast of mind, simpler and less complex that we are generally disposed to think'" (Gouhier 1924, 50). For a more recent account, see Rodis-Lewis 1995, 284–97.

he abandon the articles of his faith qua articles of faith; it required only that he not rely on faith in his search for truth. The second and related point is that his project is rationalist; his aim, so far as ethics is concerned, was not knowledge based on faith and, a fortiori, not moral knowledge based on faith; his aim was an ethics based on what can be discovered through the use of reason. So it is fitting to give a restrictive reading to the second part of the first maxim and an inclusive reading to the third part, to which I now turn.

In all matters not covered in the first two parts of the maxim, Descartes resolved to follow the example of others. This part I take to cover much of the activity governed by ordinary morality—the normal range of duties to self, to others, and within social institutions, such as the duty not to steal. It also includes not only matters of ordinary prudence but also the full range of beliefs about ourselves and the world of which we can claim moral certainty.[24]

The ostensible reason Descartes offers for deferring to the example of moderate and sensible people is that he had begun (in 1619) "to count [his] opinions as worthless." Why? "Because," he says, "I wished to submit them all to examination, and so I was sure I could do no better than follow those of the most sensible men" (6:23; 1:122). Now, this makes it look as if Descartes actually chose to divest himself of his morally certain beliefs about the world and of his pre-doubt moral beliefs, deferring instead, in the relevant areas, to the example of sensible people. To be sure, both Descartes's

24. In this first maxim, then, Descartes is, through his alleged deference to the views of sensible people, accepting certain beliefs as *morally certain*. Thus, the practical domain is insulated from the corrosive effects of methodic doubt in the theoretical domain. Referring to the three maxims, he says toward the end of part 3: "Once I had established these maxims and set them on one side together with the truths of faith . . . I judged that I could freely undertake to rid myself of all the rest of my opinions" (6:28; 1:125). In part 4 he writes: "if there are still people who are not sufficiently convinced of the existence of God and of their soul by the arguments I have proposed [he has just given his famous arguments], I would have them know that everything else of which they may think themselves more sure—such as their having a body, there being stars and an earth, and the like—is less certain. For although we have a moral certainty about these things, so that it seems we cannot doubt them without being extravagant, nevertheless when it is a question of metaphysical certainty, we cannot reasonably deny that there are adequate grounds for not being entirely sure about them. We need only observe that in sleep we may imagine . . . " (6:37–38; 1:129–30). In the French version of the *Principles* he explains that "moral certainty is certainty which is sufficient to regulate our behaviour, or which measures up to the certainty we have on matters relating to the conduct of life which we never normally doubt, though we know that it is possible, absolutely speaking, that they may be false" (8A:327; 1:289, 289n). Descartes's examples of moral certainty are restricted to beliefs about the world; he does not use the expression to refer specifically to our moral beliefs. For a good account of Descartes's notion of moral certainty, see Curley 1993, 19–20.

method and the prior argument from relativity required him to gain some critical distance from any of his prior beliefs that lacked *évidence*, including his moral opinions. But holding one's moral opinions at a critical distance is one thing, getting rid of them altogether (however this might be done) is quite another, and not something that is in the least called for by the desire to submit them to examination. Nor does the first maxim call for getting rid of them.

To see this, let us examine this part of the first maxim more closely. What would be involved in identifying a group of people as moderate and sensible? Descartes describes the sensible people whose example he chooses to follow as the most moderate in their conduct. Their opinions, which their behavior manifests, are, he says, *(a)* probably the best, *(b)* the easiest to act on, and *(c)* always closer to the right opinion than the opposing extreme. In large measure, *a*, *b*, and *c* are analytic of the evaluative term "sensible." But it is Descartes who must first determine who the sensible people are; it is he who must decide which opinions are moderate and easiest to follow. How is he to reach such a momentous decision except by relying on his own pre-doubt moral opinions? The sensible people, it would seem—those whose moral beliefs are worthy of allegiance—are those who by and large share with Descartes a common morality. If this is right, Descartes's *morale par provision*, insofar as it includes a set of first-order rules of right conduct, is continuous with his own pre-doubt morality.

And this has to be right, since the alternative is not credible. The alternative would require that the following case be fully coherent, which it is not. The case is one in which there was a notable divergence between Descartes's pre-doubt moral opinions and the moral opinions of the (so-called) sensible people in question. Suppose most members of a group, identified in some way as sensible, for example, through their manifest intelligence and their political and economic power within the larger community in which Descartes lived—suppose they rejected a precept that was embedded at a deep level in Descartes's pre-doubt morality, say, that one ought to keep promises or that one ought to help those in need. Let us call them sensible knaves. These sensible knaves appear to enjoy an agreeable style of life. In their view, keeping a promise or helping someone in need would, when such an act lacks evident prudential point, be extreme conduct (a kind of foolish moral fanaticism). Now if, as some commentators argue, Descartes's decision to follow the example of the more sensible members of his community were merely a matter of social conformism, then we could easily imagine him adopting the ways of sensible knaves. But this we cannot easily imagine. And there is nothing in the text that compels us to try.

Although Descartes has well-considered doubts about his own first-order morality, these are not of the kind to undermine moral convictions or to leave him free to follow the example of sensible knaves.

If this is a correct interpretation of Descartes's reflective understanding of his own moral convictions, however, we confront the following interpretive problem. Why does he not simply construct his *morale par provision* from his own pre-doubt moral convictions? Or, to keep our focus on the first maxim,[25] why does he say that he will follow, not his own pre-doubt moral beliefs, but rather those of the most sensible men in his society?

Perhaps he proposes to do so as a preferable alternative to continuing to rely on his pre-1620 moral convictions. But since we cannot make clear sense of the proposal so construed, we need to view his choice of moral paradigm in some other way. And what this way is should by now be clear. What Descartes is announcing in this first maxim is that he takes himself to be a member of a community of people bound together by a common morality. His policy is understandably conservative, for although he doubts that this common morality is the correct or best possible morality in all respects, he has as yet discovered no grounds for proposing or endorsing any other.[26]

Nothing in what I have argued prevents Descartes from seeking advice from sensible people, time permitting, when he faces a complex moral problem whose best resolution is not clear to him. Some moral demands may be clear and have straightforward applications—publishing the *Discourse*, for

25. I will point out below that the second maxim of the *morale par provision* does directly meet the standard of the first rule of method and can be seen, therefore, to be derived from the method in a direct and straightforward manner. It is consequently firmly established as true.

26. Descartes's first maxim bears an obvious resemblance to the following passage from Montaigne's "Apology for Raimond Sebond," which comes near the end of a comparatively sympathetic account of Pyrrhonism. "For, however much new fashions may appeal to me, I do not readily change, for fear of losing by the exchange. And since I am not capable of choosing for myself, I accept the choice of others, and remain in the state wherein God has placed me. Otherwise I could not keep from perpetual rolling. Thus, by the grace of God, I have kept wholly, without being stirred or troubled by conscience, within the ancient tenets of our religion, amidst the many sects and divisions that our times have brought forth" (Montaigne 1927, 2:14). I would make three points. First, Montaigne clearly is capable of choosing, since he embraces his religion and he voluntarily accepts the moral precepts current in his community. Second, if in so doing he is not obliged by his reason, he is nonetheless deferring to his reason in this sense, that he is able to defend his choice as not unreasonable and as most consonant with his character as formed so far. He represents his practical beliefs and attitudes as at once genuinely his and as maximally justified relative to the only standards of justification accessible to him or to anyone else. Third, Montaigne expresses the need for such beliefs and attitudes "to keep himself from rolling about incessantly." We could call these beliefs and attitudes, therefore, *une moral par provision* and see that the need for it arises from Pyrrhonian considerations. As we shall see, however, Descartes's position is not Pyrrhonian.

example—but others may not. In such cases consideration of what others who are evidently sensible would do or would advise is itself sensible. Taking sensible people as moral advisers in this sense, however, is altogether different from the wild and psychologically unrealistic suggestion that one is to uproot all one's prior moral beliefs and replace them with someone else's. We have to have confidence in those we listen to, and this confidence must itself be rooted in our own moral judgments.[27]

9. Up to this point I have taken Descartes's reasoning to have run along the following lines. Before we come to doubt our moral beliefs and see them as possibly false, we are practicing dogmatists and our beliefs have the form of precipitate conclusions and preconceptions, as beliefs passively and uncritically acquired. We are struck, however, by the diversity of social norms across cultures and are led to ask whether our own moral beliefs and attitudes may not be the product of mere custom and example.[28] Taking this point to heart, we immediately place our moral convictions at a critical distance; we cease to be dogmatists and acknowledge our liability to error, a liability we now seek to overcome through methodic inquiry. Specifically within the context of inquiry we refuse to assent to any claims, moral or otherwise, that fail to meet the standard of *évidence*; but within the larger context of everyday life, we retain our allegiance to the social norms we have previously embraced and do so with the decisiveness of one who knows them to be certified by reason.

Does Descartes's reasoning go further? If we stick to what is explicitly spelled out in Descartes's fable, perhaps not. Still, without going beyond what we can glean from relevant texts, we can extend it in an interesting way. I begin with this question: If we are beginning pure inquiry, are we justified in retaining allegiance to these social norms?

Suppose that we have had the full use of our reason from birth and that we have always been guided by it. And grant that the morality we formed

---

27. In his later correspondence with Elizabeth (August 18, 1645), commenting on Seneca, he writes: "he chides those who follow custom and example rather than reason. 'When it comes to how to live,' he says, 'people rely on mere beliefs, never on sound judgement.' Nevertheless he approves of our taking the advice of those whom we believe to be the wisest persons; though he would have us also make use of our own judgement in examining their opinions. Here I am strongly of his opinion. For although many people are incapable of finding the right path on their own, yet there are few who cannot recognize it well enough when somebody else clearly points it out to them. Moreover, provided we take care to seek the advice of the most able people, instead of allowing ourselves to be guided blindly by example, and we use all our mental powers to discover how we ought to proceed, then however things may turn out, our consciences will be at peace and we shall have the assurance that our opinions on morality are the best we could possibly have" (4:272; 3:259).

28. As Descartes engagingly puts it at one point, his opinions "may have slipped into [his] mind without having been introduced there by reason" (6:17; 1:119).

under these conditions is the perfect morality Descartes refers to in the *Principles*.[29] Since we are presently in search of the perfect morality, we acknowledge that the morality we actually have is imperfect. It is imperfect in two respects. First, even if its requirements and ideals are those that a perfect morality would contain, we do not know this to be so. For example, although we believe we should keep our promises, we do not know for certain that we should do so; for when we reflect on the matter, we see that our having acquired this belief might be explained in a manner that does not require that it be true. Second, the requirements and ideals of our de facto morality may in fact be different in content from those of the perfect morality. Even if we can scarcely imagine a perfect morality not containing the obligation to keep promises, we must admit this possibility, not to mention the further possibility that it would contain demands we have never thought of. Our question is this: how can we justify our continuing allegiance to a morality we acknowledge to be imperfect? This is a question Descartes himself does not expressly address in just this form. The question he addresses is how to justify his choice to follow the example of sensible men. But as I have argued above, what he offers in defense of this decision rests on his de facto morality. So our question cannot be set aside.

Nor does Descartes set it aside, since he decides to follow the example of those who are not only sensible but whose practical norms are moderate, easiest to follow, and probably the best (6:23; 1:122-23). Putting this together with the above conclusion—that is, that Descartes, by choosing to follow the example of sensible and moderate men, was in fact deliberately retaining allegiance to his former morality—our question becomes: How can he support the claim that his de facto morality has some antecedent probability of being true? I construct a Cartesian answer to this question in three stages.

To review the relevant points, I have argued that *(a)* Descartes retains, as part of his *morale par provision*, the substantive norms and ideals of the morality he had when he was twenty-three; *(b)* he shares this morality with the sensible and moderate members of his society; *(c)* he regards this morality as imperfect; and *(d)* he regards retaining allegiance to it as justified, imperfect as he acknowledges it to be. Now, the first stage of my answer is this: we could justify retaining our allegiance to a morality under

29. Referring to the early reflections of 1620 or thereabouts, Descartes writes: "So, too, I reflected that we were all children before being men and had to be governed for some time by our appetites and our teachers, which were often opposed to each other and neither of which, perhaps, always gave us the best advice; hence I thought it virtually impossible that our judgements should be as unclouded and firm as they would have been if we had had the full use of our reason from the moment of our birth, and if we had always been guided by it alone" (6:13; 1:117).

conditions *a*, *b*, and *c* because we have no reason to declare allegiance to another (waiving the question of how this might be possible psychologically). That is, we might justify this morality merely as our default morality. This is the Pyrrhonist position. The Pyrrhonist makes no claims that his default morality has any antecedent probability of being true and is content in his conviction that no such claims on behalf of anyone's morality can be successfully defended either. Justified probability claims must rest on background knowledge, and, says the Pyrrhonist, we have no such knowledge. But this does not appear to be Descartes's position. Although he certainly could defend his continuing allegiance to his former morality as a default morality, Descartes, unlike the Pyrrhonist, speaks credulously of antecedent probability.

This brings me to the second stage of my answer. What Descartes has and the Pyrrhonist lacks is confidence in the epistemic potential of human reason (6:2; 1:111). Descartes attributes the diversity of opinion on matters of importance to our failure to proceed slowly and methodically, a failure he would no doubt explain in terms of our ignorance of the proper method, the power of desires and traditions to influence our beliefs, and our general intellectual laziness and diffidence. Nonetheless, he takes the truths of reason to be permanent and apprehensible by those who use their reason well. This being granted, if we could pick out, among all the conflicting moral opinions we find in our history, some core of moral opinion shared by the best thinkers, then, given that human reason is a genuine cognitive power, we have some grounds for concluding that these widely shared opinions are at least approximately true—that they have some antecedent probability.

So we come to stage three. Can we not discover thinkers in this history who have done a creditable job of using their reason well, even if not perfectly, and who have bequeathed to us a body of first-order moral doctrine on which there is significant consensus? The major controversies, after all, have not been over first-order morality but over how the precepts and ideals of first-order morality are to be explained or established. Even in the midst of rehearsing the traditional skeptical arguments, Descartes praises the ancient moralists for their "useful teachings and exhortations to virtue," complaining chiefly, as we have seen, that none have provided an entirely adequate foundation for their teachings and that some have given an implausible taxonomy of the virtues. Moreover, in the earlier *Rules for the Direction of the Mind*, a work that gives us some insight into Descartes's views during the period we are considering, he writes as the good rationalist he is:

But I am convinced that certain primary seeds of truth naturally implanted in human minds thrived vigorously in that unsophisticated and

innocent age—seeds which have been stifled in us through our constantly reading and hearing all sorts of errors. So the same light of the
mind which enabled them to see (albeit without knowing why) that virtue is preferable to pleasure, the good preferable to the useful, also enabled them to grasp true ideas in philosophy and mathematics, although
they were not yet able fully to master such sciences. (10:376; 1:18)

Now, assuming that Descartes's own first-order morality is part of this overlapping consensus, I conclude that as a rationalist, he can justify his retaining allegiance to his old first-order morality not merely *faute de mieux* but
because, compared with others with which it not compatible, it has a higher
antecedent probability of being at least approximately true.

10. I turn finally to the question I raised in the beginning: What role do
the rules of method play in Descartes's formation of his *morale par provision*? In the first place, Descartes's commitment to the method is motivated by his morality, for the method is the means he has discovered for ar-
riving at truth, and truth he values as an end among other ends. His prior
value commitments are expressed in the fourth maxim and elsewhere, as I
have noted above. But how does allegiance to the four rules of method determine the remaining three maxims of the *morale par provision*?

The rule of evidence is the first rule of the method, but it is not always
the first rule to be applied. In the present case, the first to be applied is the
second rule, which requires us to analyze any problem or difficulty into its
simplest elements. If this is not an innovative rule, it is certainly a sensible
one, as far as it goes, although it is plain that we shall need practice in applying it to a variety of subject matters. The third and fourth rules are no
more precise. According to the third we are to proceed in an orderly way
in reconstructing the original complex or in solving the original difficulty,
and according to the fourth we are to review our efforts—our analyses and
step-by-step reconstruction—to make sure we have left nothing out.

The first problem we face when we take up inquiry is a practical one.
According to the second rule, we need to analyze this problem. What are its
elements? We have a declared practical aim: truth in the sciences (including morality). We have a method that promises to lead to this declared end.
It is reasonable to choose the means, other things equal, to our ends. But
the methodical search for truth is itself a practical activity which can take
place only if certain other conditions are satisfied—leisure, freedom from
interference, adequate food and shelter, help and cooperation of others,
and the like. The search itself, moreover, is not only subordinate to specific
moral aims, it is one among other practical activities with their own independent aims, and all these activities must be coordinated.

What stands out clearly, when we survey this problem, is a distinction between the domain of theory and the domain of practice. And what is equally clear, as Descartes emphasizes, is that while we must scrupulously respect the rule of evidence in the domain of theory, to do so prematurely in other areas of practice (theorizing being one practice among others) would be self-defeating. If the analysis I have offered is correct, it follows that in the affairs of everyday life we are to continue to act in the light of our moral beliefs as well as our beliefs about the world forged by ordinary experience. We are to do so because that is the best we can do in our present circumstances, that is, prior to whatever practical knowledge inquiry brings. Among those beliefs we might imagine ourselves as having, these are the ones that we judge, on grounds of overall coherence, the most likely to be correct, the most probable.

Let us assume, then, that this is the best we can do in our present circumstances and that we have in accordance with the applicable rules of method solved our first problem, which was a practical one. Then we can say that the first maxim of the *morale par provision* has been derived from the method. When it comes to the second and third maxims, however, more can be said. Take the second maxim. This maxim, as I shall argue more fully in the next chapter, follows directly from the rule of evidence. The second maxim is *évident*, as Descartes writes in the *Discourse*: "Since in everyday life we must often act without delay, it is a most certain truth that when it is not in our power to discern the truest opinions, we must follow the most probable" (6:25; 1:123). The third maxim, as I try to make plain in Chapter 3, can be seen to follow from the second by clear and evident steps, so that it too can bear the stamp of approval of the rule of evidence.

CHAPTER TWO

Descartes's Second Maxim

1. "MY second maxim," Descartes writes, "was to be as firm and decisive in my actions as I could, and to follow even the most doubtful opinions, once I had adopted them, with no less constancy than if they had been quite certain." It might appear that Descartes is simply reporting, but he goes on to justify his resolution. "It is a most certain truth that when it is not in our power to discern the truest opinions, we must follow the most probable" (6:25; 1:123). This most certain truth is a second-order practical principle; we apply it only if, pressed for time and inadequately informed as we may be, we have already adopted a considered first-order opinion about what is best to do. Many commentators do not read the maxim in this way, however. Étienne Gilson, for example, says that this maxim is "nothing more than a practical rule . . . , only an empirical rule of thumb required for use in everyday life to which we resign ourselves in the absence of theoretical certainty" (Gilson 1947, 243). And Jon Elster (1984, 54–65) takes the maxim to be a rule of thumb, although for reasons different from those of Gilson. In taking the maxim to be a rule of thumb Gilson and Elster make two mistakes. First, a rule of thumb is a first-order principle, one designed typically to save time, reduce the effect of bias, preserve valuable spontaneity, and, above all, minimize the cumulative bad effects of our limited knowledge. Descartes's second maxim, on the contrary, is a second-order rule, and its application presupposes that we have already reached a decision about what to do, whether by some rule *par provision* or in some other way. I will examine Gilson's and Elster's views below.

2. Second, and contrary to a common reading, this maxim is not restricted in its application, as a rule of thumb would be, to conditions in

which we lack time, relevant information, or, in general, certitude about what is objectively the best thing to do.[1] Descartes is explicit on this point. What he says is that we are to be firm and decisive *even* in the case of such opinions. The opinions he has in mind in the *Discourse*, of course, are admittedly doubtful first-order opinions about the truth of certain moral precepts of the first maxim and about how these apply to particular cases. But at the limit, a first-order opinion might be quite certain. The second maxim applies in either case. Typically, our first-order opinions are doubtful. And in the context of the *Discourse* it is only to doubtful opinions that the maxim is being applied, since, *ex hypothesi*, doubtful opinions are the only opinions we have; for the opinions directly in question include our first-order moral beliefs about good and bad, right and wrong—beliefs at the center of attention in the first maxim. What the second maxim enjoins is that we be firm, decisive, and constant, even when it is on these beliefs, in conjunction with other probable beliefs, that we rely. But it also enjoins us to be decisive, firm, and constant even when the beliefs we rely on are certain. Whether we are ever in such a situation, of course, is another matter.

I shall return to consider why this maxim is commonly thought to have a restricted application. But first we need to get clear what it means to be firm and decisive in our actions.

3. Let us begin with an ideal case, one in which we know for certain *(a)* what is the best thing to do in our present circumstances and *(b)* that the time for action is right now. Examples that would come close to this ideal, assuming appropriate background knowledge, would be my taking an aspirin to alleviate an excruciating headache or my not stepping on another's gouty toes. In such cases, on Descartes's view, we will freely do what we judge is best forthwith, without hesitation or second thoughts.[2] Where my

---

1. In interpreting this maxim, we may ascribe to Descartes the view that there are objectively correct answers to such questions, whether or not these answers fall within our cognitive competence.

2. At the conclusion of his presentation of the *morale par provision*, Descartes summarizes: "For since our will tends to pursue or avoid only what our intellect represents as good or bad, we need only to judge well in order to act well, and to judge as well as we can in order to do our best" (6:27; 1:125). Commenting on this passage in a letter to Mersenne written in late May 1637, he writes: "You reject my statement that in order to do well it is sufficient to judge well; yet it seems to me that the common scholastic doctrine is that 'the will does not tend towards evil except in so far as it is presented to it by the intellect under some aspect of goodness'—so that if the intellect never represented anything to the will as good without its actually being so, the will could never go wrong in its choice. But the intellect often represents different things to the will at the same time; and that is why they say 'I see and praise the better, but I follow the worse,' which applies only to weak minds" (1:366; 3:56). He expresses the same position later in his replies to the second set of objections to his *Meditations*: "The will of a thinking thing is drawn voluntarily and freely (for this is the essence of will), but nevertheless inevitably, towards a clearly known good" (7:166; 2:117).

best judgment amounts to certain knowledge, my will effortlessly follows my judgment. I judge that my taking the aspirin is the very best thing to do in the present circumstances and, firmly and decisively, I take the aspirin.

In the ideal case there is no slippage between the intellect and the will; the will executes what the intellect illuminates to be best. The second maxim asks that we approximate this ideal even in the nonideal case in which full intellectual illumination is absent. We are to make up in volitional effort what is lacking in intellectual certainty. To be firm and decisive in the non-ideal case is to judge as well as possible and to treat the resultant opinion as if it were clear and certain. In correspondence Descartes gives the example of a man who may starve if he does not eat but whose will is para-lyzed by the worry that the only food available may be poisoned. Suppose the food is poisoned. In this case his eating it would be quite bad. People can dwell on possibilities of this kind and become anxious to the point of not taking decisive action. One who adheres to the second maxim, how-ever, is guided by his estimate of what is probably the best thing to do— eat or starve. Once he judges that the food is very probably safe, he acts decisively, just as if he knew this for certain. What his judgment may lack in certainty his will makes up for in resolve and constancy.

4. Being firm, decisive, and constant, however, does not rule out chang-ing our minds. We are to be firm, decisive, and constant in *following* an opin-ion, once we have judged as well as we can, given our limited information and the constraints of time; but this does not imply that we must be firm and constant in this very judgment, which, in the light of new information, might then be seen as mistaken. Descartes makes this point in a clarifying letter for Alphonse Pollot.

> If I had said without qualification that one should hold to opinions that one has once decided to follow, even though they are doubtful, I should indeed have been no less to blame than if I had said that one should be opinionated and stubborn; because holding to an opinion is the same as being persistent in a judgement that one had made. But I said something quite different. I said that one must be decisive in one's actions even when one was undecided in one's judgements, and that one should fol-low the most doubtful opinions with no less constancy than if they were quite certain. By this I meant that once one has settled on opinions which one judges doubtful—that is, once one has decided that there are no others that one judges better or more certain—one should act on them with no less constancy than if one knew that they were the best, which indeed they are when so considered. There is no danger that this constancy in action will lead us further into error or vice, since there can be error only in the intellect which, I am supposing, remains free

throughout and regards what is doubtful as doubtful. Moreover, I apply this rule[3] mainly to actions in life which admit of no delay, and I use it only provisionally [*par provision*], intending to change my opinions as soon as I can find better, and to lose no opportunity of looking for them. (2:34–35; 3:97)

Indeed, in taking up inquiry he is taking advantage of the opportunity to discover a more perfect morality than that to which he is presently, if sincerely, committed.

5. Although the second maxim applies whether or not our practical judgment is certain, as I have remarked above, commentators often take it to apply only when our judgment is not certain. That only doubtful moral opinions are in play in the *morale par provision* lends itself to this interpretation. So too does Descartes's illustration. In adhering to the second maxim, Descartes says, "I would be imitating a traveller who, upon finding himself lost in a forest, should not wander about turning this way and that, and still less stay in one place, but should keep walking as straight as he can in one direction, never changing it for slight reasons even if mere chance made him choose it in the first place; for in this way, even if he does not go exactly where he wishes, he will at least end up in a place where he is likely to be better off than in the middle of a forest" (6:24; 1:123).

The traveler chooses in a condition of ignorance, ignorance specifically about the quickest safe way out of the forest. He is, however, intelligent and only comparatively ignorant. In Descartes's example, on its most natural construction, he wants to survive; he believes there is a very low probability he will survive if he remains where he is, because, among other things, there is little chance of being rescued; he believes there is a slightly greater probability that he will survive if he wanders about, for in this way he might by chance find himself on the edge of the forest; he believes there is a high probability he will survive if he walks in a straight line. If survival has a utility of 1 and he can reasonably assign probabilities of, say, .1 to surviving by staying put, .2 to surviving by wandering about, and .7 to surviving by walking in a straight line, then the rational choice is clearly the last, which has an expected utility of .7, as compared to .1 or .2. The maxim does not imply that this decision is irrevocable; it holds only that it would be irrational for the traveler to deviate from his chosen course for slight reasons; it does not say that he should not deviate for clear and evident reasons, such as a well-marked trail or signpost might provide. It requires solely

---

3. "This rule" must be understood to refer to the specific practical rule to be followed, not to the second maxim itself. For example, in the case of a man lost in the forest, the rule would be to walk in a straight line.

and simply that he ought to continue walking in a straight line once he has deliberated and decided that, relative to the information he has available, that is the best thing to do, the action with the highest probability of a successful outcome. But of course he ought to be firm and constant and to continue walking in a straight line, as if he knew for certain that the probability of success was 1. Certainty at the level of first-order opinion is just a special case.

A further reason why the second maxim might be thought to be restricted to choice not grounded in certainty is that only when we lack certainty is it possible that we may not act as we judge best. But at the time of the *Discourse* Descartes's view is represented by the following letter to Denis Mesland of May 2, 1644, setting out the view expressed in the *Meditations* and in an earlier letter to Marin Mersenne in 1637: "For it seems to me certain that a great light in the intellect is followed by a great inclination in the will; so that if we see very clearly that a thing is good for us, it is very difficult—and, on my view, impossible, as long as one continues in the same thought—to stop the course of our desire." Yet the letter continues: "But the nature of the soul is such that it hardly attends for more than a moment to a single thing; hence, as soon as our attention turns from the reasons which show us that the thing is good for us, and we merely keep in our memory the thought that it appeared desirable to us, we can call up before our mind some other reason to make us doubt it, and so suspend our judgement, and perhaps even form a contrary judgement" (4:116; 3:233–34).

Descartes's view, then, is that a clear and distinct perception that some plan of action is best does not alone assure firmness and constancy of the will beyond the moment of this perception.[4] Even if we do not have the liberty of perversity, we still need the second maxim. It would read as follows: Once we have deliberated and decided on the best plan of action, we must

---

4. If, however, one ascribes to Descartes a conception of free will according to which we have the power not to do what we clearly and distinctly judge to be best, then there is even less reason to object to the universal applicability of the second maxim. But the reason to ascribe this conception to Descartes is found only in a single letter. In it Descartes writes: "For it is always open to us to hold back from pursuing a clearly known good, or from admitting a clearly perceived truth, provided we consider it a good thing to demonstrate the freedom of our will by so doing" (4:173; 3:245). Anthony Kenny argues that the precise date and intended recipient are not known and that this fact alone is one reason for us not to place great weight on this passage. Kenny goes on to argue that Descartes does not strictly allow what he calls the liberty of perversity. Alquié, on the other hand, thinks that this letter clearly indicates that Descartes changed his view about free will. My claim that the second maxim applies universally, however, does not depend on which of these accounts of free will we ascribe to Descartes. Both writers agree, of course, about what conception of free will Descartes endorsed at the time of the *Discourse* (see Kenny 1972; Alquié 1987, chap. 14). Relevant to this topic also is a letter to Elizabeth, dated September 15, 1645, on the need for good habits.

adhere to this decision throughout the period of its execution, just as if at every moment we clearly and distinctly apprehended that it was the best.

6. There is no reason to deny, then, that the maxim applies regardless of the confidence we have in our opinion. It is, however, restricted in a different way. It applies only on the condition that our opinion is as well-considered as time and accessible information permit. Then and only then does it enjoin that we stick to a course of action. "Since in everyday life we must often act without delay, it is a most certain truth that when it is not in our power to discern the truest opinions, we must follow the most probable" (6:25; 1:123).

A detail should be noted. As stated, the maxim requires that when necessary we act without delay, but, presumably, only when further delay would be counterproductive. After all, many cases admit some delay. And although assessing whether a delay is reasonable is no doubt a delicate matter, one that requires that we be good judges of how much time we should spend deliberating or trying to extend our informational base, we need to interpret the maxim to allow for this complexity. Reasonable first-order judgments, then, are reasonable along two dimensions: they combine a reasonable judgment about how much time to give to deliberation and a reasonable judgment about what is best to do, given the information accessible within that interval.

Now, the maxim allows reasonable decisions to be in some respects arbitrary. "Even when no opinions appear more probable than any others, we must still adopt some; and having done so we must then regard them not as doubtful, from a practical point of view, but as most true and certain, on the grounds that the reason which made us adopt them is itself true and certain" (6:25; 1:123). Although the traveler's choice of direction may be arbitrary, he is then to act just *as if* this choice had been based on good evidence. The maxim itself, to be sure, gives no guidance about how initially to decide or how long to deliberate. It says only that we must be firm and constant once we have deliberated well and decided.

7. Descartes justifies his adopting the second maxim by an appeal to the most certain truth "that when it is not in our power to discern the truest opinions,[5] we must follow the most probable." Descartes's view is that our own reason demands that when we cannot know for certain what is the best thing to do, "we must follow the most probable." The view might be set out this way, in terms of first-order and second-order evaluation. A first-order question might be: Should I eat this food? With respect to this question, I am unable entirely to eliminate the possibility that this food is poi-

---

5. "That is to say, those that would be *absolutely speaking* the best" (Gilson 1947, 244).

soned. If I could have certain knowledge, then I would freely choose to eat, my will being in this case determined to follow my clear and evident perception of the good. As it happens, I cannot entirely eliminate this possibility. If I cannot attain certainty at this level, I can attain certainty at a higher level. If I cannot know for certain that x is the best thing to do here and now, yet I reasonably believe that x is probably the best thing to do, then I can know for certain that I ought to do x. We move from first-order uncertainty to second-order certainty. What we may know for certain is that the best thing to do in conditions of uncertainty is to do that which we reasonably believe is most probably the best.

Descartes's thought is that if we always knew for certain what is best in every circumstance of life, we would unfailingly do that thing. As rational agents, we would then all be firm and decisive in our actions. But we are not like this. Nor is Descartes, the pure inquirer, like this, for he is a person with a life to lead while he meditates. What is a pure inquirer to do? What are *we* to do? Dither, wallow in uncertainty, starve? Self-evidently not. While we may not be able to rid ourselves of doubts at the level of our first-order judgments, we can rationally resolve the practical question, What should we do? at the second level. If I can doubt at the first level whether x is the best thing to do, I can resolve this doubt *as a practical matter* at the second level; at this level, if I reasonably judge that x is most probably the best thing to do, then I know that x is, from a practical point of view and from the point of view of reason, the best I can possibly do in the circumstances. Even if I should, *per accidens*, do what is in fact the best thing to do while violating the second maxim, I do not escape remorse and regret, nor do I act well.

What could stand in the way of our doing what we judge to be most probably the best thing to do? We might dwell on the possibility that we may be making a first-order mistake, that doing x may in fact be bad; or we might dwell on the desirable aspects of the alternative after we have rejected it. Such second thoughts are the cause of irresolution, weakness, indecisiveness. They are contrary to reason, since they are the dispositions of someone who does not take to heart the truth on which Descartes's maxim is based, namely, that when certainty is not in the offing, we must make do with probability, even in the case where the probability is quite low. And truth is seldom if ever in the offing. First, we often lack sufficient information to determine what is in fact the best thing to do. Second, even when sufficient information is accessible, we often do not have the cognitive capacity to make the best use of it. Third, we typically lack sufficient time to make the best use of what information we have ready to hand. Finally, time itself is of the essence; the ends we seek are indexed to time and the necessary means to these ends indexed to an earlier time. So to the question, What is the best thing to do? is added the further question, What is the optimal duration for deliberation? In the theoretical domain of pure inquiry, we have the luxury of delaying as long as it takes to arrive at certain knowledge. In everyday life, by contrast, we have no such luxury. And here, Descartes argues, our own reason requires that we own up to the fact of these epistemic, informational, and temporal limits on our practical reasoning.

8. So far I have considered the second maxim mainly as it applies to action in the immediate present. In this case, it gives the rational response to the common human fault of irresolution in the face of first-order uncertainty concerning what should be done here and now. But this maxim has a more general application. It also applies when we deliberate about what to do at some future time, or about a plan of action that will take time to carry out, or about a general rule of action to be followed in certain types of circumstance. Significantly, Descartes's own choice in the first maxim, to follow local custom and example, involves a precommitment to such general rules.

Descartes's traveler lost in the forest cannot determine for certain which is the most expeditious route to his intended destination; indeed, he cannot say of any particular route that it is probably the most expeditious. On the other hand, among the alternative plans of staying put, wandering around this way and that, or walking in a straight line, the last is most likely to improve his position and move him toward his destination. Even if the direction he takes is not selected as probably the most expeditious—indeed, even if it is selected arbitrarily or only for the weakest reasons—continuing to walk in this direction is most probably the best thing to do in the circumstances.

How, precisely, are we to understand this illustration? The correct answer, I believe, is straightforwardly. Descartes takes himself to be such a traveler; while engaged in pure enquiry, he is a traveler in everyday life. The general rule for those who travel in terrain where the best path has no certain marks is to choose the most probably correct path and to stay on it. Staying on the path is precisely what following reason in conditions of uncertainty amounts to. Indeed, staying on a path of which the traveler knows for certain that it is best is what following reason in conditions of certainty amounts to. But following reason in conditions of uncertainty is rather more difficult and requires a special act of will to control the sort of irresolution and vacillation that attends the condition of uncertainty. We are to make up with strength of will what we lack in cognitive competence.

9. The example can, however, lead one to a different interpretation of the second maxim. At one point in his *Commentary*, as I remarked above,

Gilson writes that "considered from the perspective proper to the *Discourse*," the second maxim is "nothing more than a practical rule . . . , only an empirical rule of thumb [*procédé*] required for use in everyday life to which we resign ourselves in the absence of theoretical certainty" (Gilson 1947, 243). While we must, if we are lost in a forest, resign ourselves to a rule of thumb as recommended in the example, the general maxim under which we subsume this rule is not itself a rule of thumb, nor is it based on empirical considerations. It would be a mistake, therefore, to see a direct analogy between the traveler's rule of thumb and the second maxim itself, both being provisional in the same sense. It is not as if Descartes's decision, expressed in the second maxim, relies on the probabilistic judgment that resolution is the best general policy. It is true, of course, that the rule of thumb for travelers lost in a forest could be abandoned under conditions of certainty. If the traveler comes on a clearly marked trail out of the forest, he may alter his present course and follow a new one. And it is also true that if Descartes were to achieve certainty in the science of ethics, he could abandon his earlier decision to follow custom and good example and instead follow the clearly lit path of his reason.[6] Nonetheless, the second maxim is itself not based on empirical knowledge of probabilities. Nor is resolution recommended strictly on the basis of its being the most probably effective means to an agent's intended goals. It is not resolution itself, after all, that is maximally useful to the agent in conditions of uncertainty. Resolution without good judgment is not useful. To be sure, good judgment without the strength of will to follow it is not maximally useful either. Both are needed. But the rule of reason, namely, to follow our best judgment, is not itself empirically based or justified in terms of its being the most probably effective practical rule. It is, as Descartes says, self-evident.

10. Jon Elster, guided, it seems, by the traveler example, reads Descartes's second maxim as an empirically justified procedure for achieving rationality by indirect means. Elster sees Descartes as a critic of so-called "instant rationality." The question posed is this: Should we try to decide

6. I do not mean to suggest that even at the time of the *Discourse* Descartes believed such a science of first-order ethics was possible. He certainly did not think that in matters of ordinary prudence, where the crucial governing beliefs are beliefs about future consequences of action, we could have clear and distinct knowledge of what is best to do. And for the same reasons we must lack clear and distinct knowledge in the application of some moral rules. In his letter to Hyperaspistes, dated August 1641, he expresses a view that it is only reasonable to suppose he always held. "It would indeed be desirable to have as much certainty for the conduct of our lives as is needed for the acquisition of knowledge; but it is easily shown that in such matters so much is not to be sought or hoped for. This can be shown *a priori* from the fact that a human, being a composite entity, is naturally corruptible, while the mind is incorruptible and immortal. It can be shown even more easily *a posteriori* from the consequences that would follow" (3:422; 3:189). Here he gives the example, cited above, of the man who would starve if he refused to act until he had certain knowledge that his food was not poisoned.

on every occasion of choice what is the best thing to do—the thesis of instant rationality—or should we, rather, commit ourselves to follow certain rules for certain circumstances? He interprets Descartes as advocating rules of thumb by arguing that the policy of instant rationality is not, all things considered, cost effective.[7] There is little in the *Discourse* itself, however, to suggest that Descartes's aims to reject instant rationality.[8] In his example of the traveler in the forest Descartes does say that the traveler would be better off walking than pondering. More generally, he says that "we must often act without delay." Now, if instant rationality were the policy of not acting until we achieved certainty, then it would be, by Descartes's lights, about the worst policy we could have. But if the policy of instant rationality is that of trying to decide each particular case as it arises rather than relying on standing rules that are insensitive to the particulars of every case, then the second maxim itself does not favor the one policy over the other. Perhaps it is better for travelers to adopt a standard policy for occasions when they are lost in a forest, but there are other contexts of action where we may have no standing policies or where having standing policies would not serve us better than trying to evaluate the situation. Standing policies no doubt save time, but it is an open question, so far as the second maxim itself is concerned, whether the time saved might not have been better spent evaluating the case at hand before acting.

Descartes's other principal examples, in connection with the second maxim, do not give secondary rules a prominent role. In one case, a man has before him food of which he has not the slightest reason to be suspicious, and the question is whether he should satisfy his hunger by eating it. Descartes says that he should do so without vacillation, even though he believes it is possible that the food is poisoned. In another case, a man should travel on the road that is least frequented by robbers and do so without vacillation once he has determined that it is probably the safest route. In both cases—as in example of the traveler lost in the forest—the point is the same: we are to do with dispatch, with firmness and resolution, what we judge to be the best thing to do, even though we acknowledge that our judgment about what is best may be in error. Whether we should adopt

---

7. This discussion is found in Elster 1984. Elster offers two "Cartesian" arguments in favor of rules of thumb. The first is that "a continuous evaluation and reevaluation requires so much time that it can be expected to more than outweigh the time gained by the improved direction that issues from the evaluation," and the second is that "not only [is] the *time* spent getting out of the forest . . . increased if the traveller constantly stops to reevaluate the situation, but . . . instant rationality actually makes the *path* itself longer than it would have been along an arbitrarily (or at least along an optimally) chosen straight line" (Elster 1984, 57, 60).

8. "Cartesian" arguments of these kinds can be found, however, in the *Passions of the Soul*. There he argues, for example, that our having standard policies for specific sorts of circumstances is optimal, because it saves us from lost opportunity costs.

standing policies for certain kinds of circumstances is a matter to be decided in the same general way that a traveler decides to follow a straight course through the forest.

Sometimes, to be sure, we should firmly and resolutely adhere to a rule, but when this is so, it is because we had judged earlier that, all things considered, the best thing to do if we anticipate finding ourselves in certain situations is to adopt a general rule of conduct. In other cases, it may be that no rule to which we are in this way precommitted applies. Then we must try to determine, so far as time permits, what is most probably the best thing to do and then do that thing, with the resolution of one who had certain knowledge of it. In either case, the emphasis falls on what the maxim presupposes, namely, that the initial decision was best in the circumstances and that these circumstances have not changed in any relevant respect.

11. In concluding his brief commentary on this maxim Descartes remarks: "By following this maxim I could free myself from all the regrets [*repentirs*] and remorse [*remords*] which usually trouble the consciences of those weak and faltering spirits who allow themselves to set out on some supposedly good course of action which later, in their inconstancy, they judge to be bad" (6:25; 1:123). Self-evidently, Descartes says,[9] reason demands *(a)* that we judge as well as we can and *(b)* that we act in accordance with our very best judgment (while recognizing that this may be objectively in error). In the domain of practice, once we have met these two conditions, we have done as well as we possibly can. Having this demand embedded in our conative and affective dispositions is what being firm and resolute amounts to. And this, in turn, frees us, not from sadness in general, but from the burden of remorse and repentance. This is so because remorse and repentance, on Descartes's view, are the forms that irresoluteness takes retrospectively; they are the passions that attend second-thoughts. If we are firm, decisive and resolute, we do not have such second thoughts. This is not to say that in deciding to take the road that is probably the safest we forthwith become absolutely certain there we will meet no robbers. Not having second thoughts about how we should act does not involve any kind of self-deception about our liability to error. Nonetheless, being firm, decisive, and resolute, in the sense Descartes intends, is to have the same

---

9. In the *Discourse* he says that this is a most certain truth; in the letter of 1641 to Hyperaspistes, discussing the man who hesitates to eat on the off chance that his food is poisoned, Descartes writes: "Suppose further that he could not obtain any food that was not poisoned, and that his nature was such that fasting was beneficial to him; none the less, if the food had appeared harmless and healthy, and fasting appeared likely to have its usual harmful effects, he would be bound to eat the food and thus follow the apparently beneficial course of action rather than the actually beneficial one. *This is so self-evident to all that I am surprised that anyone could think otherwise*" (3:423; 3:189; my italics).

affective and conative dispositions connected to one's judgment of what is probably the best as one would have if all one's first-order evaluations of action were *les plus vraies*.[10]

Contrary to some commentators, I believe we should take Descartes's remark not as expressing the point or rationale of the second maxim but as pointing out the effect of our taking the maxim to heart. For when we have met its demands—when we have made first-order decisions with care and without undue delay and then stuck to them as if we were absolutely certain of them—we have acted as well as we possibly could; as rational agents we cannot ask more of ourselves. And since we cannot reasonably ask more, we should be free of regret and remorse, even if we were to discover retrospectively that our first-order judgment was mistaken.

In the ideal case, of course, we have certain knowledge that *x* is the best thing to do and we chose to do it. Here we have both perfect judgment and perfect willing, and there can be no occasion for remorse or repentance.[11] Owing to the imperfection of our cognitive powers (itself a reflection of our composite nature), we often cannot determine with certainty what is objectively the best thing to do; we do not always have perfect judg-

---

10. Descartes returns to examine the passion of irresolution in the *Passions of the Soul*: "an excess of irresolution results from too great a desire to do well and from a weakness of the intellect, which contains only a lot of confused notions, and none that are clear and distinct. That is why the remedy against such excess is to become accustomed to form certain and determinate judgements regarding everything that comes before us, and to believe that we always do our duty when we do what we judge to be best, even though our judgement may perhaps be a very bad one" (11:460; 1:390–91).

11. Of course, there can be plenty of occasion for regret or sorrow in the sense that the world may be filled with unavoidable evils. Even if I could be absolutely certain that I ought to do *x*, it may still occur that *x* turns out to be a contributing cause of some outcome, *y*, which is evil. I may judge, indeed, judge rightly, that such evil was in the circumstances absolutely unavoidable, but it is nonetheless evil. If, in order to save my fellow spelunkers from drowning in the rising water, I will have to blast out a member of the party who, in no danger of drowning himself, is stuck in the only available exit from the cave, I may rightly judge that blasting is the best thing to do in the circumstances. The death of my innocent friend is an evil to which I cannot be indifferent; such evil is the stuff of tragedy. But this evil of which I am the instrument, although the occasion for sorrow or sadness of some kind, is not the proper occasion of *remords* and *repentirs* in the Cartesian sense. "Remorse of conscience," Descartes writes in the *Passions of the Soul*, "is a kind of sadness which results from our doubting that something we are doing, or have done, is good. It necessarily presupposes doubt" (11:464; 1:392). Repentance results from our believing that we have done some evil deed (11:472; 1:396). Descartes argues that all these passions—remorse, repentance, and irresolution—have their proper uses, but they may also be improper or excessive. The remedy against them is the same, "to accustom ourselves to form firm and determinate judgments . . . and to believe that we always do our duty when we do what we judge to be best, even though our judgment may perhaps be a very bad one" (11:460; 1:391). We feel remorse when we doubt that what we do is good, and we feel repentance when we believe what we did was evil. We may feel both sentiments in connection with the very same action, on Descartes's analysis, for so long as we are in doubt, we see our action as at once good in one respect and evil in another and dwell in an anxiety of irresolution. These passions are forms of anxiety that derive pointlessly from

ment. On the other hand we do have the power to will perfectly, as in the ideal case. So even if we cannot overcome our finitude and achieve perfection in our judgment, we can achieve perfection in our willing. The point of the second maxim is to set this standard; it is the standard for both the ideal of perfect judgment and the nonideal case.

It must be understood, however, that if—in the interval between our decision to act and our action—we have good reason to reconsider and possibly to revise our judgment, then, time permitting, we should do so. The rule applies only to the cases in which there is no good reason to revise our judgment. It holds that if there is no rational basis for doing so, then there is no rational basis (in our judgment) for revising our will or intention. In the forest example, I am acting irrationally if I change my direction without express reason for changing my prior judgment. From a practical point of view, I am to act as if my prior judgment were certain. That there is a lapse of time between the time of acting and time of the relevant judgment is not itself a reason for reconsidering or revising the judgment. What such a lapse may occasion, however, is my inability to recall with sufficient vivacity the reasons that originally led me to judge as I did, so that I may be tempted on the occasion of action by "some slight reason" or impulse to think my prior judgment was flawed, which may give rise in turn to the illusion that I should reconsider and possibly revise my intention. The rule holds simply that I am bound by those of my past rational intentions that apply to actions in the present.[12]

We are, then, to deliberate as well as we can within the time allowed and henceforth honor our rational prior intention. Descartes goes on to say that in acting in this way we shall avoid remorse (*remords*) and regret (*repentir*). The terms *remords* and *repentirs* are understood by Descartes in a special way, which the natural translations "remorse" and "regret" may not capture. Both derive from irresolution in judgment, where the tantalizing but vague thought that I might hit upon a better solution prevents me from acting decisively. In advance of action, it is my fear of mistake or error that prevents my definitely resolving the matter as well as I can, where "mistake"

---

our refusal to accept our limitations as human agents, particularly limitations on our knowledge and our time, and our consequent failure to make determinate judgments in the absence of full information. In his discussion of Descartes's second maxim Elster writes: "It is hard to read the correspondence of Descartes without being struck by this 'grand seigneur' aspect of his character; never explain, never apologize" (Elster 1984, 60). There is some truth in this remark, but the comment as it stands does not take into proper account Descartes's insistence that we must also judge as well as we can.

12. Descartes does not address the case in which my prior judgment was not my best judgment and my prior intention not, in the defined sense, rational. If without reason I reconsider and then revise my judgment, I may in fact judge better and, correspondingly, improve the prospects of my course of conduct. Do I act rationally or not in such a case?

and "error" are given a comparatively objective or even absolute sense. Remorse and regret refer to painful reflections arising after having made some mistake or error. Suppose I retrospectively judge that I made an error in judgment, in consequence of which I have failed to attain a good that (I erroneously believe) was within my grasp. For "weak and faltering spirits" this is the occasion for regret and remorse.[13] Fear of error or mistake, prospectively, and remorse and regret, retrospectively, derive equally from an unrealistic and effective refusal to accept our finitude and the imperfection of our power of judgment. In sum, we act irrationally when our intention does not match our best judgment, and our regrets are irrational so long as we have not acted irrationally.

12. Looking back at this maxim from the viewpoint of Descartes's later work, we see it as the nascent form of the fundamental principle of virtue. Descartes says as much in his important letter to Elizabeth, where, expressly referring back to the *morale par provision* of the *Discourse*, he tells her that the second rule of living the best life possible is "to have a firm and constant resolution to carry out whatever reason recommends without being diverted by passion or appetite. Virtue, I believe, consists precisely in firmness in this resolution; though I do not know that anyone has ever so described it" (4:265; 3:257–58). By this time Descartes had also argued that being virtuous and living well are the same. The point to make here, however, is that the second maxim of the *morale par provision* not only survives further critical reflection, it emerges as a central part of the principle of virtue in Descartes's final morality.[14]

13. As Descartes writes in the *Passions of the Soul*, "The weakest souls of all are those whose will is not determined in this way to follow such judgement, but constantly allows itself to be carried away by present passions. The latter, being often opposed to one another, pull the will first to one side and then to the others, thus making it battle against itself and so putting the soul in the most deplorable state possible. Thus, when fear represents death as an extreme evil which can be avoided only by flight, while ambition on the other hand depicts the dishonour of flight as an evil worse than death, these two passions jostle the will in opposite ways; and since the will obeys first the one and then the other, it is continually opposed to itself, and so it renders the soul enslaved and miserable" (11:367; 1:347).

14. In the final statement of this *morale* Descartes writes in the *Passions of the Soul*: "Thus I believe that true generosity, which causes a person's self-esteem to be as great as it may legitimately be, has only two components. The first consists in his knowing that nothing truly belongs to him but his freedom to dispose his volitions, and that he ought to be praised or blamed for no other reason than his using this freedom well or badly. The second consists in his feeling within himself a firm and constant resolution to use it well—that is, never to lack the will to undertake and carry out whatever he judges to be best. To do that is to pursue virtue in a perfect manner" (11:445–46; 1:384). The first part is anticipated in the third maxim of the provisional morality, as we shall see; the second part is a development of the second maxim. With respect to the second and third maxims, then, there is no radical difference between Descartes's final or mature ethics and his early ethics.

CHAPTER THREE

The Third Maxim

1. IT may appear from the third maxim of his *morale par provision* that Descartes sought to align himself with the moral doctrines of Justus Lipsius and Guillaume Du Vair, neo-Stoics of the period, who were developing a line of moral thought succinctly formulated by Epictetus: "Do not seek to have events happen as you want them to, but instead want them to happen as they do happen, and your life will go well" (Epictetus 1983, 13). "My third maxim," Descartes writes, "was to try to master myself rather than fortune, and change my desires rather than the order of the world. In general I would become accustomed to believing that nothing lies entirely within our power except our thoughts, so that after doing our best in dealing with matters external to us, whatever we fail to achieve is absolutely impossible so far as we are concerned" (6:25; 1:123).[1] This maxim differs noticeably from the famous Epictetan injunction, which strikes a note of quietism or resignation. Descartes's maxim is, however, quite close Epictetus's interpreter Du Vair, who writes in *The Moral Philosophy of the Stoics*:

> When we doe anything, though we doe it neuer so wisely, take all aduantages, chuse all opportunities, vse all possible diligence: yet for all this we must know that the greatest part of the euent is altogether ouermsastered by Fortune. Wee are lords and masters of our counsels and determinations, but all the rest dependeth vpon other matters which are not in our power. And therefore we can doe no more but vndertake a mat-

---

1. Descartes gives a nice commentary on this maxim in his letter to Reneri for Pollot, April or May 1638. See also Gilson 1947, 247–48.

ter with wisedome, pursue it with hope, and be readie to suffer whateuer shall happen with patience. If good enterprises haue bad successe, the answere which the noble man of Persia made, may serue for an excuse to all them which are wise, but vnfortunat. One was desirous to know of him wherefore (seeing that he knew him to bee a very wise, & valiant gentleman) his affayres went no better forward. Because (quoth hee) in my affayres I can but giue good counsell, that is all I can doe, the successe belongeth altogether vnto us, that is, if wee attempt nothing but with a good end, and follow it not but by lawfull and honest means. (Du Vair 1951, 127)

The striking similarity between this passage (and many like it in Lipsius and Du Vair) and Descartes's third maxim should not, however, lead us to the view that Descartes simply borrowed his maxim from the neo-Stoic texts with which he was familiar, texts ready to hand and suited to the temperament of a pure inquirer. In the first place, it was very far from Descartes's style as a thinker to be tempted to put together the congenial thoughts of others in a syncretic pastiche. Moreover, we know from the central role that Epictetus's celebrated distinction plays in Descartes's later writings on ethics that this maxim was not one he adopted casually, nor, I would add, primarily as an aid to his research.[2] Yet if we are not to see this maxim as simply taken over from, say, Du Vair, do we not need some more internal or systematic explanation for its inclusion? One might reply that this is too much to ask. As readers of an autobiography described at one point as a fable, we should not expect the narrative to mirror a rigorous sequence of thought. To be sure, the tone of this maxim is more personal than that of the second maxim. Since the maxim seems more personal, it may also seem more optional. After all, it was not in fact necessary for Descartes to become a Stoic sage, or even some reasonable approximation of one, in order for him to get on with his project. And while we may grant that the Stoic ideal appealed to him, this would not account for any systematic connection between this maxim and the two preceding. Is it, then, required to complete Descartes's *morale par provision*?

2. As to the much debated question of Descartes's intellectual indebtedness to Stoic and neo-Stoic writers or of the degree to which he was a Stoic, it would be premature to consider it here. For a good discussion of the question, see D'Angers 1976. It will not be my aim to consider this question directly or as a special topic; I treat it indirectly and in the context of other issues throughout the remainder of the book. What we shall find, in sum, is that Descartes gives a definite rationale for Epictetus's distinction within the framework of his metaphysics, defines virtue in terms of what is entirely in our power, and makes virtue sufficient for happiness. On the non-Stoic side of the ledger, he rejects the traditional Stoic theory of the emotions, and he identifies happiness with contentment, not with virtue itself.

2. The second maxim, we have seen, is a second-order principle; it is also presented as self-evident. The third maxim is also a second-order principle; and if it is not quite self-evident, it is systematically connected with the second maxim in such a way as to justify it and its inclusion in the *morale par provision*. I say that these are second-order principles since they bind whatever might be the content of the precepts and values of our first-order morality. The third maxim would hold that, whatever our specific ends, we need to acknowledge that they are never entirely in our power; if we do not realize them despite out best efforts, we are not responsible. In this way, we might see the third maxim as a variant of the principle that *ought* implies *can*, which principle is neutral among competing accounts of what we ought to do or try to achieve. And being neutral, this maxim could be asserted with confidence by someone who was, comparatively speaking, in doubt about his own first-order moral convictions. Indeed, following this line of thought, one might be led to see the third maxim as self-evident or at least as a principle one must accept if one accepts any morality at all.

But this line of argument—even if we accept it as a plausible reconstruction of Descartes's thinking—would not get us all the way to the third maxim as formulated. Although it is neutral about what specific ends are worth pursuing, the maxim nonetheless requires that we regulate our desires in such a way that we do not, in some full-fledged or robust sense, desire those otherwise acceptable ends we seek under the guidance of our first-order morality.

3. An example may help. Suppose I become a doctor and join Les Médecins sans Frontières with the principal aim of bringing medical care to those in the world who are most in need. Suppose also that I think this is worth doing because I think that human suffering is an evil which cries out to be alleviated. These are thoughts included in my first-order morality. Perhaps, as I go about my task, I am often aware that I risk my life by exposing myself to disease and other dangers. Suppose I say the risk is worth it, since the end I am promoting is more important than my own life. The focus of my attention is on the evil to be eliminated. But whether it is eliminated is not entirely in my power. According to the third maxim, I should discipline my desiring in such a way that my desires—or my strongest desires—fix on what is in my power and not on the external good I am trying to achieve.

What this maxim requires is, on the face of it, paradoxical, if not self-defeating. It seems to demand that at one and the same time I desire and not desire to eliminate the evil of disease.[3] Certainly, part of the problem

---

3. The paradox is familiar from ancient Stoicism. The Stoics would classify the end, in this case, as at once indifferent and preferred. The only true good, they would argue—good in the sense of being in accord with nature or reason—is the manner of acting, not the state of affairs or end sought. Critics deny that the Stoics can successfully overcome the following diffi-

lies with the variable use of the term "desire." One line of thought is this: if I seek some end as itself choiceworthy and justify my acting in terms of its value, I can be said to desire it. According to another line of thought, I cannot rationally desire what I judge to be impossible. Both are present in Descartes's commentary on the third maxim. We may follow them up to the point where they seem to collide, starting with the second.

"Our will," Descartes writes,

> naturally tends to desire only what our intellect represents to it as some-how possible; and so it is certain that if we consider all external goods as equally beyond our power, we shall not regret the absence of goods which seem to be our birthright when we are deprived of them through no fault of our own, any more than we regret not possessing the kingdom of China or of Mexico. Making a virtue of necessity, as they say, we shall not de-sire to be healthy when ill or free when imprisoned, any more than we now desire to have bodies of a material as indestructible as diamond or wings to fly like the birds. (6:26; 1:124)

In speaking specifically of the will, in this passage, Descartes limits the dis-cussion to outcomes we might conceive as objects of our will, that is, to abstractly possible states of the world whose existence we could conceiv-ably influence through carrying out some plan of action, where the con-straints on conceivability are those of our own reason and experience. Thus, for any state of the world whose value is given, if we can trace no credible causal series of events that would both require some voluntary actions of our own and lead to that state, then this state is not a possible object of de-sire, or, more accurately, of rational desire. Granting that it would be a good thing for me to possess China, it would not be possible, or in any case, ra-tional for me to desire to do so, because there is no conceivable causal se-ries of events that would lead me from where I am to this outcome.

To return to my example, if I am trying to alleviate the suffering of oth-ers, I certainly believe that what I am doing increases the likelihood that

---

culty. If the end is not truly of positive value, then the claim that the manner of acting has positive value is empty. In the example of the doctor, it is as if disease is not an evil, but try-ing to eliminate it is nonetheless good. The objection is that this account does not make clear sense. Looking at the matter from the point of view of the doctor, he can make sense of his efforts only on the supposition that what he is trying to accomplish is genuinely worthwhile; he must presuppose that a world in which he conquers disease, even to some limited degree, is better than one in which he does not, where the difference in value is in part simply a func-tion of the reduced incidence of disease. If, on the other hand, he thought the end was with-out any value whatever and that a world with less disease was not a better world, he could hardly think that a world in which he sought to eliminate disease was better than one in which he did not, the disease itself being of no value or disvalue. There is no doubt that Descartes inherits a similar problem, which he does not successfully resolve in the *Discourse*. Whether he resolves it later, using the resources of his theory of the passions, remains to be seen.

those I am treating will be returned to good health and freed from pain. And my reason and experience tell me that I may expect many of my efforts to be successful. Suppose, however, that I come to believe in a particular case that whatever I do will have no effect on whether or not my patient is cured or delivered from pain. Then, if my desire follows reason, I no longer desire the good in question, while continuing to believe it is a good. It is just that under the stipulated conditions this good can no longer be an object of my will. So, following the first of the above lines of thought about desire, I cannot be said to desire that this patient of mine not suffer. In this particular case, the first line of thought about desire coincides with the second. Are there cases in which they would collide, as I have suggested?

If we follow the reasoning behind the third maxim, the answer will be that they collide only in cases in which I am confused. Consider the case in which I believe that a patient's return to health does depend on my continuing efforts to cure him. I acknowledge, of course, that his health does not depend only on my own efforts; it depends in part on other factors that are entirely beyond my control. Indeed, when I reflect on the case, I see clearly that the good in question, if it comes about at all, will do so as a consequence of causal factors of which some are entirely in my control and others not at all. This reflection, however, will bring the second case into line with the first. In the first case I come to believe that whether my patient returns to health depends entirely on factors beyond my control. In the second case I also know that after I have done what I believe is necessary and within my power, whether health is restored will depend on factors entirely beyond my power. Now, the good in question is a patient's health in both cases. In the first case, we see that this outcome cannot be an object of my will and hence cannot be an object of my desire. But the second case is essentially no different with respect to the patient's health, because once I have done everything I can, what happens next is not at all in my power. His health, should it be restored, is among things which happen that are, given what I have done, entirely beyond my control. It follows that my will cannot be directed at such objects, any more than it can be directed at health in the first case. And according to the first line of reasoning concerning desire, it follows that I cannot desire any objects that are not entirely in my power. I must judge things not entirely in my power as, relative to my will, absolutely impossible and, accordingly, as goods that I cannot rationally desire. In sum, a desire for an object not entirely in my power is an irrational desire. So far as we are perfectly rational, therefore, we desire nothing that is not entirely in our power. And so far as we are perfectly rational, "we shall not regret the absence of goods which seem to be our birthright when we are deprived of them through no fault of our own."

4. In the final analysis, things entirely in our power are restricted to our own acts of will. And the only goods entirely in our power are *good* acts of will. In his commentary and defense of the third maxim Descartes does not tell us what makes good acts of will good, although he suggests that an act of will is good when it is willed as a necessary condition within a causal series whose issue is something of value, say, the easing of another's pain. Moreover, he hints—it is only a hint—that such acts of will are good not simply as means but as having value in themselves. The hint lies in his remark that even without our achieving external goods whose value explains our undertakings, we should find contentment simply in our acting well; it lies also in his comment on the ideal of the Stoic sage. It takes long practice and meditation, he says, to take the third maxim fully to heart, however compelling it is to the intellect. In doing so

> lay the secret of those philosophers who in earlier times were able to escape from the dominion of fortune and, despite suffering and poverty, rival their gods in happiness. Through constant reflection upon the limits prescribed for them by nature, they became perfectly convinced that nothing was in their power but their thoughts, and this alone was sufficient to prevent them from being attracted to other things. Their mastery over their thoughts was so absolute that they had reason to count themselves richer, more powerful, freer and happier than other men who, because they lack this philosophy, never achieve such mastery over all their desires, however favoured by nature and fortune they may be. (6:26; 1:124)

The third maxim, then, is not simply borrowed from the Stoics. It is presented, rather, as the conclusion of an argument that takes as its point of departure the notions of rational desire and of what is impossible (relative to us). These concepts are neutral among competing first-order moralities, and if the argument succeeds, the self-mastery it commends could be defended as a desideratum within any morality. In this sense, this maxim could be defended as a formal demand. And like the second maxim, I should add, it is not to be conceived as provisional in a pejorative sense, that is, as a candidate for possible replacement with something better—something that might be discovered at the end of inquiry.

5. In addition to their being neutral among competing first-order moralities, the second and third maxims are presented to us as demands of our own reason, commended to our *bon sens* on the basis of clear conceptions and clear lines of argument. In fact, they would seem to meet the requirements of Descartes's method, the second maxim being declared self-evident, the third being deduced from clear and evident concepts. Beyond this, the sec-

ond and third maxims share an important common feature; both are parasitic on the idea of a correct first-order morality. Here they too become vulnerable to the Pyrrhonist's weapons. The Pyrrhonist argues that although there are correct moral directives and correct answers to moral problems, what appears correct to us is determined not by what is correct in some absolute sense but rather by socializing forces that vary from culture to culture and that seem to swing free from the moral facts. Whether this argument weakens the defenses of either the second or third maxims depends on what these maxims presuppose. They do presuppose that there is a correct first-order morality. But the Pyrrhonist argument shares this presupposition. The question is this: Do these maxims also presuppose that we can in principle gain genuine knowledge of the correct directives and correct answers to practical problems, at least on some occasions? If they do, the Pyrrhonist argument is a threat even to them.

Descartes's answer to this question, I believe, would run along the following lines. First, the Pyrrhonist argument may succeed in undermining our commonsense or naive view that our deepest moral convictions amount to knowledge at the level of theory, but it does not or need not succeed in undermining our confidence in them at the level of practice. Second, since we can expect to gain epistemic access to the true moral directives at the end of methodic inquiry, we may look forward to meeting the Pyrrhonist's argument then at the level of theory. For the moment, however, confidence is sufficient—sufficient, that is, for the second and third maxims to be applicable. To illustrate the need for confidence, consider our doctor once more.

Even if I am enlightened and subscribe to the third maxim, so that what I will is entirely in my own power, nonetheless what accounts for my acts of will is my conviction that another's suffering is a real evil. If I lost all confidence in this conviction, I would have to see my own acts of will as pointless, however much they may be entirely in my power. Moreover, if it is true, as Descartes hints, that my own contentment follows on the heels of my doing all entirely in my power to alleviate your suffering, this too is conditional on my conviction that what I am doing is worthwhile, which is conditional on my confidence in my conviction that your suffering is an evil. A point that is scarcely discernible in the *Discourse* but which comes into prominence in later writings is that acting well, as I have described it, is virtue, the supreme good in Descartes's developed theory. And he argues later that what gives the sweetest and most durable contentment is our awareness of our own virtue. If Descartes is right, then even amid the most trying and uncomfortable circumstances, my consciousness will be suffused with the highest and most solid contentment that a human being can feel. Still, the focus of my attention is on the evil to be eliminated, not on my own virtue or on my own contentment. But it is crucial both to my contentment and to my conception of my supreme good that the evil I seek to eliminate is a genuine evil. If truly it is not a real evil, because in truth there is no real distinction between good and evil, then I am deluded, and my virtue is compromised—one might be inclined to say it is bankrupt. If I am right, on the other hand, and there is a real distinction between good and evil, then my virtue is transparently genuine. It is important for the theory of virtue itself that this evil be real, for it is a mark of my virtue—indeed, it is constitutive of my virtue—not only that I stick to my task but that I judge the end to be worth promoting. The point, I concede, is delicate, since we need not insist on moral infallibility in this area in order to ground a theory of virtue. But we do need a theory that shows that, in favorable conditions of judgment, when I take something to be a real good or a real evil, I am at least following the scent of true good and evil.

How can I be confident that I am following the right scent? In the end, Descartes cannot keep the levels of theory and of practice apart. The confidence that is requisite for practice looks forward to the real possibility of our coming to know that the moral appearances accurately mirror moral reality. At least, this is the position of the young Descartes. If I am at once a practicing doctor and a Cartesian inquirer who has not yet met the Pyrrhonist challenge, it will be my cognitive optimism that keeps the level of my confidence up and that validates the second and third maxims.

6. To close this first part of the book on a further note of optimism, although Descartes did not leave us with a full account of objective value, which his theory requires, he left enough material for us to reconstruct a good part of such a theory on his behalf; and this theory will show (providing we grant some of his premises) that disease and suffering are genuine evils that I can know to be such and that I am not mistaken about the value of my work. But, to return to the third maxim, the point of the example here is that when I seek a true external good in my action, I should limit my desire to what is entirely in my power, namely, my intention to help the needy.[4]

---

4. As we shall see in later chapters, this third maxim is the centerpiece of Descartes's more developed moral theory. The argument I have sketched in this chapter is fully set out, with the aid of a theory of the passions in the *Passions of the Soul*, particularly in articles 143–46.

Part 2

DESCARTES'S FINAL
MORALITY

SINCE Descartes himself refers to the morality of the *Discourse* as *une morale par provision* and not, as he might have done, as *une morale provisoire*, there is no basis in the text for our referring to Descartes's provisional morality, a pejorative term that suggests something makeshift which one expects later to discard. To be sure, given the particular context in which his *morale par provision* is formed, however deeply embedded it is in Descartes's character and however respectful he is of its norms and ideals, this *morale* is at the same time bound to be conceived as imperfect in some respects. It is, after all, a reasonable supposition that both metaphysics and science may have some bearing on moral questions and on moral theory, so that any morality we embrace is likely to inherit some of the imperfections that may infect our beliefs in these other areas. But although the *morale par provision* may be regarded as imperfect in this respect, it does not follow that it is to be succeeded by something quite different. Now, we have seen already that the *Discourse* is not the only place where Descartes refers to the morality to which he subscribed in the early years of his search for truth. In the letter-preface to the French edition of the *Principles*, where he describes this morality as sufficient to regulate the actions of life, he says expressly that it is imperfect and that he follows it only *par provision* until he knows a better one. We should not infer more from these descriptions than the texts support, however, and all they support is some distinction between *une morale par provision* and a "perfect moral system." But they do not give us a clear understanding of this distinction. Nonetheless, commentators tend to argue that the *morale par provision* of the *Discourse* is a provisional morality, where this description is read—quite naturally—in a pejorative sense.

This tendency is, no doubt, encouraged by the famous passage from the letter-preface: "Thus the whole of philosophy is like a tree. The roots are metaphysics, the trunk is physics, and the branches emerging from the trunk are all the other sciences, which may be reduced to three principal ones, namely medicine, mechanics and morals. By 'morals' I understand the highest and most perfect moral system, which presupposes a complete knowledge of the other sciences and is the ultimate level of wisdom" (1:186; 9B:14).

Here again, if we do not go beyond what the text supports, we can say only that the perfect moral system would be one formed in the context of relevant knowledge of metaphysics, physics, mechanics, and medicine. This leaves some very large questions: How much of this knowledge is relevant? How is it relevant? and What would a perfect moral system look like? Note that he does not say that we need knowledge of all the other sciences in order to derive, much less deduce, a perfect moral system, nor does he assert anything that would, on the face of it, compromise the autonomy of morality. In short, this famous passage is not very helpful. The best way to interpret it, in my view, is in the light of Descartes's correspondence with Elizabeth and his *Passions of the Soul*. If this is right, however, then—at least so I will argue—we will not find any radical shift in his conception of morality between, say, 1630 and 1650, nor any radical departure from the *morale par provision*.

If the letter-preface should whet our appetite for the morality to come, neither in it nor anywhere else does Descartes give even a general outline of his conception of such a system, much less spell it out in detail. But of course, we are hardly totally in the dark. For we should expect its main outline to be very familiar. We expect a full Cartesian moral system, like any other, to contain the following elements: *(a)* a set of moral precepts of the sort familiar from commonsense morality (or some functional equivalent), *(b)* a defense of these precepts (presumably sufficient to meet skeptical doubts), *(c)* an account of practical deliberation and practical judgment in which these precepts play a role, *(d)* an account of moral virtue, and *(e)* an account of the good life in which moral virtue has its proper place.

In the correspondence and the *Passions of the Soul* Descartes treats systematically and at length *d* and *e*; indeed, he gives a well-developed account of virtue and of its place in the good life. Descartes does not anywhere treat *a*, *b*, or *c* with a like thoroughness. In this second part of my study I will set out Descartes's theory of virtue and of the good or happy life. In the third part I will construct a Cartesian theory of the good and offer some suggestions about what a Cartesian theory of the right—a first-order morality—might look like.

CHAPTER FOUR

The Summum Bonum

1. BETWEEN the *morale par provision* of the *Discourse* and the final morality of the correspondence and the *Passions* lie the metaphysics and the physics of the *Meditations* and the *Principles*. The metaphysics is important principally because it provides the framework within which we can work out the answer to the basic ethical question of how we are to live happily. If we fail to get our metaphysics right, Descartes implies, we are almost bound to fail to get our morality right. The physics is important since it is through knowledge of physics and the special sciences that we can best gain control both of the world and of our own character and temperament. Descartes stresses the role of metaphysics in a letter to Elizabeth of September 15, 1645. After remarking that "nobody except God knows everything perfectly,"[1] he writes that "we have to content ourselves with knowing the truths most useful to us." He lists the following: we should accept calmly everything that

---

1. This point, perhaps obvious in itself, has special significance within Descartes's moral theory and is one he makes repeatedly. Its significance for moral theory is brought out in a letter to Elizabeth of October 6, 1645. "I think also that there is nothing to repent of when we have done what we judged best at the time when we had to decide to act, even though later, thinking it over at our leisure, we judge that we made a mistake. There would be more ground for repentance if we had acted against our conscience, even though we realized afterwards that we had done better than we thought. For we are responsible only for our thoughts, and it does not belong to human nature to be omniscient, or always to judge as well on the spur of the moment as when there is plenty of time to deliberate. . . . it is true that we lack the infinite knowledge which would be necessary for a perfect acquaintance with all the goods between which we have to choose in the various situations of our lives. We must, I think, be contented with a modest knowledge of the most necessary truths such as those I listed in my last letter [of September 15]" (4:307–08; 3:269).

happens to us "as expressly sent by God"; our soul is a substance nobler than and independent of the body; the universe is vast, and the earth has no privileged place or status in it; and we cannot subsist entirely alone and are essentially dependent beings, part of "the earth, the State, the society, and the family to which we belong by our domicile, our oath of allegiance and our birth." Although he does not spell out the connecting argument, he seems to infer from our being dependent on these various wholes that the interest of the whole must always be preferred to our own (4:290–96; 3:265–67).[2] Oddly, he omits from this list a fifth metaphysical truth that is most useful to know, namely, that we have free will of unlimited scope. This truth bears importantly on the question of what our supreme good is, for in Descartes's view it implies that our greatest perfection, in which we approximate to the greatest possible degree the perfection of God, is the right use of our free will. That this is so, moreover, we can know clearly and distinctly, and among things useful to know it is perhaps the most useful, since our happiness depends on it.

2. Leaving aside the question of how our happiness depends on our free will until later, we may begin with Descartes's account of what he means by happiness. For the most part, what Descartes has to say on this topic is to be found in his correspondence with Princess Elizabeth,[3] of which nearly two-thirds is taken up with morality. Early on in their moral correspondence (July 21, 1645) Descartes proposed that they read Seneca's *De vita beata* together, so that together they might clarify their thoughts about morality and determine "the means which philosophy provides for acquiring that supreme felicity which common souls vainly expect from fortune, but which can be acquired only from ourselves" (4:252; 3:256). Only a few days later (August 4), however, he expressed second thoughts about his choice of text. In choosing it, he explained, he had taken account "only of the reputation of the author and the importance of his topic."[4] With Seneca's open-

2. In Descartes's era this was a moral commonplace, one with ancient roots. The plausibility of this claim, however, varies depending on which whole is in question. What foundations it has in Descartes's theory of value I consider in Chapter 8.

3. Princess Elizabeth (1618–80) was the daughter of Frederick V of Bohemia and niece of Charles I of England. Frederick, who was king of Bohemia only for one winter, was defeated in 1620 by the Austrians, whereupon his family went into exile in Holland, protected by the Prince of Orange. Descartes's correspondence with Elizabeth began in 1642. Descartes dedicated the *Principles of Philosophy* (1644) to her and wrote for her his *Traité* on the passions of the soul in 1646.

4. Several writers believe that Descartes had been introduced to the writings of Seneca at La Flèche (Mesnard 1936, 4; D'Angers 1954, 453–59; Sirven 1928, 38). As to his reputation, Seneca was very widely read in the late sixteenth and early seventeenth centuries in France. For a list of studies that document the influence of Seneca on the writers of this period, see Julien Eymard D'Angers, *Recherches sur le Stoïcisme aux XVIE et XVIIE siècles* (New York: Georg Olms Verlag, 1976).

ing remark, "All men want to live happily [*vivere beata*], but do not see clearly what makes a life happy," Descartes agrees. But he objects that Seneca fails to have defined happiness or told us how to achieve it. So, postponing further comment on Seneca,[5] Descartes confidently expresses his own views.[6]

> I would translate ["vivere beata"] into French as "vivre heureusement," if there were not a difference between *l'heur* and *la béatitude*. The former depends only on outward things: we are thought more fortunate (*heureux*) than wise if some good happens to us without our own effort; but happiness (*béatitude*) consists, it seems to me, in a perfect contentment of mind and inner satisfaction, which is not commonly possessed by those who are most favoured by fortune, and which is acquired by the wise without fortune's favour. So *vivere beata*, to live happily, is to have a perfectly content and satisfied mind. (4:263–64; 3:257)[7]

Descartes raises two traditional issues: What is the place of external goods—health, wealth, beauty, friends, etc.—in the happy life? and What is the relation between being wise and being content? He responds to the second question in his next letter (August 18, 1645). To answer the first, he begins by distinguishing between two classes of things which "can give us this supreme contentment, . . . those which depend on us, like virtue and wisdom, and those which do not, like honours, riches and health" (4:264; 3:257). Virtue and wisdom are sufficient for full contentment, he says, but external goods are necessary for more perfect contentment. It is therefore within the power of each of us to live a fully happy or contented life even if we are not well-favored by fortune.

> It is certain that a person of good birth who is not ill, and who lacks nothing, can enjoy a more perfect contentment than another who is poor, un-

5. He resumes his commentary, unfairly critical in my view, in his next letter, but there again he grows impatient with Seneca and elects to state his own view. To be sure, Seneca's discussion does not have the economy of Cartesian prose, and one can see why a reader like Descartes might have become impatient. Seneca's essay is repetitious and imprecise. On the other hand, a charitable reader could have profited from it more than Descartes claims to have done. Indeed, I believe that had Descartes taken more pains with his chosen text, he might have appreciated some distinctions that would have helped him to make clearer than he does what his own view is—as we shall see directly.

6. That he does so without much hesitation, and that the views he expresses are not only consistent with those hinted at in the *Discourse* but adhered to throughout his later correspondence and in his *Passions of the Soul*, strongly suggest that Descartes had given some thought to these very questions before proposing to Elizabeth that they read Seneca together. I do not agree with Alquié, therefore, who infers from the manner in which Descartes suggests to Elizabeth that they read Seneca that Descartes did not have firm or clear views about ethics (see Alquié 1989, 3:585n).

7. See also *Discourse* 6:26 (1:124) and *Principles* 9B:4 (1:180).

healthy and deformed, provided the two are equally wise and virtuous. Nevertheless, a small vessel may be just as full as a large one, although it contains less liquid; and similarly if we regard each person's contentment as the full satisfaction of all his desires duly regulated by reason, I do not doubt that the poorest people, least blest by nature and fortune, can be entirely content and satisfied just as much as everyone else, although they do not enjoy as many good things. It is only this sort of contentment which is here in question; to seek the other sort would be a waste of time, since it is not in our own power. (4:264; 3:257)

It has been suggested that Descartes has two conceptions of happiness, which he cannot combine into a single, coherent view.[8] According to one, the full-contentment conception, virtue and wisdom are sufficient for happiness; according to the other, the perfect-contentment conception, they are not. But some of the conceptual tension might be eased in the following way. We can distinguish between the third-person perspective and the first-person perspective of the deliberating agent. In speaking of full contentment, Descartes adopts the first-person point of view of an agent. From this perspective, full contentment is all that matters. When, on the other hand, he implies that some can be more perfectly content than others, he adopts a third-person point of view, not the point of view of a deliberating agent. And from this third-person perspective we can very well compare the degree of contentment of two sages, one in robust health, intellectually acute, and wealthy and the other poor, sickly, and dull. Moreover, that we can take this point of view and make such comparative judgments is, in fact, a corollary of the prescription to seek our own full contentment; for in seeking our own full contentment we try to enjoy as many of the gifts of fortune as we can. What we are not to do, however, is allow our own contentment to become a hostage to fortune. For Descartes, as we shall see later in this same letter, living happily is essentially a matter of having rational aims, acting with firm resolution, and taking to heart that what we do not attain was, given our well-informed efforts, impossible for us; living happily does not entail self-denial, nor is it a matter, for example, of a sick sage not being able to see the value of good health. Of the two conceptions of happiness distinguished above, that of full contentment is dominant. Indeed, in the only context in which the distinction has practical import—in

---

8. I have in mind Alquié, who writes: "Descartes seems here to reject the idea that the happiness of the sage is perfect and to grant possible degrees of his own happiness: a sage in good health is happier than one who is sick. Things that do not depend on us, therefore, contribute to happiness. But he is going then to invoke another principle, defining happiness in terms of the plenitude of desires regulated by reason. One is to desire only the possible. Accordingly, each can render himself fully content" (Alquié 1989, 3:588n).

the act of deliberation or during the formation of one's own character—the two conceptions are extensionally equivalent. One's own perfect contentment just *is* one's own full contentment. If, then, we are to live happily and be perfectly content, we must first of all become virtuous, but we should by no means forego the contentment of gifts of fortune so long as we do not allow our satisfaction of mind to become a hostage to such gifts as may be denied us.[9]

Let us grant that virtue and wisdom are necessary for happiness and turn to the second question, How are these related to full contentment? Later, when we examine the rules we need to follow in order to live happily, we shall see the basis of a clear distinction between virtue and wisdom; for the moment we may treat them as the same and speak simply of virtue as the necessary condition of happiness. Virtue, on Descartes's account—to give a brief sketch—is the disposition always to judge as well as we can what is the best plan of action and to adhere strictly to that plan. How, then, are we to understand the connection Descartes has in mind when he implies that virtue is a necessary condition for full contentment?

When he turns specifically to this question in his letter of August 18, 1645, his first observation is that

> there is a difference between happiness, the supreme good, and the final end or goal toward which our actions ought to tend. For happiness is not the supreme good, but presupposes it, being the contentment or satisfaction of mind which results from possessing it. The end of our actions, however, can be understood to be one or the other; for the supreme good is undoubtedly the thing we ought to set ourselves as the goal of all our actions, and the resulting contentment of the mind is also rightly

9. In the text on which Descartes is commenting, Seneca writes of the wise and virtuous person's attitude toward the gifts of fortune as follows: "Who, however, can doubt that the wise man finds in riches, rather than in poverty, this ampler material for displaying his powers, since in poverty there is room for only one kind of virtue—not to be bowed down and crushed by it—while in riches moderation and liberality and diligence and orderliness and grandeur all have a wide field? The wise man will not despise himself even if he has the stature of a dwarf, but nevertheless he will wish to be tall. And if he is feeble in body, or deprived of one eye, he will still be strong, but nevertheless he will prefer to have strength of body, and this too, though he knows that there is something else in him that is stronger than body. If his health is bad he will endure it, but he will wish for good health. For certain things, even if they are trifles in comparison with the whole, and can be withdrawn without destroying the essential good, nevertheless contribute something to the perpetual joy that springs from virtue. . . . And besides, who among wise men—I mean those of our school, who count virtue the sole good—denies that even those things which we call 'indifferent' do have some inherent value, and that some are more desirable than others" (Seneca 1965, 155–57). If we deleted Seneca's talk of one's wishing for things we cannot have, we would have in this passage a view very close to Descartes's own. Neither is orthodox Stoicism.

called our end, since it is the attraction which makes us seek the supreme good. (4:275; 3:261)

The term "end" (*fin*) is, then, ambiguous; it may refer to the supreme good as the end we seek to achieve in all our actions, or it may refer to the contentment which, Descartes asserts, results from our achieving this end. In both distinguishing the supreme good from happiness and connecting them in this way, he hopes to reconcile two respectable lines of thought, Stoicism and Epicureanism. He is explicit about this. Indeed, the specific occasion for his taking up this issue is Seneca's critique of Epicurus and defense of Stoicism in *The Happy Life*. Seneca is at pains to identify happiness and virtue with each other and with the supreme good, leaving the contentment of mind that follows on the heels of virtue as a separate value that, strictly speaking, does not add to the value of happiness. It may be that Seneca does not represent the classic Stoic position of Zeno and his immediate successors, but he certainly adopts a position that cannot be reconciled with that of Epicurus. For this reason, as we shall see, we cannot agree with Descartes when he says of the views of Epicurus, Zeno, and Aristotle that, if interpreted favorably, they can be "accepted as true and consistent with each other."

Descartes adds to his first preliminary observation a second, "that the word 'pleasure' was understood in a different sense by Epicurus from those who argued against him. For all his opponents restricted the meaning of the word to the pleasures of the senses; whereas he, by contrast, extended it to every contentment of mind, as can easily be judged from what Seneca and others have written about him." What Descartes says here is true only in part. If many critics of Epicurus mistakenly suppose that all pleasures were of the sort Epicurus called kinetic pleasures, others, Seneca among them, appreciate that Epicurus sought to extend the concept of pleasure to cover static pleasure, the state of being without bodily pain or mental anxiety. Nonetheless, Seneca sees himself as an opponent of Epicurus. He does not fault Epicurus for the kind of life he led, which, he concedes, was in accordance with virtue. It is Epicurus's account the supreme good he objects to. He upbraids him for putting pleasure first in his theory and for making of pleasure itself the final good, even in the extended sense of tranquillity.[10] Seneca's objection is that Epicurus has made of living a virtuous life a mere means to the final good, not the good itself. And to the sugges-

---

10. An incidental reason for upbraiding Epicurus is that by putting pleasure at the center of his theory, he encourages others to moral laxity under the guise of a philosopher's theory. "The reason why your praise of pleasure is pernicious is that what is honourable in your teaching lies hid within, what corrupts is plainly visible" (Seneca 1965, 131).

tion of compromise, that the highest good (*summum bonum*) could be a union of virtue and pleasure, Seneca responds that the supreme good can have no part that is not good. "Even the joy that springs from virtue, although it is a good, is not nevertheless a part of the absolute good, any more than are cheerfulness and tranquillity, although they spring from the noblest origins; for goods they are, yet they only attend on the highest good but do not consummate it" (Seneca 1965, 137). Seneca refers to the ancient Stoic doctrine of indifferents in this connection, arguing expressly that the pleasure that attends the consciousness of one's own virtue is "indifferent" to one's moral goodness and, hence, to one's living happily. Where does Descartes stand? He may appear to reject this Stoic devaluation of pleasure; indeed, he may appear to be defending the Epicurean view that virtue is a mere means to contentment (i.e., happiness, *béatitude*). In fact, however, it is not easy to interpret Descartes's letter on this point. In the first place, not only does he not assert, with Epicurus, that virtue has value only as a means to perfect contentment, he says explicitly that virtue has supreme value as an end. Evidently, if there is a consistent view to be extracted from this letter, it is not easy to come by. And earlier commentators are not much help.[11]

---

11. One writes: "How, therefore, must we characterize the Cartesian morality? It is not a form of utilitarianism; not even perhaps a form of eudaimonism, since pleasure is reduced to the role of means of achieving the supreme good: it is as it were a path that nature uses to direct us to perfection" (Hamelin 1921, 384). Another writes: "In accepting this union of virtue and happiness, Descartes inherits the eudaimonism of the ancients. This is accompanied, however, by an effort to make clear the basis of rather vague doctrines and to overcome the differences, superficial according to Descartes, among the peripatetics, the Stoics and the Epicureans. The goods of the body to be sure have their value. . . . But not being at the disposal of each, these goods cannot define a happiness open to everyone. The Stoics saw clearly that the control of our thoughts alone is in our power and that this constitutes virtue; but they were mistaken to make virtue 'so severe and inimical to pleasure': to make clear that *béatitude* is obtained through virtue permits reconciling Stoicism, to which it confines itself, and Epicureanism, which subordinates all morality to the pursuit of pleasure" (Rodis-Lewis 1970, 43). And in contrast to these, Alquié suggests that in seeing there is no strictly analytic connection between virtue and happiness and that these need to be joined synthetically, Descartes here anticipates Kant (Alquié 1989, 3:596n). But if Descartes anticipates Kant in denying the analytic connection, he affirms, while Kant denies, that contentment is within reach of every virtuous person in this life. In so doing, however, it is far from clear that Descartes's conception of happiness (*béatitude*) is the same as Kant's conception of *Glückseligkeit*, which is a rationally constructed ideal of imagination, roughly, the notion of the optimum satisfaction of all our desires. Between Descartes and Kant came the empiricists and with them a highly distinctive conception of happiness (anticipated by the Cyrenaics); this was a conception of happiness, however, that is not at the same time a conception of a final end, in the classical sense of a *summum bonum*. The comparison of Descartes with Kant, on this particular point anyway, is of very limited value.

In a letter in which, in general, he suggests Descartes is much overrated as a philosopher and particularly as a scientist, Leibniz gives him very low marks also as a moral philosopher. "His

Let us return to the letter. Descartes continues: "Aristotle considered the sovereign good of all human nature in general, that is to say, the sovereign good that can be had by the most accomplished of all men. Thus he had reason to compose it from all the perfections of which human nature is capable; but that does not serve our purpose." The principal debate between the Stoics and the Aristotelians was whether external goods such as wealth, health, friends, and family are parts of one's own happiness. Descartes may have this question in mind here, since it follows from Aristotle's doctrine that it is not always within one's power to attain the supreme good—happiness. But Descartes seems to have a further point in mind: Aristotle projects an ideal of the supreme good as the having of all the excellences both of intellect and character that one can have, as well as an abundance of external goods. The supreme good in this sense is even further out of reach for most of us. In any event, it is puzzling how Descartes thinks he can reconcile Aristotle and the others. He does, however, agree with Aristotle that external goods can make a contribution to one's happiness, something strict Stoics deny. On the other hand, he diverges from Aristotle and approaches the Stoics in affirming that happiness is attainable even by the least fortunate. We see this in his image of the vessels of different sizes.

The letter continues:

> Zeno, on the contrary, considered that which each man in particular can possess; that is why he also had very good reason for saying it consists in virtue, because, from among the goods we can possess, only virtue entirely depends upon our free decision. But, by making all vices equal, Zeno has represented this virtue as so stern, and as such an enemy of pleasure, that it seems to me it must have been only melancholics, or minds entirely detached from bodies, who were able to be his disciples.[12]

---

morality is a composite of the opinions of the Stoics and Epicureans—something not very difficult to do, for Seneca had already reconciled them quite well" (Ariew and Garber 1989, 241).

12. This is a common complaint, but it is not worthy of Descartes. It may indicate that he was not an attentive reader of Seneca, Epictetus, or Cicero or that he was not speaking seriously. But there is, in this comment, an anticipation of a deep doctrinal difference between him and the classic Stoics. Like the Stoics, Descartes takes the mind to be single, but in contrast to the Stoics he asserts that the passions have a vital role to play in human happiness. This doctrinal difference is worked out on the basis of his theory of the mind-body *ingenium* in his *Passions of the Soul*. The title of the closing article expresses a view that would be anathema to the Stoic: "It is on the passions alone that all the good and evil of this life depends" (11:488; 1:404). A point that he ignores in the Stoics, but which Seneca makes in the text Descartes is commenting on, is that joy supervenes on virtue. This joy (*eupatheiai*) is very similar, it would seem, to the *plaisirs à part* that Descartes posits in his *Passions of the Soul*. Referring to this letter, D'Angers points out that Descartes clearly separates himself from his contemporary Christian humanists, who held the following trio inseparable—beatitude, supreme good, and final end—but who denied that virtue itself is the final end. He summarizes Descartes's view as follows: "Virtue being inseparable from pleasure, understood in its true, spiritual sense, the Stoics were seriously mistaken in presenting virtue to us as without joy. . . . Thus, with

Lastly, when Epicurus considered what happiness consists in and to what purpose or end our actions tend, he was not wrong to say that it is pleasure in general—that is to say, contentment of the mind. For although the mere knowledge of our duty might oblige us to do good actions, yet this would not cause us to enjoy any happiness if we got no pleasure from it. But because we often give the name "delight" to false pleasures, which are accompanied or followed by worry, anxiety and repentance, many have believed that this view of Epicurus inculcates vice. Indeed, it does not inculcate virtue. Suppose there is a prize for hitting a bull's-eye: you can make people want to hit the bull's-eye by showing them the prize, but they cannot win the prize if they do not see the bull's-eye; conversely, those who see the bull's-eye are not thereby induced to fire at it if they do not know there is a prize to be won. So too virtue, which is the bull's-eye, does not come to be strongly desired when it is seen all on its own; and contentment, like the prize, cannot be gained unless it is pursued.[13]

That is why I believe I can conclude that happiness consists solely in the contentment of mind—that is to say, in contentment in general. For although some contentment depends upon the body, and some does not, there is none anywhere but in the mind. But in order to achieve a contentment which is solid, we need to pursue virtue—that is to say, to

---

Descartes, and despite his deep and sincere Catholicism, with Descartes a new spirit appears. Man is summoned to find his contentment in himself, in the achievement pure and simple of his duty, independently of any recompense in the beyond" (D'Angers 1976, 468–69).

13. This is a variation on a classic Stoic image. Descartes is trying to distinguish the final end, the supreme good, virtue, and contentment. He wishes to argue that virtue is the supreme good, that contentment results from our attaining the supreme good, even if some forms of true contentment can have other sources as well. He is not, therefore, a good Stoic. In *De finibus bonorum et malorum*, Cicero has Cato say: "A possible source of error must be removed here: could it not be assumed that it follows that there are *two* supreme goods? Not at all, if we compare the supreme good to the case of a man who has set himself to aim at some mark with a spear or arrow: in such an illustration the man has to do everything possible to shoot straight, nevertheless the actual doing of all he can to accomplish his purpose is in this instance *his* supreme good (comparable to what we call the chief good in life), whereas his hitting of the target is 'to be chosen,' and not 'to be desired'" (Cicero 1991, 3.22). Descartes follows Cato in arguing that virtue is the supreme good, but unlike Cato, he takes virtue to be the target rather than the man's doing everything possible to hit the target. The fact is that Descartes shares Cato's view that it is the striving to shoot straight that is virtue. And we might well say that Cato has got better control of the image than Descartes, given his understanding of virtue, for Descartes's virtuous person needs a target other than virtue itself, say, another's well-being. In the final paragraph of the letter Descartes alludes to the needed distinction between the target and the striving to hit it, where the latter is what is best to do (the appropriate action). Now, Cato might agree that there is a prize that awaits those who attain virtue. If, however, Descartes means to say that the prize is the motive, then, in Cato's view, virtue would be lost. On the other hand, if being virtuous involves not only trying to hit various appropriate targets but doing so for the right reasons, and if right reasons exclude thoughts about resulting contentment, then the distance between Cato and Descartes is considerably reduced.

maintain a firm and constant will to bring about everything we judge to
be the best, and to use all the power of our intellect in judging well.
(4:275–77; 3:261–62)

As I noted above, it is not clear that we can extract a clear and coherent
account of happiness from this letter. The letter raises a number of questions without providing clear, definite, and mutually consistent answers.
We may begin with the question whether, on Descartes's view, virtue is a
mere means to happiness.[14] The simple and, so far as it goes, correct answer—this the letter makes explicit—is that virtue is not merely a means
to contentment; virtue is, Descartes and Zeno agree, the supreme good,
"the thing we ought to set ourselves as the goal of all our actions." As we
shall see below, setting virtue as our goal amounts to following three rules
of morality (related to those of the *morale par provision* of the *Discourse*).
Having virtue as our goal, then, is not like having some specific end in
mind—say, saving a friend from drowning—and adopting the means to
virtue is not like choosing an action as the appropriate means to such an
end. To speak in terms of Descartes's image, aiming at virtue is not well understood on the model of aiming at a target. Nor, so far as we can conceive
virtue as a means, is this relation to be conceived on the model of a causal
relation between a specific action and its effect. Morality is not, then, like
medicine. We may conceive a science in terms of which we can relate certain medical procedures (seen as means) to the curing of a disease (effect),
but this is not a possible model for the relationship between virtue and
contentment. It is not one's virtuous actions that procure contentment, on
Descartes's view, but the knowledge that one is virtuous that does so.[15]
    Up to this point, then, we might see Descartes as aligned with Zeno.
How, then, does he accommodate himself to Epicurus? We can't say precisely, because he does not go into enough detail concerning Epicurus's
theory of pleasure. Still, he may say enough to make us doubt that the ac-

14. This is the interpretation given by Martial Gueroult. Central to his reading is his claim
that for Descartes morality is "the technique that must determine in what way I must act in
this life in order for my soul to be full of contentment. . . . We see immediately that morality,
like medicine, can only be a technique that makes use of a theoretical science" (Gueroult 1985,
179). Referring to the present letter he writes: "Virtue is the goal only subsidiarily, as is the
bull's eye in a target shoot: we aim for it only to win the prize, meaning pleasure" (184). I discuss Gueroult's interpretation in Chapter 6.
    15. This remark should be qualified. Descartes speaks of contentment in two ways. Content-
ment can be a passion, the passion called joy, but it can also be a state of mind distinct from
a passion, a *plaisir à part*, in this case a contentment that supervenes simply on the reflective
knowledge that one is virtuous. As a passion, contentment or joy is intermittent, the contentment in question here arising from the awareness that one is performing a virtuous action from the proper motive.

commodation he suggests is possible. The problem has to do with the precise role contentment plays in the practical deliberation of Descartes's virtuous agent. What the letter strongly suggests is that unless one sees supreme contentment in the offing, one will not be motivated to become virtuous. The apparent difficulty lies in trying to combine three things: a theory of the will according to which it is moved by a conception of the good, a theory of value that is not hedonistic, and a theory of motivation that is hedonistic. To begin to sort things out, we need to distinguish between two contexts—a context in which someone aims at virtue as a target and a context in which someone who is virtuous aims at some good distinct from virtue. In the latter, the agent who is already virtuous acts for the sake of the value of the target, this value being at once such an agent's motive or reason for acting. But how precisely are we to conceive the former case? Perhaps the idea is that agents who lack virtue are typically motivated primarily by thoughts of their own pleasure and that in order to put them on the path of virtue and true happiness we must praise virtue in motivational language they can understand and respond to.[16] In any event, the letter does not contain the doctrine that the virtuous person is motivated by thoughts of contentment, and it is quite consistent with the view Descartes endorses elsewhere that contentment is what follows on one's being characteristically motivated by judgments of the good.

   To the reader of John Stuart Mill this letter will give rise to another question. Is the contentment that results from the awareness of one's own virtue of a qualitatively different order from contentment derived from our awareness of possessing other goods? And if so, is this contentment commensurable with other varieties? If not, is virtue the supreme good only in that it produces more contentment, or more certain and durable contentment, than other sources? The Cartesian answers to these questions, whose defense I hope to provide in the following chapters, are as follows. The contentment supervenient on virtue is not only sweeter, more certain, and more durable than contentment from gifts of fortune,[17] it is qualitatively

16. The discussion in the *Passions of the Soul* sheds little light on Descartes's thinking on this motivational matter. Joy, he says there, is the sentiment that follows directly on the belief that we possess some good. In the case of the good of virtue, which is, in Descartes's taxonomy, an intellectual good as distinct from a sensory good, our knowledge that we possess virtue is itself clear and distinct, and the joy that follows is, in the first instance, an intellectual joy. Because we are embodied and therefore passionate, however, intellectual joy must, as a matter of fact, reverberate in our passional life. At the level of phenomenology, Descartes assures us, this passionate joy or contentment is not only the most durable, it is the sweetest. This account, until the passions are introduced, is in accord with Zeno.

17. For example, Descartes writes in his letter of November 1647 to Queen Christina: "the peace of mind and inner satisfaction felt by those who know they always do their best to discover what is good and to acquire it is . . . a pleasure incomparably sweeter, more lasting and more solid than all those which come from elsewhere" (5:85; 3:326).

different and phenomenologically of a higher order, so that even at the level of experience, there could arise no question of a trade-off. Descartes appears to be working with a theory of value that is not, at its base, hedonistic at all. Of the goods we can possess, virtue is supreme. But the measure of the value of goods is not the degree or kind of contentment our thought of possessing them produces. Indeed, as I shall detail later, the level and kind of contentment is both explained and evaluated in terms of an antecedent judgment of the value of the goods we possess. Accordingly, in the case of virtue, it is in terms of its being supreme among goods we can possess that the contentment it produces is a higher form of contentment.[18]

In the letter just quoted, then, Descartes should not be seen as endorsing hedonism when he objects to the rigor of Zeno's first account of virtue. Rather, he is pointing out that virtue is one thing, contentment another, and that virtue carries with it its own reward. There is, of course, the strong but highly problematic suggestion that were it not for this reward, virtue would have fewer votaries.[19] This suggestion threatens incoherence, however, if it is taken to imply that the virtuous person's motive for pursuing moral ends is dependent on this very contentment. For what is essential to virtue is our judging as well as we can and sticking to the chosen plan. Our targets, if we are virtuous agents, are such goods as the well-being of others, knowledge, and health; judging well involves our deciding how best to achieve these and other, often competing, ends in the circumstances in which we find ourselves. As I interpret Descartes, such ends have genuine and objective value; they are worth pursuing for their own sakes, and our reason for acting depends on our seeing these ends as having such value. Accordingly, the entire justification for our acting well can be told without reference to the contentment that supervenes on our reflective awareness that we have acted well. It would seem, then, that no true votary of virtue needs the prospects of contentment as a motive. If this is so, and on grounds that Descartes accepts, the suggestion in this letter that the virtuous are moved by the offer of a prize is hard to reconcile with the rest of Descartes's account of virtue as the supreme good.

18. In this respect Descartes's accommodation of pleasure within the good life is similar to Aristotle's.

19. Pierre Mesnard seems to think that, according to Descartes, virtue would have no votaries at all if it were not for the prize. "Zeno made perhaps a greater mistake when he separated categorically the supreme good from beatitude. Descartes reproaches him for that which Kant was later to be reproached: that virtuous actions from pure duty have little allure and risk being rarely performed. However, our philosopher intends to make duty as attractive as possible: it is by pleasure that he wished to lead to virtue" (Mesnard 1936, 155).

CHAPTER FIVE

The Rules of Morality

1. DESCARTES's use of *béatitude* and *bonheur* corresponds to a distinction between goods that depend entirely on us and those that do not. Virtue and wisdom are goods of the first kind; riches, honors, and health are of the second kind.[1] Virtue is sufficient for *béatitude*, that is, for full contentment, whether we are otherwise favored by fortune or not. "It seems to me," Descartes writes to Elizabeth in his letter of August 4, 1645,

> that every man can make himself content without any external assistance, provided that he respects three conditions, which are related to the three rules of morality which I put in the *Discourse on the Method*.
>
> The first is always to employ his mind as well as he can to discover what he should or should not do in all the circumstances of life.
>
> The second is to have a firm and constant resolution to carry out whatever reason recommends without being diverted by passion or appetite. Virtue, I believe, consists precisely in firmness in this resolution; though I do not know that anyone has ever so described it.[2]

---

1. The terms *béatitude* and *bonheur* do not, perhaps, have modern translations that capture the precise sense they had for Descartes. As Descartes makes clear in the letter to Elizabeth in which he comments on Seneca's *De vita beata*, the term *bonheur* had the sense of good fortune, which in modern French has been largely lost. On the other hand, the term *béatitude* is not nowadays commonly used and has in any case the flavor of religious ecstasy, a flavor quite foreign to Descartes's intention. What Descartes had in mind was a blend of contentment (a positive affect) and tranquillity (an unperturbed state).

2. Anthony Levi suggests, on the contrary, that Descartes's account of virtue was fairly commonplace at the time. Without suggesting that Descartes was not sincere in his claim to originality, Levi notes that his definition of virtue is close to Du Vair's and to Charron's defi-

The third is to bear in mind that while one thus guides oneself, as far as one can, by reason, all the good things which one does not possess are all equally outside one's power. In this way one will accustom oneself not to desire them. Nothing can impede our contentment except desire, regret, and repentance; but if we always do what reason tells us, even if events show us afterwards that we were mistaken, we will never have any grounds for repentance, because it was not our own fault. (6:265–66; 3:257–58)

2. Descartes speaks of virtue *and* wisdom (*sagesse*). Although the two are not quite equivalent in meaning, they are in Descartes's theory inseparable and, at least within the domain of practice as distinct from pure theory, designate different aspects of one and the same character trait. Thus, in the second rule Descartes uses the term "virtue" to refer narrowly to firmness of resolution. Correspondingly, we might take "wisdom" to refer narrowly to the capacity to judge well, but Descartes elsewhere expressly denies that firmness of resolution alone is sufficient for virtue; good judgment is also necessary. In any case, when Descartes says that both virtue and human wisdom are alone entirely in our power, I take him to be referring to a single, complex character trait with these distinguishable aspects. I say "human wisdom," not the perfect wisdom that only God could have.[3]

---

nition of *preud'hommie* . As DuVair writes in the *Moral Philosophy of the Stoics*, "The good . . . of man will consist in the use of right reason, that is to say, in virtue, which is nothing other than the firm disposition to do what is virtuous [*honnête*] and appropriate [*convenable*]" (Levi 1964, 286–87).

3. In the first rule of his *Rules for the Direction of the Mind* Descartes seems to suggest that we could achieve perfect wisdom. Since all the sciences are interconnected, he says, one should not focus on one in particular to the exclusion of the others. "He should, rather, consider simply how to increase the natural light of his reason, not with a view to solving this or that scholastic problem, but in order that his intellect should show his will what decision it ought to make in each of life's contingencies." But this passage need not be taken to imply that with perfect knowledge in all the sciences—the topic of the first rule—we would be able to determine with certainty in each particular circumstance what is the best thing to do. And since it is very obvious that scientific knowledge would not lead to such "perfect" practical knowledge, it would be uncharitable to read the young Descartes as if he thought it would.

In the "Dedicatory Letter to Elizabeth" Descartes speaks of "pure and genuine virtues, which proceed solely from knowledge of what is right," and which "have one and the same nature and are included under the single term 'wisdom.' For whoever possesses the firm and powerful resolve always to use his reasoning powers correctly, as far as he can, and to carry out whatever he knows to be best, is truly wise, so far as his nature permits. And simply because of this, he will possess justice, courage, temperance, and all the other virtues; but they will be linked in such a way that no one virtue stands out among the others." This theme of the unity of virtue is emphasized in the later *Passions of the Soul*. Descartes concedes, however, by nature some have more powerful intellectual vision than others, yet all "achieve wisdom according to their lights" (8A:2–3; 1:191).

We should accordingly see the above three rules as spelling out the full conception of human virtue or practical wisdom. The first two rules refer to the two aspects I have just mentioned. One is the strength and firmness of will to execute the plans we judge to be best; this power to act well is one we develop to its maximum degree through our understanding of the nature and use of the passions. The other is the power to judge well (*bien juger*). The third rule completes the conception, since we have perfect virtue only when our desires are well ordered. Without the addition of the third rule, we would have only what Aristotle called continence, but not perfect virtue.

3. The first rule, which has to do with judging well, applies in two contexts. In the conduct of our daily lives, we are called upon to decide what specific actions to perform in particular circumstances. If we go by the few examples Descartes offers of practical decision making, he appears to assume that well-formed practical questions about what is appropriate to do have an objectively right answer, even if we are poorly equipped to determine what this answer is. Sometimes the appropriate thing may also be the best; at other times it may be the only thing permitted. So it might be said that, so far as such practical choice is concerned, we are wise in proportion as our disciplined practical judgments tend to approximate what is, objectively speaking, appropriate.[4] Perfect wisdom in this area, however, is beyond our competence.[5]

In the second context, our judgments are not practical decisions about particular acts in particular circumstances but decisions that bear on longer range projects, including that of forming our own character. And here something approaching perfect knowledge is not beyond our competence. Indeed, it is this knowledge that Descartes is concerned to impart and to cultivate. These two domains are of course connected; to achieve wisdom in the second way, we must be striving to achieve wisdom in the first.[6] As

---

4. In speaking of "appropriate action," I have in mind the Stoic notion of *kathékon*, the notion at the center of Cicero's *De officiis*. This is a useful concept, since it ranges over actions that are morally required, at one extreme, through those that are morally best, to those that are just all right or natural, and which raise no moral issue. There is no express reference to moral rules in Descartes's discussion of good judgment. But we have seen in the *Discourse* that he is not reluctant to speak of moral laws, for example, the law that we ought to serve mankind.

5. In his letter of September 15, 1645, he writes to Elizabeth: "In order to be always disposed to judge well, only two things seem to me necessary. One is knowledge of the truth; the other is practice in remembering and assenting to this knowledge whenever the occasion demands. But because nobody except God knows everything perfectly, we have to content ourselves with knowing the truths most useful to us" (4:291; 3:265). This is, however, overstated. The list of these truths does not include first-order morality.

6. If mistake in this domain is unavoidable for us, how can we any longer maintain that God is no deceiver? The answer, first, is that full contentment depends not on our never mak-

Descartes says reassuringly in this same letter, "It is . . . not necessary [for *béatitude*] that our reason should be free from error; it is sufficient if our conscience testifies that we have never lacked resolution and virtue to carry out whatever we judge the best course. So virtue by itself is sufficient to make us happy in this life."

Nevertheless, the letter may seem to betray a certain ambivalence.[7] For while he asserts quite straightforwardly that full contentment does not presuppose freedom from practical error, later in the letter he writes: "Virtue unenlightened by intellect can be false," and in order to prevent virtue from being false, we require the "use of reason," which will yield a "true knowledge of the good."[8] Only if we have true knowledge of the good, moreover, will "the contentment which virtue brings be solid." Here Descartes might be making the familiar point that even when we judge as well as we can, we may be mistaken, a mistake we may later discover. Yet if we have judged as well as we could have, then even if we later discover error, we know that it was not our fault. That we judged well and acted well, so far as it might affect our contentment, could only contribute to it. It is not easy to see, therefore, what could be meant by saying that the possibility of our making a blameless error somehow undermines our contentment. The best to made of it, perhaps, is that we can see ourselves as causally, although not morally, responsible for some bad outcome. In any event, Descartes's final view is quite clear; it is the one he expresses in his letter to Queen Christina of November 20, 1647: "I do not see how it is possible to dispose [the will] better than by a firm and constant resolution to carry out to the letter all the things which one judges to be best, and to employ all the powers of one's mind in finding out what these are. This by itself constitutes all the virtues; this alone really deserves praise and glory; this alone, finally, pro-

---

ing a mistake but on our trying—so far as our finite intellect allows—to determine what is appropriate; second, as we see from the second rule, we are not acting under the delusion that what we so choose is clearly and distinctly right, but we act *as if* we had such knowledge. In short, we can attain full contentment even if we have no clear and distinct knowledge of what is objectively right *or if we mistakenly believe we have such knowledge*; and so far as we believe we have chosen as wisely as possible, we make no *practical* error.

7. Alquié, remarking a difference between the *morale par provision* and the "new" rules, writes: "Descartes seems to hesitate between two conceptions of the good use of reason: one anticipates the good will, in the Kantian sense; the other presupposes the knowledge of true goods" (Alquié 1989, 3:589n).

8. He appears to express a similarly extreme position in article 49 of the *Passions of the Soul*, where he says that strength of soul amounts to virtue only when our practical judgments are based not on "some false opinion" but "solely on knowledge of the truth" (1:347; 9:368). But the context of this claim is special. He is speaking of "determinate judgments," rules of thumb to be applied in repeatable types of circumstances. Here what is generally called for is not a fine-tuned judgment but a checking of the influence of our passions on our judgment.

duces the greatest and most solid contentment in life. So I conclude that it is this which constitutes the supreme good" (5:83; 3:325).

4. Descartes says that these rules state conditions that relate to the first three maxims of his *morale par provision*. These are, in fact, the very conditions that would be satisfied by anyone who adhered to the earlier maxims. There is, then, no difference in content or thrust between the earlier and the later morality. There is, however, an apparent difference, as is often remarked, between the first maxim of the earlier morality and the first rule of the later. The contrast is supposed to be this: according to one (the first maxim) Descartes resolved to follow the example of others, and according to the other he enjoins us to follow our own reason. Still, as I argued in Chapter 1, the decision to follow the example of sensible members of one's own society must itself be based on one's own reason; our decision is supported by the best reasoning available in the context of doubt, namely, reasoning from probabilities—reasoning at lower levels of *sagesse* than knowledge from first causes.[9] Accordingly, in taking local custom and the example of sensible people as his guide in this context, Descartes was doing precisely what the "new" first rule prescribes, namely, following his own reason. In this respect, then, Descartes does not amend the principal import of the "old" first rule.

5. Of course there is this difference: by the time of this correspondence the credentials of our own reason have been established (at least to Descartes's and Elizabeth's satisfaction). And with this point in mind, one might look back on Descartes's quandary in the *Discourse* and question whether he had any right to consult his own reason in the way I have just indicated. The issue is a bit complicated. In the first place, the Descartes of the *Discourse* did not question the credentials of his own reason or, more

---

9. Descartes distinguishes levels of wisdom in the letter-preface to the *Principles*. Philosophy, or knowledge from first causes, is the fifth degree of wisdom; Descartes's four rules were to lead us to this level. The first level, he says, "contains only notions which are so clear in themselves that they can be acquired without meditation." The second takes in all that we acquire through sense experience; the third and fourth embrace what we acquire from others, either by conversation or by reading their instructive books. As a pure inquirer, Descartes denies that wisdom at these levels amounts to certain knowledge, yet in the practical domain, since he cannot afford to await such knowledge, he must accept the probable—that is, the best that can be gleaned from the ordinary sources of knowledge concerning how to act and to live— *as if* it were certain. Some commentators argue that in his own philosophy he never achieved the fifth level of wisdom in the practical domain. To be sure, he did not achieve it at the level of ordinary practical decisions about what to do and what not to do. But as I have argued, this was never in the offing at any time in Descartes's thought, since it would require something approaching divine wisdom. On the other hand, he did show how we could actually achieve wisdom in the practical domain that really matters, namely the wisdom sufficient for virtue and happiness. This is the story I am following in this chapter.

particularly, his standard of *évidence*. His complaint was that so few claims to knowledge truly meet this standard. Our possible skepticism about the standard itself is a feature of the *Meditations*, not of the *Discourse*. In the *Discourse* Descartes begins, however boldly, with the assumption that each of us has reason and that this is a genuine cognitive power. What we need to do to gain knowledge — or such knowledge as is within our competence — is to use it well. The first maxim of the *morale par provision*, therefore, is not the maxim of someone who is skeptical about reason's claim to be a genuine cognitive power. It is the maxim of someone who does not have certain knowledge of first-order morality. Now, even if reason's credentials as a genuine cognitive power have in the meantime been secured, the Descartes of the correspondence with Elizabeth does not claim to have a surer grip on first-order morality than he did a decade or more earlier. Moreover, as we shall see shortly, he continues to show similar respect for common public morality.

But, to return to Descartes of the *Discourse* and his right to defer to his own reason, we might put the matter as follows. Call "reason" the power we exercise when we try to distinguish the true from the false and the good from the bad, or the better from the worse. That we have such a power — or that we act as if we do — is implicit in our making these distinctions, indeed, in our asking practical questions at all. In the context of the most radical kind of doubt, to be sure, it is an open question whether this power, so understood, is a true power, such that, when operating as well as possible, it tends to lead us to the goals we seek — the true and the good.[10] After the *Meditations* (I am assuming) reason as a true power has been validated. Indeed, in this change of epistemic status lies one main difference

---

10. In this connection, we may note that Descartes never questions our capacity to understand certain primitive notions, even within the context of doubt. Indeed, unless we had such an understanding, the method of doubt could not even get launched. What is more, in the *Meditations*, having isolated some propositions we apprehend clearly and distinctly, he says that so long as we attend only to these, we cannot but give them our assent. Here Descartes discovers the perfect epistemic marriage between our best cognitive faculty and its object, truth. The problem posed by metaphysical doubt is that of showing that our best cognitive faculty is genuinely cognitive — that our clear and distinct ideas accurately represent existent beings as they truly and essentially are.

To be sure, in validating reason in the *Meditations* Descartes seemed concerned only to validate our clear and distinct ideas as veridically representing reality. And yet, as I have several times emphasized, at the level of first-order decisions about what it is best to do, all things considered, we do not have clear and distinct apprehension — at least, not in Descartes's view. Evidently, therefore, when he speaks of using our mind as well as we can or of relying on our reason in practical contexts, he must be authorizing its use in areas where we have no access to clear and distinct knowledge and where, moreover, we are in some measure under the guidance of our passions, which are intrinsically obscure. I shall examine the role of reason in Cartesian first-order morality in Part Three.

between the old and the new morality; nonetheless, it is not a difference in content but one of reason's own credentials. And as I have just noted, the Descartes of the correspondence is not significantly nearer to certain knowledge in the domain of first-order morality than before.

There is a further reason why we should not take the apparent difference in content of the two first rules too seriously. As I argued earlier, it is a bit misleading of Descartes to say that he elected to follow the example of the most sensible members of his community, for the decision to follow good example was necessarily of a piece with his retaining his pretheoretical moral convictions. The point of the first rule (as I analyzed it) was to explain how someone engaged in pure inquiry could be thoroughly critical of one's own moral convictions while at the same time retaining them as deep moral convictions. I will not repeat the analysis here but only recall its conclusion: throughout the project of pure enquiry, Descartes retains both his (pretheoretical) moral convictions and his respect for custom and good example as his most reasonable practical policy.

Now, this policy has not in the least been shown unreasonable by anything that has occurred in the transition from Cartesian doubt to post-*Meditations* enlightenment. What is more, in the few texts that bear specifically on this matter, Descartes continues to express this respect for local custom. For example, in his letter to Elizabeth of September 15, 1645, he adds to the several things it is most useful to know the following: "I have only this to add, that one must also examine minutely all the customs of one's place of abode to see how far they should be followed. Though we cannot have certain demonstrations of everything, still we must take sides, and in matters of custom embrace the opinions that seem the most probable, so that we may never be irresolute when we need to act. For nothing causes regret and remorse except irresolution" (4:295; 3:267).

But what, it may be asked, establishes even the antecedent probability that local customs, the laws of one's society, and, most of all, one's deepest moral convictions are worthy of the respect of one whose final authority is one's own reason? Why is Descartes's self-confessed morally conservative strategy rational? About one's moral convictions I have already given my answer in Chapter 1. But two further points may be added that cover the customs and laws of one's society. First, there is an argument grounded in Cartesian metaphysics, specifically in the principle of the best. Earlier in this same letter, Descartes had written that

> though each of us is a person distinct from others, whose interests are accordingly in some way different from those of the rest of the world, we must still think that none of us could subsist alone and each one of us is

really one of the many parts of the universe, and more particularly a part of the earth, the State, the society, and the family to which we belong by our domicile, our oath of allegiance, and our birth. And the interests of the whole, of which each of us is a part, must always be preferred to those of our individual personality. (4:293; 3:266)

We are rooted, then, not just in the physical world, but in a social world with a particular structure and history. From the perspective of God, these facts—of our being lodged in a body not as a pilot in a ship and of our being located in a particular social world—are perfectly ordered and for the best. We may know that the conditions in which we live are divinely ordered and for the best even when they do not so appear. Accordingly, we have some basis for interpreting our own social practices, including our local commonsense morality, as naturally good, as we also interpret our passions—but with this caution: to neither passions nor social directives are we to subordinate our reason.

In addition to this theological argument in defense of the common laws of society, however, Descartes offers an entirely nontheological argument. At the end of his letter to Elizabeth of January 1646, he defends the common laws of society as tending on the whole not only to the public good but also to the private good. Those who depart from these laws, he says, may sometimes do better for themselves, even at the expense of others, but their occasional success, which it is not reasonable for them to expect, is due either to the ignorance of others or to luck.[11] As for himself, Descartes says, "the maxim I have I have observed in all my conduct has been to follow the main road [*le grand chemin*], and to believe that the utmost cleverness is not to be too clever [*de croire que la principale finesse est de ne vouloir point du tout user de finesse*]" (4:357).[12] This abiding thought echoes a passage from the *Discourse* where he speaks of established public institutions:

These large bodies are too difficult to raise up once overthrown, or even to hold up once they begin to totter, and their fall cannot but be a hard one. Moreover, any imperfections they may possess—and their very diversity suffices to ensure that many do possess them—have doubtless been much smoothed over by custom; and custom has even prevented or imperceptibly corrected many imperfections that prudence could not so well provide against. Finally, it is almost always easier to put up with

11. I shall examine this very interesting passage in more detail in Chapter 9. Suffice it to say here that Descartes seems to be anticipating Hobbes's reply to the fool in *Leviathan*, pt. 1, chap. 14.

12. The volume and page reference here is to *Oeuvres de Descartes*. This part of the letter is not translated in *The Philosophical Writings of Descartes*.

their imperfections than to change them, just as it is much better to follow the main roads that wind through the mountains, which have gradually become smooth and convenient through frequent use, than to try
to take a more direct route by clambering over rocks and descending to
the foot of precipices. (6:14; 1:118)

And in the *Passions of the Soul*, speaking of pride, he says that it is a "kind
of joy based on the love we have for ourselves and resulting from the belief
or hope we have of being praised by certain other persons." Pride and its
opposing passion, shame, share the useful function of moving us "to virtue,
the one through hope and the other through anxiety" (11:482; 1:401). It is
not good, he says, to try to rid ourselves of these passions, even if, absolutely
speaking, solid contentment does not depend on what others think of us. In
sum, there are several reasons Descartes suggests for a moral conservatism,
reasons that are in place after the validation of reason in the *Meditations*.

6. I conclude that we satisfy the first condition of virtue and full contentment when we adhere to the first maxim of the *morale par provision*.
So it is in the case of the second condition; we satisfy it when we adhere
to the second maxim of the earlier *morale*. This maxim, however, should
benefit from the validation of reason. If it meets the standard of *évidence*,
as I have argued above, the maxim gains epistemologically in that this standard has in the meantime been validated. In this respect, the second maxim
is like a truth in arithmetic; both are indubitable so long as they alone are
clearly and distinctly at the center of our cognitive focus. The second
maxim, therefore, survives the full methodic doubt of the *Meditations* and
emerges essentially unaltered in the final morality of the correspondence.

Here again there is a superficial change. In the correspondence the second maxim is presented as the principle primarily constitutive of virtue.
Virtue, he implies, is strength of will, capable of withstanding the appetites
and passions that oppose it. In the *Discourse*, to be sure, Descartes does not
speak explicitly of virtue in connection with the second maxim, and he
does not dwell on the motivational influences that oppose our steady adherence to it. It is clear, nevertheless, that we do satisfy the first and second conditions of full contentment just when we judge as well as we can
and when we steadily adhere to our best judgments, whatever may oppose
this steady adherence. For to be virtuous, on Descartes's view, is to have a
firm and constant resolution to do what reason requires—reason demand-
ing this very firmness—in conditions of both certainty and uncertainty
about what is appropriate. Where we are not certain what is appropriate,
however, we are especially vulnerable to the distorting effects of our passions, whose tendency is to make objects appear better than they actually

are. Here not only must we be on our guard in our practical deliberation, we need considerable strength of will to adhere to our best judgment—which is more strength than we typically require when we know for certain what we ought to do. Strength of will is needed to overcome irresolution, on the one hand, and undisciplined appetite and excessive fear, on the other. In the *Discourse*, as we have seen in Part One, Descartes had irresolution—especially irresolution bred by cognitive uncertainty—in his sights as the enemy of constancy. In the correspondence but especially in the *Passions of the Soul*, he turns his attention to the distractions of appetite and fear. Still, the conception of virtue is essentially unchanged from the *Discourse* on.

7. Descartes comments on both the first and second rules throughout the correspondence and in several articles of the *Passions of the Soul*. In the later works, however, he shifts the emphasis away from vacillation of will owing to uncertainty to vacillation owing to unregulated passions. Yet beyond this shift of emphasis, Descartes adds a new and distinctive element, "determinate judgments bearing upon the knowledge of good and evil" (11:367; 1:347). There are three ways, he says, we can prevent our passions from diverting us from the right path.[13] First, we can produce an opposing passion indirectly, by directly representing to ourselves something with which the opposing passion we wish to have is usually joined.[14] The value of this method, however, is limited; it may simply leave us with two passions which "jostle the will in opposite ways . . . rendering the soul enslaved and miserable" (11:367; 1:347). Second, we may by an act of will resist the movement of the body to which, unresisted, the passion would otherwise lead, as when we resolve not to run from an object that excites fear in us. Third, knowing that we will find ourselves in circumstances of various kinds in which our passions will likely be aroused—anger caused by an insult, indignation caused by an injustice—we may arm ourselves with "firm and determinate judgments bearing upon the knowledge of good and evil" (11:367; 1:347). Such judgments, he says, are the "proper weapons" for the will to employ in this conflict, and they are in fact the weapon of choice of most people. Few are so weak, he says, that they always must follow their strongest passion; most take guidance from *some* determinate

13. Among them is not the possibility of willing an opposing passion, since the concept of willing a passion is a contradiction in terms. In the case of a weak passion, Descartes does say that we can simply choose to ignore it by attending to something else, in the way we can ignore a slight noise by concentration (11:363–64; 1:345).

14. "For example, in order to arouse boldness and suppress fear in ourselves, it is not sufficient to have the volition to do so. We must apply ourselves to consider the reasons, objects, or precedents which persuade us that the danger is not great; that there is always more security in defence than in flight; that we shall gain glory and joy if we conquer, where we can expect nothing but regret and shame if we flee; and so on" (11:363; 1:345).

judgments or other. Yet just as we may err in our practical judgments about what is appropriate here and now, we may also err in forming these more general practical judgments, designed for occasions of certain kinds. In forming "determinate judgments," it is especially important therefore to judge well. For these are practical judgments destined to become embedded in our habitual responses to situations where we are most likely to err through haste or bias; if we go wrong in forming them, we lay ourselves open to a life vulnerable to remorse, even though we may overcome our present irresolution.

Descartes's introduction of determinate practical judgments as constituents of good deliberative practice might seem to require that we amend our interpretation of both the second maxim of the *morale par provision* and the second rule of the "new" morality. To see whether this is so, consider Descartes's case of the man lost in the forest, a case of decision under conditions of uncertainty. When we are uncertain about the quickest way out of the forest and decide to walk in a straight line from where we are, we may be said to have judged well (even if falsely). Indeed, as Descartes presents the case, the directive to follow a single straight line out of the forest seems to be recommended as a good rule of thumb to follow in such circumstances. In one respect, this directive is like a Cartesian determinate judgment, for it is a general rule with sound empirical credentials. But whether it qualifies as a Cartesian determinate judgment or not, it is not paradigmatic of what, I believe, Descartes has specifically in mind in the *Passions*. Cartesian determinate judgments seem rather to be settled policies or practical maxims having general and repeated applicability and designed expressly as proper "weapons" of the will in its conflict with strong passions. Indeed, the theory of the passions—which Descartes writes as a physicist (*en physicien*)—has its chief practical utility in showing how we may embed determinate judgments in our own emotional structure, a topic I shall treat below.

Let us suppose that we can formulate and then embed determinate judgments in our character in the form of conative dispositions. We become, say, the sort of person who does not respond inappropriately to insults, however angry they may make us. Why bind ourselves to general rules, when in particular circumstances we may discover good grounds to make exceptions? On our way out of the forest we may run across a well-marked trail and signpost that give us excellent reason for changing course. We would be irrational not to respond to this new evidence. Might not determinate judgments likewise lead to irrational action? Might they not preclude practical deliberation leading, say, to the conclusion that in a particular case it is appropriate to respond angrily to an insult?

The answer to this question will depend on what form the determinate judgment takes. As I noted, deciding whether we should commit ourselves to general maxims or policies and what specific form these should take requires sound judgment in the light of available information about the relevant probabilities. But it is certainly up to us to leave our judgments somewhat open-ended. Indeed, in one sense the model for such judgments might well be the decisions made by someone lost in a forest, since they may take the form of policy judgments, which in certain specific cases are defeasible. Descartes, to be sure, unfortunately for his commentators, does not concern himself with these details, leaving such matters to be settled by our experience and commonsense. Such is the spirit of his rather off-putting response to Princess Elizabeth, who, having asked how we are to determine when we have done enough to promote the well-being of others, was told unhelpfully to let her conscience be her guide.

I have already noted that determinate judgments are destined to take the form of habits. So they are a subclass, if an important one, of policy judgments. They are also designed with an eye to our occasional liability to strong emotional reactions, which tend to distort our ability to deliberate well. In general, they will be dispositions for dealing with anger, fear, lust, envy, and *amour-propre*—the usual passions that tend to deflect us from pursuit of the right and the good. Accordingly, many of them will be, in the narrow sense, moral judgments concerning what is, at least presumptively, inappropriate.[15]

8. Finally, we satisfy the third condition for full contentment when we have followed the third maxim of the earlier *morale*. We are to control our own emotional life so as to be unperturbed by evils entirely beyond our power to prevent. Our happiness depends entirely on our own virtue and on our possessing goods within our power. The enemies of full contentment are remorse, repentance, and desires we cannot satisfy. By following the first two rules we gain mastery over repentance and remorse, and by following the third we gain mastery over our desires.[16] In particular, we are to rid ourselves of desires that have no instrumental value for us and to retain only desires that do have such value, for the effect of having a desire for some object is to make it more likely that we will try to attain that object, other things being equal. A desire for x enhances our motivational

---

15. Descartes is nowhere explicit about the form an ideal first-order morality would take.

16. "Desire" in this context means passion in Descartes's sense. This is a somewhat restricted use of the term. We might have conative dispositions directed toward ends without these ends being objects of desire in this sense. Indeed, many of our actions will be directed toward ends that it is proper—rational—to have without these ends being objects of desire. I discuss Descartes's account of the passions in the next chapter.

tendency to try to get *y*. Now if, assuming we are free from remorse and repentance, we are not fully content, this must be because we have desires that cause us impatience or sadness; and desires of this sort are in every case desires based on some false belief, either about the value of the object or about the possibility of our attaining it. "We do not desire to have more arms or more tongues than we have," Descartes writes, "and yet we do desire to have more health or more riches. The reason is simply that we imagine that the latter, unlike the former, can be acquired by our exertions, or are due to our nature. We can rid ourselves of that opinion by bearing in mind that since we have always followed the advice of our reason, we have left undone nothing that was in our power; and that sickness and misfortune are no less natural to man than prosperity and health" (4:266; 3:258).

The line of thought here is precisely that found in the *Discourse* (cited above), where he writes that once we see clearly that external goods are beyond our power, we shall not regret their absence "any more than we regret not possessing the kingdom of China or Mexico" (6:26; 1:124). We shall meet this idea again in several articles in the *Passions of the Soul*. In brief, it says that we should limit our desires to objects that are entirely in our power. In the case of things that seem only in part to be in our power, for example, objects we can attain only through acting, we should limit our desire to that part, leaving the rest to Providence. To be agitated by desires that range more widely is to suffer uselessly. Suppose I judge well and pick the safest route to a worthy destination. My desire—that is, my passion of desire—should be limited to my taking this route; it should not be fixed on my reaching my destination. If "Providence" decrees that I shall be set upon by robbers on this route, then I discover that my original goal was not possible.

> Reason insists that we choose the route which is usually the safer, and our desire in this case must be fulfilled when we have followed this route, whatever evil may befall us; for, since any such evil was inevitable from our point of view, we had no reason to wish to be exempt from it: we had reason only to do the best that our intellect was able to recognize, as I am supposing that we did. And it is certain that when we apply ourselves to distinguish Fatality from Fortune in this way, we easily acquire the habit of governing our desires so that their fulfillment depends only on us, making it possible for them always to give us complete satisfaction. (11:440; 1:381)

As here sketched, this may not seem a compelling line of thought. One might ask, somewhat in the spirit of William James, whether we might not profit from desires in cases in which having the desire in question is itself a necessary condition of our being able to attain its object. I leave further discussion of this matter to the next chapter. My chief concern here has been to demonstrate the continuity—indeed, the near identity—of the earlier and later moralities. Nothing in the correspondence hints that Descartes ever altered his conception of virtue or of what we must do to achieve it.

CHAPTER SIX

Gueroult's Account
of Descartes's Ethics

1. IN the second volume of his study of Descartes's philosophy, Martial Gueroult devotes two substantial chapters to Descartes's ethics.[1] In the first, he argues that according to Descartes morality is a mere technique. I shall set out below what this interpretative claim amounts to. In the second, having pointed out that we can identify three different conceptions of morality in the development of Descartes's thinking—the provisional morality of the *Discourse*, a perfect morality enabling one to determine the best thing to do on each occasion of rational choice, and a conception of morality as a striving for virtue or as a kind of morality of intention—Gueroult argues that after trying to achieve a perfect morality according to the second conception and finding it impossible, Descartes eventually settled for a final morality according to the third, a morality surprisingly similar in content to the provisional morality. I think that neither interpretative claim gives us the best reading of the Cartesian texts. I do not believe that Descartes ever conceived morality as a mere technique, nor do I think that anything in the relevant texts obliges us to suppose that Descartes changed his conception of an ideal morality for human beings in any essential way between 1637 and his death.

2. Let us begin with the first interpretative claim—that Cartesian morality is a mere technique. What does this claim amount to? It has two distinct

---

1. Gueroult 1985, chaps. 19, 20. Until very recently these two chapters contained the only comprehensive discussion by an established scholar and available in English of Descartes's treatment of moral subjects. They merit a critical assessment.

elements: moral virtue is a mere means, and the end that morality serves is the agent's maximum pleasure.[2]

According to Gueroult, at least at the time of the *Discourse*, Descartes conceived morality as a technique "comparable to medicine" (Gueroult 1985, 2:178). Just as it is given to medicine that its end is "to heal the sick and to preserve health," so it is given to morality that its end is happiness. And just as medicine is properly conceived as a technique or applied science, so too is Cartesian morality. To be sure, it might seem that one business of the moral theorist is to determine the proper end of human action. But according to Gueroult, Descartes simply dismisses this problem, or rather simply presupposes that we already know by the natural light what our proper end is and need only to discover how to realize it.[3] Morality, then, is comparable to medicine. Both are mere techniques and both are concerned to promote the final ends of man as man. Medicine aims to preserve the integrity of the body, and morality aims to promote maximum contentment of the embodied mind. For Gueroult, "Morality is therefore the technique that must determine in what way I must act in this life in order for my soul to be full of contentment, in spite of the fact that this soul is not only pure mind, but is also substantially united to a body that plunges it into a natural and social world whose vicissitudes are infinite. We see immediately that morality, like medicine, can only be a technique that makes use of a theoretical science" (2:179). On Gueroult's interpretation, then, Cartesian morality is to contentment as medicine is to health. And just as medicine may be seen as applied science (physiology), so morality may be seen as the ap-

---

2. If morality is a technique, then a perfect morality would be an infallible, perfectly effective technique. Accordingly, one who had knowledge and command of a perfect morality in this sense would be armed with an effective decision procedure for deciding on and electing the very best thing to do in any particular set of circumstances in which the practical question, What should I do? might arise. Of course, one might well conceive morality as a technique but also believe that no such perfect morality could be within the competence of any human being. As we shall see, Gueroult suggests that Descartes did think at one time that he might achieve a perfect morality of this sort, just as he thought at one time that he might achieve a perfect medicine.

3. "Natural light, along with natural instinct (both guaranteed by divine veracity), reveal to us immediately, without the least doubt, that our end is happiness in the present life. It remains for morality only to furnish the technique capable of realizing this: 'There is no person who does not desire happiness, but there are some who do not have the means'" (Gueroult 1985, 2:178). This quoted passage is from Descartes's letter to Elizabeth, September 1, 1645, the letter in which Descartes examines Seneca's *De vitae beata*. I shall give reasons below why I disagree with Gueroult's reading of Descartes. I note here only that it does not follow from Descartes's remark in this letter to Elizabeth. No doubt all of us desire happiness, but it does not follow that happiness is or should be the sole or final end of all our actions. What is more, whether or not happiness is an end realizable by a "technique" depends on how we conceive it.

plication of those sciences that set out the causes of contentment (mechanics, physiology, and psychology).[4] Summarizing this part of his discussion, Gueroult concludes: "Since it is turned toward an end external to virtue, and since it requires an action modifying material nature as much as my own nature, asking the exact sciences to illuminate these means, Cartesian morality is truly a technique, an applied science" (2:187).

3. As I said above, I do not think we should interpret Cartesian morality—early or late—as a mere technique in the sense Gueroult intends. But let us suppose that Gueroult is correct. Then the idea naturally suggests itself that the intended successor to a provisional morality would be a perfect scientific morality consisting of what Kant called assertoric hypothetical imperatives (counsels of prudence) with the definiteness and effectiveness of what Kant called problematic hypothetical imperatives (rules of skill). A perfect morality, so conceived, would evidently be a morality in the broad sense.

Morality conceived as a mere technique—as a set of technical imperatives—would be an applied science. Which one? Medical science, suggests a famous passage from part 6 of the *Discourse*—at least a medical science such as Descartes hoped at the time he would be able to develop. The maintenance of health, Descartes writes, "is undoubtedly the chief good and the foundation of all the other goods in this life. For even the mind depends so much on the temperament and disposition of the bodily organs that if it is possible to find some means of making men in general wiser and more skillful than they have been up till now, I believe we must look for it in medicine" (6:62; 1:143). Descartes's expectations for rapid progress in medicine were, of course, disappointed, and his developing anthropology also altered his view of medicine itself; yet he did not feel required to retract what he actually says in this passage, which is that good medical science would be a vitally important human good. For where bad health takes away our capacity to reason, Descartes says later to Princess Elizabeth, a remedy to restore health would be indispensable for contentment.[5]

But if improved medical science could deliver more effective counsels of prudence, only fantasy could produce the thought that a perfect medicine will someday supply an effective algorithm for maximum contentment whenever the question of contentment arises. The above passage, of course,

4. To anticipate in some measure the argument below, I should note that the complex causal relation in Descartes's theory between moral action (in the sense of action expressive of virtue) and contentment is not straightforwardly one of means to end. In the first place, it is a connection necessarily mediated by a judgment of value; second, what is judged to have value *as an end* is virtue itself.

5. Letter of September 1, 1645 (4:282; 3:262).

implies no such promise. And the same could be said of any natural science, not only of the two other sciences on Descartes list, physics and mechanics. What is more, not even physiological psychology, as Descartes came to conceive it, could supply such a prudential algorithm.[6] What it can provide is important for morality as Descartes conceived it, but its application, as we shall see, is not principally prudential casuistry. Indeed, what we are to learn from this science, at least the part of it having to do specifically with the passions, is that these can be very poor casuistical guides in particular cases. The plain fact is that all the sciences together could not in principle give us knowledge of the sort that would always save us from first-order practical error—for the obvious reasons Kant pointed out: counsels of prudence are not rules of skill. It would be uncharitable, then, to interpret Descartes as holding otherwise, even should we (in my view mistakenly) read him as conceiving morality as a technique.

4. Nevertheless, Gueroult appears to believe that it was just such a perfect morality that Descartes was heralding in the *Discourse* and referring to in the letter-preface to the *Principles*. Thus, he sees the question Descartes faced in his scientific work to be "whether this morality-science (*morale-science*) can be constituted, whether the technique of happiness can suffice for its end, can furnish every man whatsoever a practical law indicating to him what it is suitable for him to do or not to do in every circumstance, 'encompassing in all cases and for all reasonable beings the same determining principle of the will'" (Gueroult 1985, 2:191).[7] In Gueroult's reading, as we shall see shortly, Descartes abandoned hopes for achieving a morality so conceived. But as I noted, only when we are led to think of Cartesian morality as a technique do we ask whether a "morality-science" of this sort can be formulated.

5. I now return to the original question of whether we should think of Cartesian morality as a mere technique in the first place. Is virtue a mere means, on Descartes's view? Here we have to ask, How does Descartes come down on the question of whether our proper final end is virtue or happi-

---

6. Gueroult makes this point, to be sure, but he does so in the context of trying to show that, owing to this very fact, Descartes had to depart from his original ideal of a perfect morality. In fact, on Gueroult's account, this was Descartes's second departure from his earlier ideal.

7. The quotation is from Kant, *Critique of Practical Reason*, theorem 3, scholium 3, sec. 3. That Gueroult chooses to quote Kant in this context indicates very well how he interprets Descartes's conception of morality as a technique. On this conception, the principles of a morality would all be assertoric, hypothetical imperatives. On the contrary, as I shall contend, Descartes does not construe first-order moral precepts as imperatives of precisely this kind. What is more, contrary to Gueroult's interpretation, I read Descartes as declaring that virtue itself is the proper end of action, not a mere means to contentment.

ness? Gueroult believes Descartes firmly commits himself to Epicurus's answer, not to the Stoic's. Descartes does argue that we need to detach ourselves from "pleasures arising from the body," to be sure, but as Gueroult
reads Descartes, this is because in so doing and in devoting our energies to
"pleasures arising from the soul," we realize more pleasure in the long run
(Gueroult 1985, 2:186). It is because our greatest contentment arises from
the consciousness of our own "strength of soul" that Descartes endorses
stoic detachment. The essential point, however, is that, for Gueroult's Descartes, contentment, not virtue itself, is the end. "Virtue is the goal only
subsidiarily, as is the bull's eye in a target shoot: we aim for it only to win
the prize, meaning pleasure" (2:184). Evidently, the question of whether
virtue is a mere means is closely connected in Gueroult's understanding to
the question of Descartes's hedonism. Let me deal briefly with this latter
question and then return to the former. Did Descartes hold a hedonistic
ethical theory? He certainly sings the praises of contentment. But the question is whether he took contentment to be the sole intrinsic good toward
which our actions should aim—or do aim. As I have several times pointed
out, principally in Chapter 4, the answer is unequivocal: he did not. I have
already noted several of Descartes's texts which imply that contentment is
not the only intrinsic good, much less the supreme good. Gueroult puts
Descartes squarely into Epicurus's camp, but this is correct only if, in Descartes's view, the contentment that supervenes on virtue is the end toward
which the virtuous person strives. Although in his letter on this topic
Descartes does make remarks that might lead to Gueroult's interpretation,
we are nonetheless bound to reject it, since it is at odds with the central
doctrine of Descartes's theory of value, namely, that virtue is the supreme
good. Moreover, it is at odds with the motivational view implicit in his account of virtue, according to which the virtuous agent's primary intention
is to promote goods other than his own contentment, even if his own contentment is the crown of his achievement. Here I add one further argument against taking Descartes to be an egoist hedonist. The contentment
said to supervene on virtue presupposes the value of virtue as an end. It
would be incoherent for Descartes to argue that virtue is a mere means.
But he does not argue this way. Rather, he claims that virtue is a true good
for us (a perfection), that we can know this to be so, and that it is from our
knowledge that we are virtuous that our sweetest and most durable contentment arises. This remarks holds both for intellectual contentment and
for the passion Descartes labels *générosité*. If virtue were not an intrinsic
good, this contentment would not, on Descartes's view, be possible. This
last point, concerned specifically with virtue as a good, can be generalized.
Descartes holds that we achieve contentment, as distinct from the bodily

sensation of pleasure, through our believing that we are suitably joined (either by love or possession) to some true good. The reason our highest contentment derives from our being and knowing that we are virtuous is that being virtuous is our greatest possible perfection and the only perfection entirely within our control.[8]

6. So much, then, for the interpretative claim that Cartesian morality is a mere technique. Let us turn to Gueroult's second main interpretative claim. It is that, at first, Descartes had hoped to achieve a "morality-science" along the lines sketched above but that this effort finally miscarried to a large extent; in the end, Gueroult argues, we find Descartes turning away from a moral science conceived in terms of rules for the direction of the will, telling us what to do and not to do in every circumstance, and toward a kind of morality of intention—from a morality conceived materially to one conceived formally. "That will be the drama of Cartesian morality, which is played across the inextricable complication of a provisional doctrine which heralds a definitive doctrine that must replace it, and of a definitive doctrine, which, on the contrary, confirms and consolidates, once and for all, the morality that we thought to be provided" (Gueroult 1985, 2:192). This passage concludes the first of Gueroult's two chapters on ethics. The next picks up its theme in its title: "Some Consequences concerning Medicine and Morality: Three Ideas of Medicine and Morality." Suppose we begin, as Descartes appears to do in the *Discourse*, by conceiving of morality as a "science of life" which, in Descartes's words, allows "man to distinguish the true from the false in order to see clearly with respect to his actions, and to walk with assurance in this life" (6:10; 1:115). Then we shall discover that in the strictest sense of Cartesian science, such a science of life is impossible: on the one hand, such a science would be re-

---

8. Two more items can be mentioned here. In his letter to Elizabeth of October 6, 1645, Descartes clearly rejects pure hedonism, arguing that it is better to have knowledge than to have pleasure. "If I thought joy the supreme good, I should not doubt that one should try to make oneself joyful at any price, and I should approve the brutishness of those who drown their sorrows in wine, or assuage them with tobacco. But I make a distinction between the supreme good—which consists in the exercise of virtue, or what comes to the same, the possession of all those goods whose acquisition depends on our free will—and the satisfaction of mind which results from that acquisition. Consequently, seeing that it is a greater perfection to know the truth than to be ignorant of it, even when it is to our disadvantage, I must conclude that it is better to have less cheer and more knowledge" (4:305; 3:268). And this from the early *Rules for the Direction of the Mind*: "But I am convinced that certain primary seeds of truth naturally implanted in human minds thrived vigorously in that unsophisticated and innocent age—seeds which have been stifled in us through our constantly reading and hearing all sorts of errors. So the same light of the mind which enabled them to see (albeit without knowing why) *that virtue is preferable to pleasure, the good preferable to the useful*, also enabled them to grasp true ideas in philosophy and mathematics, although they were not yet able fully to master such sciences" (10:376; 1:18; my italics).

stricted to knowledge through clear and distinct ideas; on the other, practical deliberation has to do not with essences but with "existences and exis-
tential circumstances known by means of the senses" (Gueroult 1985, 193).
So there can be no practical *science* in this strict sense. Nonetheless, we can
know, in this sense, what the role of sensation is and how sense experience
may be reliably brought to bear to help us to "walk with assurance" in this
life. Now, one science that may inform practical choice is mechanics. Another, which has to do not with an essence but with the substantial union
of mind and body, is the science of psychology, as set out in the *Passions of
the Soul*. From this science, we can learn that the passions are in their nature good and, when properly regulated, serve as reliable guides to action;
and we can also learn the available techniques for regulating our passions.
But this knowledge cannot entirely satisfy the will. "For this, it would have
to attain more than mere general rules. It would have to furnish us, with
respect to *each case* likely to occur in daily experience, the means to discover the exactly appropriate formula for action, that is, the knowledge of
what is useful to do in order to assure both the preservation and happiness
of our life" (Gueroult 1985, 2:197). From knowledge of such general rules
we cannot derive knowledge of what is best to do in every circumstance of
our lives. If we are to act in the light of reason, our finite reason does not
give us full illumination. Although, as Descartes puts it in the *Discourse*,
those who judge well act well, in our practical judgments we can at best
only approximate judging well.

7. In looking over the development of Descartes's ethics, Gueroult finds
three distinct conceptions, of which two are set out in the early *Discourse*.
According to the first, morality is conceived as "an exact science."[9] Such a
science, following on the heels of the similarly exact sciences of mechanis-
tic physics and medicine, would be the final fruit of the tree of philosophy.
"Wisdom, which is its aim and ultimate principle, depends on the Supreme
Good. The latter is the knowledge of the truth through first causes. This
knowledge, to which the *Principles of Cartesian Philosophy* gives us the
means to accede, must allow us to reach the highest degree of wisdom,
meaning the fifth degree. That is the first idea of morality" (Gueroult 1985,
2:201). The second conception is that of a provisional morality, a set of
maxims to serve us until such time as we are able to establish a definitive
morality according to the first idea. Descartes, as we know, never set out
such a perfect or definitive morality. And although some have suggested
that he never abandoned the belief that such a morality could be worked

---

9. Gueroult finds this conception also in the letter-preface to the *Principles*. Indeed, he
refers expressly to this preface when he uses the term "exact science."

out, Gueroult thinks this unlikely. In the first place, a morality of this kind would "violate the interdiction against applying the understanding alone to the substantial composite." "He must therefore, for metaphysical reasons, and not for external reasons renounce the idea of a perfect morality, meaning an exact morality, having for object only clear and distinct mathematico-deductive ideas drawn from physics"(Gueroult 1985, 2:201–2). In the *Passions of the Soul*, however, we find, not a morality as an exact science of some pure essence, but a scientific morality of the substantial union. In this late work, Gueroult notes, Descartes "wished to explicate the passions not as a rhetorician nor as a moral philosopher but as a natural philosopher" (Gueroult 1985, 2:202). This science "assembles items of evidence of different kinds, some purely rational ones concerning either extension alone (physiological mechanisms), or the soul alone (various functions of the soul, the emotions stemming from it alone, such as contentment, which comes solely from within), and others that are above all sensible, concerning the sensation of passion itself" (2:203). Now, this third conception of morality—the morality of the *Passions* and of the correspondence—is one Descartes did substantially realize and also offered as the replacement for the provisional morality. Evidently, if this is Descartes's final morality, a morality presented, moreover, as a "technique" sufficient for our maximum felicity in this life, it does not fit the ideal of a scientific morality according to the first conception. In its content, furthermore, it matches the provisional morality. Indeed, it is essentially the provisional morality placed on a secure foundations, both metaphysical and scientific.

Morality conceived as an exact science would remove all uncertainty from practice. But we learn from metaphysics—the metaphysics of the substantial union—that uncertainty in this domain as to what is materially the best thing to do on each occasion can never be overcome. The new or final morality, however, teaches us how to cope with and overcome this uncertainty, or rather it teaches us how to assure maximum felicity in this life in the face of such uncertainty.[10]

10. Here I should mention an especially puzzling feature of Gueroult's interpretation. He speaks of three separate conceptions of morality in Descartes's works. In fact, however, he seems to be dealing with *four* conceptions of morality: (1) morality as an exact science, (2) provisional morality, (3) morality as an exact science of the substantial union, a science that eliminates practical uncertainty, and (4) that of a morality that teaches us how to gain felicity in the midst of uncertainty. In his discussion—and this is the puzzling feature—he tends to run together the first and the third. The letter-preface of the *Principles* is the main text which seems to express conception 1. The passage from the *Discourse* in which Descartes speaks of walking with assurance in this life suggests conception 3 (as does the passage quoted in note 8 above from the *Rules for the Direction of the Mind*). On the reading I prefer, there is no discontinuity between the second and fourth conceptions; indeed, the fourth, as expressed in the correspondence and in the *Passions*, is simply a more mature, better grounded form of the second. If Gueroult is indeed dealing with four conceptions of morality, he can be seen as ar-

Since no science, neither mathematico-deductive nor psychophysical and empirical, can reveal to us what is the true good in each case, there remains the science that furnishes a general principle that is always within reach and that teaches us what we have to do in this state of ignorance. . . . Virtue and the beatitude that accompanies it—in brief, the supreme good—no longer therefore reside in the possession of the true, from which good action would invincibly result, but in the effort to attain it. (Gueroult 1985, 2:206)

8. The final morality, therefore, is revealed as a kind of ethics of intention. We do not need to know what is the best thing to do in each circumstance of this life in order to achieve maximum contentment, we need only try to determine what is best. Gueroult puts this—very obscurely—as follows: "Since the supreme good does not consist for us in the possession of the absolutely good in itself, but in the effort to attain it, the principle of the goodness of action no longer resides in the excellence of the matter of the act, meaning in the thing it realizes, but in the excellence of the intention that animates the will, meaning in the intention to realize the best" (2:207). In settling for this third conception of morality, Gueroult says, Descartes "seems to have changed its orientation radically." [11]

[Cartesian morality] was first conceived as a technique derived directly from the scientific knowledge of the universe, and the value of an action was consequently placed wholly in its *matter*, since the action is not good except in virtue of the excellence of its results—the excellence of its results being guaranteed by the possession of what is true. . . . Virtue and good, which until now were tightly linked to the truth of judgment, from which good action depends, meaning the matter of the action determined by the knowledge of the true good, are now dissociated from the nature of the matter and reported under the form of action. Whatever the various occurrences, the possible degree of our error, our virtue remains whole once our *intention* is good: the action may be good even though its matter is intrinsically bad and rests on error. (Gueroult 1985, 2:207–8) [12]

---

guing that since Descartes could realize neither the first conception nor the third, he finally settled for the fourth as the final "substitute" for the first.

11. Later, in setting out three difficulties of Cartesian ethics, he writes: "Descartes is led to reverse, almost completely, the fundamental principles of his morality. . . . A morality of the form of the action is substituted for the technical truth of its matter, as a necessary and sufficient condition of beatitude. In some respects the reversal is complete, since virtue is compatible with error, and good action is compatible with a bad theoretical judgment" (2:213).

12. Throughout, in my view, Gueroult seems never to take into account the distinction between morality in the broad and narrow senses. When he speaks of morality as a technique, he must mean morality in the broad sense. Here moral injunctions are hypothetical imperatives—assertoric imperatives. But the moral knowledge sought by the Cartesian agent is not knowledge of such an imperative. The Cartesian agent strives to discover what is the right

We do not, of course, end up with a "morality of pure intention," because we still have to do with morality that is conceived in terms of contentment and justified by its effectiveness as a means to contentment. What has altered is this. Our contentment is seen to be a function not of our doing the best thing in the circumstances but of our firm intention to do the best thing.[13] Now, it is clear that this notion of virtue as a firm intention to do the best requires that we keep the idea of the best—materially conceived—alive. "The value of the virtuous action remains attached to the true by the intermediary of the intention that gives it its value, since virtue is virtue only through permanent effort toward the highest approximation of the true" (2:209).

9. Although we can accept much in Gueroult's account, we cannot assent to some of its central theses. First and perhaps foremost, we should not accept the background assumption that, for Descartes, morality is a mere technique and virtue a mere means. Second, we need to highlight a vital distinction that this account leaves hidden, the distinction noted above between morality in the broad and narrow senses. Insofar as morality is construed as a technique, it is morality in the broad sense, where the agent's happiness is the end and morality is made up of whatever precepts or dispositions are necessary to this end. But the practice of virtue presupposes precepts of a radically different sort, namely, those of a first-order morality

---

thing to do, where the notion of the right thing to do is a notion that figures within the concept of morality in the narrow sense. In this context, "right" does not mean "most optimific for me." It means, simply, right or best thing to do, objectively speaking. I believe Descartes's view is that I will realize my own maximum contentment in trying to discover what is the best thing to do and always have a firm resolution to do what I so judge. But the judgment presupposes that the idea of the best thing to do is not identical to the idea of what will bring my maximum contentment. Think of my example of the doctor who devotes his life to promoting the well-being of those in underdeveloped countries at great risk to his own health. The good he seeks is the good of *others*. Only on the condition that their good is a genuine good— or that he believes that it is—does his conduct make good sense. The contentment comes from his reflection that he is, to the best of his ability, judging and acting well. This contentment would vanish with the thought that what he was doing was maximizing his own contentment and that the well-being of others was a mere means.

13. Gueroult reads Descartes as holding that our contentment is in no way compromised by our not having knowledge of the best. Thus, on his reading, retrospectively discovered error should not disturb our contentment. Later he identifies the fact that "moral good can coexist with total theoretical error" as one of the inextricable difficulties of Cartesian ethics (2:211–12). I quite agree that, in the absence of a well-founded theory of value, this would be a serious difficulty for Cartesian ethics. But if I am right, Descartes can reply to this criticism that we do know not only what sorts of things are objectively good but also how, in a general way, these things can be ordered. While this knowledge is not sufficient to preclude all theoretical error in our practical judgments, it may be sufficient to preclude "total theoretical error" (whatever Gueroult means by this). I think it is reasonable to say that our doctor who dedicates his life to alleviating human misery in foreign lands is not totally off base. Indeed, if he were totally off base, then God would be a deceiver. For more on these topics, see Chapter 8.

in the narrow sense. Descartes's virtuous agent is not, in deliberating, trying to discover what course of action will maximize his own contentment. He is trying to decide, for example, whether to publish his book, to help a friend in distress (with the possible risk of his own life), to join the army and to fight for his sovereign (again with the risk of his life), to join Les Médecins sans Frontières and fight disease and poverty in foreign lands (once again with the risk of life), and the like. These practical, everyday decisions, however, presuppose objective values, or a belief that there are objective values in play among which one has to choose. These are the values projected by or constitutive of first-order morality, values without which the virtuous life would be entirely empty—without value itself. Now, as I have said, it is important to be aware of this distinction and of the role it plays in Descartes's account of virtue. It is equally important to appreciate that the first-order morality that this account presupposes—unspecified and underdeveloped as it is—is radically different from a set of Kantian assertoric hypothetical imperatives. But such a set of imperatives is what Gueroult has in mind when he speaks of a "morality-science" and claims that such a science was what Descartes had initially hoped to achieve, a hope he later abandoned. I do not think that Descartes ever had such a hope, for reasons I have already given. Indeed, many of these reasons Gueroult himself has very well set out, but he draws from them the wrong conclusion.

Did Descartes in any basic way change his conception of what an ideal morality would be after the *Discourse*? We have already seen that the morality he settled for—or, at least, the morality he was urging on Princess Elizabeth eight years later—was essentially the same in content as the earlier *morale par provision*, differing from it mainly in the security of its foundations. Still, were we to think that Descartes initially conceived of the ideal morality as a perfect scientifically based algorithm that would determine the objectively correct conduct in every circumstance and guarantee that one could walk with assurance in this life, then it is clear that Descartes never achieved such a morality and that what he settled for was something not only less but altogether different. Fine points aside, it is Gueroult's view that Descartes did have in mind such an ideal and did come to settle for less. The scientific project was not advancing apace, the mind-body *ingenium* proved an obstacle to a rigorously scientific medicine, and the theory of the passions, although scientific, could produce no such algorithm. But if I am right, it was never Descartes's view that the path to true happiness was through objectively right conduct; his view was always that the path went through moral virtue. What leads me to this view, among other things already noted, is that we find in the *Passions*, supported by the contemporaneous correspondence, a more thoroughly developed form of what we met in the *Discourse* under the rubric *une morale par provision*.

CHAPTER SEVEN

The Moral Theory of the Passions

1. AS we should expect, the moral theory that appears in Descartes's *Passions of the Soul* conforms to that of the contemporaneous correspondence and continues that of the *Discourse*. The *Passions* develops and defines several familiar lines of argument. In its examination of the essence and function of the passions we get for the first time an account of how we can effect desirable changes in our passional structure. Nonetheless, the moral theory of this work is not fully developed; it is not, therefore, the perfect morality projected in the letter-preface to the *Principles*. Although it offers a much richer account of virtue than we have met so far and culminates in a compelling analysis of *générosité*, it still lacks an explicitly formulated first-order morality and at best only sketches a theory of value.[1] I shall have more to

---

1. According to Stephen Gaukroger's account of Descartes's instruction in moral philosophy at La Flèche, little attention was given to these topics. He writes: "Aristotle's *Nicomachean Ethics*, together with the detailed Coimbra commentary on his work, formed the basis for the moral philosophy course, but there were in fact two different kinds of approach to ethics pursued, and the *Ratio studiorum* was particularly explicit in its insistence on a proper balance between the two. The first approach was that of speculative moral theology of the sort that one finds in Aquinas' *Summa Theologica*. The second was practical casuistry, which promoted a view of moral philosophy not in terms of adherence to general and universal principles, but rather in terms of developing practical guidance for resolving moral problems, guidance that may not be generalizable beyond the particular case. Such an approach had its origins in the writings of the Stoics, and its first full presentation in Cicero, and it fitted well with the kind of practical advice one might expect of a priest. The focus of such teaching was 'cases of conscience' and there were firm strictures against trying to resolve such cases from general principles. The cases themselves ranged from private matters of personal conduct to very public disputes: an important treatise in the latter category, Francisco Vitoria's *Relecto de Indis et de Jure Belli* (1539), for example, looks at the question of the status and rights of the indigenous peoples of Central and South America. There was no shortage of textbooks in the area of ca-

say about Cartesian first-order morality and the associated theory of the good in the final part of this study.

2.   Central to Descartes's theory of virtue is the Stoic distinction between what does and what does not depend entirely on us, although in Descartes's version this is more precisely the distinction between what does and what does not depend entirely on our own free will. This distinction dominates Descartes's thinking about virtue and happiness, as we have seen. It is connected, moreover, through his metaphysics, to another important distinction, that between what happens by necessity (or by Providence) and what does not; indeed, these are shown to be extensionally equivalent. Given these distinctions, it follows that everything we judge to be good is either entirely in our power or not at all in our power. If someone should object that there is a middle ground—things at least partially in our power—Descartes replies that things that seem partially in our power are simply things in which there is a causal division of labor between the part that is and the part that is not entirely in our power—the part charged to Providence. This leads to the most important question of whether our own happiness is entirely in our power. Descartes answers that it is.

3.   Descartes's instructions for attaining happiness are by now familiar; we need only assiduously follow three rules: deliberate well, have a firm and constant resolution to carry out what our reason recommends, and keep in mind that if we do so we shall always have all the goods that are truly in our power.[2] It will help to secure allegiance to these rules if we keep in mind a couple of basic truths of metaphysics: everything that is not entirely in our power is directly sent by God, and the perfections of the mind are greater perfections than the perfections of the body.[3] It will also help if we bring

---

suistry, both on specific issues and on the nature of casuistry itself, one of the most famous texts in the latter genre being Toletus' *Summma Casuum Conscientiae* (1569), and it is hard to believe that Descartes would not have been familiar with this, as the Jesuits made casuistry very much their own. . . . We have every reason to think, given the Jesuit focus on casuistry, that the young Descartes would have thought of morality above all in terms of casuistry, and a training in the subject would have served him well in the kind of political, administrative, or legal career that the Jesuits envisaged their students entering" (Gaukroger 1995, 61). In this speculation—that the young Descartes thought of morality above all as casuistry—I suspect Gaukroger goes too far. Evidently reflecting on his instruction at La Flèche, the young Descartes does not speak of casuistry but complains of the ancient moralists'—the Stoics'— taxonomy of the virtues and more emphatically of their lacking good theoretical foundations. For an account of the curriculum in moral philosophy that seems to fit better Descartes's discussion in the *Discourse*, see Rodis-Lewis 1995, 33–37.

2. To be sure, that we can follow these rules at all presupposes that we have a first-order morality in which we have reasonable confidence. I outline what I think such a morality would contain in the final chapter.

3. Alquié, among others, has complained that while Descartes makes use of the notion of perfection, it remains very obscure. I will make some efforts to clarify the concept in Part

our passions under the control of our will. How we can manage this is one useful product of the theory of the passions.

Although Descartes's account of the passions presupposes his dualistic metaphysics, it is not a direct derivative from it. It rests on a further truth that is found directly in our own experience of the quasi-substantial union of our own mind and body. It is the truth that we are not lodged in our body as a pilot is in a ship, the truth vouchsafed to us, not through clear and distinct ideas, but through two sorts of confused ideas, bodily sensations and passions. Thus it is through bodily sensations and passions that we know ourselves to be a true union of mind and body. And through Descartes's theory of the passions we finally meet the true subject, the moral agent of Cartesian ethics. This is the self, whose virtue and happiness have all along been the topic of our discussion.[4]

One final preliminary remark before turning to the theory of the passions. The theory bears on all three of the rules of morality, although most especially on the third rule. It bears on the first rule in showing us that because our passions tend to exaggerate the value of what they represent to us as good, we must correct for this deceptive appearance if we are to judge well. It bears on the second rule in showing us how we can best cope with obstacles to steadily adhering to what we judge to be best. It bears on the third rule in showing us how to become so thoroughly masters of our desires that our happiness cannot be held hostage to events not entirely within our power. In this sense, but without the least suggestion that we should retreat from an active life in the pursuit of external goods, it discloses the secret of the ancients.

4. In his treatise on the passions, Descartes seeks to answer these questions: What are passions? How are they defined and distinguished from other psychological states? Do they have a distinctive function or use in

---

Three. But it certainly seems that in using this notion, Descartes is building on intuitions formed in the tradition of the great chain of being, which speaks of degrees of reality and corresponding degrees of perfection (or value).

4. Amélie Rorty (1986) doubts that Descartes succeeds in formulating a unified account of this moral agent. Assuming that the will wills what the understanding represents to us as good for us (*convenable*), what conception of the good, she asks, does Descartes offer that is specifically a good for us as individual mind-body substantial unions? It is clear enough that health and bodily strength are perfections of the body, and it is also clear that knowledge is a perfection of the soul. But suppose I am faced with a choice between doing something that will achieve a good for my body and something that, while it is likely to harm my body, will achieve a good of the soul. Which of these is good for me as a mortal moral agent? The problem is acute in those cases in which promoting the welfare of a friend—highly approved by Descartes—requires that we risk our lives. This is certainly not good for the body. What is required is a unified account of what is good for us, not an account in which what is good for the body competes with what is good for the soul; for the moral theory in question is a moral theory for us as embodied minds, and the happiness in question is our happiness as mortal moral agents. I go some way toward responding to Rorty's doubts in Part Three.

our psychological economy? Do they admit a useful taxonomy? Why is it desirable to have a theory of the passions?

States of the soul, Descartes begins, that is, *pensées* or modes of thought, are of two kinds, actions of the soul and passions of the soul. Actions of the soul are its acts of volition, which terminate either in the soul, for example, when we voluntarily call to mind the idea of God, or in the body, for example, when we voluntarily raise our hand. Passions of the soul are states considered as effects, which are divided into those produced by actions of the soul and those caused by movements within the brain. The idea of God, for example, would be a passion of the soul, as the effect of a prior volition. Passions caused by movements in the brain are again divided into those we refer to external objects (sensory perceptions), those we refer to states of our body (bodily sensations), and those we do not refer to anything physical at all; these last are the passions in the specific sense of emotion-passions, and they are, as Descartes puts it, felt "as being in the soul itself" (9:346; 1:337).[5]

In addition to the above, nominal, definition of the passions, Descartes gives an instrumental definition and a real definition.[6] The principal effect

---

5. He sums up his first definition of emotion-passion in article 27: They are "perceptions or sensations or excitations of the soul which are referred to it in particular and which are caused, maintained, and strengthened by some movement of the spirits" (11:349; 1:338–39). This definition calls for some comment. Although it is clear, at least in a rough, intuitive way, what is meant by our referring sensory perceptions to external objects—those we naturally and spontaneously take to be their causes—and by our referring bodily sensations to regions of our body, it is not similarly clear what is meant by an emotion-passion's being felt in the soul itself. But if the meaning of this expression is not itself clear, it is clear enough what Descartes's view is. In the case of sensory states, we spontaneously take these to be caused in us by the action of external objects, and the objects in turn to have the properties they appear to us to have. In the case of bodily sensations, we take these to be caused by states of the body and to be located in the region of these bodily states. In the case of the passions, we do not spontaneously identify something physical as their salient, remote cause, nor do we spontaneously take an apparent feature of the cause to be a real feature of it. Rather, we take the passion to be a real feature of the soul itself. Of course, it is strictly speaking an error, on Descartes's view, to ascribe either a color or a pain to something physical, although we are not wrong in judging that something physical is the remote, salient cause of our perception or bodily sensation, as the case may be. In the case of the passions (in the narrow sense), while we are correct in our natural judgment that they are states of the soul, we may be inclined to think, falsely, that they are also produced by the soul itself. We may be so inclined simply because there is nothing in their phenomenology that suggests to us a physical origin.

As we shall see, Descartes later introduces a different but closely related psychological state, an intellectual emotion. These bear a phenomenological resemblance to emotion-passions, but they are not produced or maintained by physiological states. They are, in principle, emotions that a disembodied soul could experience. Such states will be found to play a significant role in Descartes's final account of human happiness (see especially articles 147, 148, and 212). They do so because through the mediation of the pineal gland they set up passional resonances.

6. Here I follow a suggestion of Jules Vuillemin (1988, 19–23).

of the passions, he writes in article 40, is to "dispose the soul to want the things for which they prepare the body. Thus the feeling of fear moves the soul to want to flee, that of courage to want to fight, and similarly with the others" (11:359; 1:343). As to the use of the passions, he writes in article 52 that it "consists in this alone: they dispose the soul to will the things nature tells us are useful and to persist in this volition" (11:372; 1:349). According to their instrumental definition, the passions dispose us to want certain things; and according to the real definition, these things are (in general) true goods. Although in both definitions the emphasis falls on the instrumental role the passions play in protecting the integrity and health of the body—the real definition adding that the effects of the passions are true goods[7]—it later emerges that they have an even more significant role in promoting true goods of the soul. In this connection, the passions have not only instrumental value but value as an end.

To take a standard case,[8] a passion arises in us on the occasion of our perceiving some object. What happens when we see an animal coming toward us, for example, is that light is reflected from its body, which in turn sets up motions in the eyes, then in the optic nerves, then in the brain, registering finally as a set of motions in the pineal gland, these motions constituting the image of the moving animal. If the image bears a close resemblance to images of animals that have been harmful to us in the past, it excites the passion of apprehension and (in some cases) the passion of fear. These same motions in the gland that produce apprehension also propel animal spirits both into the nerves that produce the bodily motion of running away and into the heart, which in turn propels animal spirits back to the brain, subsequently moving the gland in a manner that sustains the initial apprehension and fear.[9]

Just as the body has the power to affect states of the soul, so the soul has power to affect states of the body, in both cases through motions of the pineal gland. Although I cannot directly move the pineal gland by willing to do so, I can, merely by willing to run, make it move in the way required

---

7. The "real" definition presupposes Descartes's view that God has benevolently instituted basic connections between movements in the pineal gland and our passions, in such a way that the volitions these movements and their associated passions support are, in general, beneficial, at least to the body. If Descartes held a simple preference theory of value, he could infer directly from the instrumental definition of the passions that their effects were (in general) good. Since, however, these connections are interpreted as expressions of divine benevolence, the volitional effects they project are correspondingly to be interpreted as having more than subjective value.

8. There are nonstandard cases, as in dreams, reveries, dramatic presentations, and objectless passions. Passions also arise in connection with bodily sensations. The standard cases are used later for taxonomical purposes.

9. This summarizes the account Descartes gives in articles 35 and 36 (11:355–57; 1:341–42).

for running (11:360; 1:343). The effect of volition on this gland is part of my
natural heritage; some motions of my body I can naturally will, others I
cannot. By habituation, however, I can establish new connections between
volition and movements of the gland. In learning to speak a language, for
example, I establish new connections between willing to say something
meaningful and appropriate motions of the mouth and tongue. Similarly,
just as I cannot by mere willing directly produce motions in the gland, I
cannot by mere willing produce or inhibit my passions. But I can do so indirectly, by willing some thought that is usually joined to some passion I
would have or opposed to present passion I would not have. "Thus, in order to excite boldness and displace fear in oneself, it is not sufficient to have
the volition to do so—one must apply oneself to attend to reasons, objects, or precedents that convince [one] that the peril is not great, that
there is always more security in defense than in flight, that one will have
glory and joy from having conquered, whereas one can expect only regret
and shame from having fled, and similar things" (11:362–63; 1:345). Calling these thoughts to mind, however, may have only momentary and limited effect if the present passion we wish to oppose is strong, since such a
passion is being produced by physiological mechanisms that we cannot oppose directly and which have natural momentum. What we can do in such
a case is simply refuse to act in the way our present passion inclines us. "For
example, if anger makes the hand rise in order to strike, the will can ordinarily restrain it" (11:364; 1:345). The measure of our strength of will is
precisely that of the strength of the passions we can oppose in this way, that
is, by stopping the bodily motions they prompt us to. To test our strength,
however, we should use our best weapons, namely, "firm and decisive
judgments concerning the knowledge of good and evil." If these give us
strength to subdue present passion, unless they themselves are based on
good judgment, they will not render us less vulnerable to regret and repentance than we would be if we were weak-willed (11:367–68; 1:347). To gain
complete control over our passions, therefore, we need prior judgments
concerning what is beneficial, judgments at once firm, decisive, and well
founded.

   In closing the first part of the *Passions* Descartes reminds us of a different
procedure for bringing both our passions and our conduct into line with
our considered judgments about how to live. Noting again, as he had argued in article 44, that by habituation we can alter an established connection between particular motions of the pineal gland and particular passions
of the soul, as occurs when we learn to speak a language, he concludes:

   It is useful to know that although the movements—both of the gland
   and of the spirits and brain—which represent certain objects to the soul

are naturally joined with those [movements] which excite certain passions
in it, they can nevertheless by habituation be separated from them and
joined with other quite different ones . . . . Even those who have the weakest souls could acquire a quite absolute dominion over all their passions
if one employed enough skill in training and guiding them. (11:369–70;
1:348)

There are, then, two principal ways we can gain control of our passions—
through firm, decisive, and sound judgments of value and through bringing our passional dispositions themselves into line with considered judgments concerning good and evil—so that we are appropriately passionate
only about those things that truly merit the passion in question. The critical case is that of desire, since this is the passion that directly inclines the
will. What Descartes claims is that habitual connections between the passion of desire and only those objects truly warranting it can be effected in
each of us. His argument is that we should ideally limit the passion of desire to a single object, namely, the cultivation of the disposition always to
judge as well as we can concerning what is appropriate to do and firmly to
adhere to such judgments. This object is, in a word, virtue.

5. At the beginning of the second part of the *Passions* Descartes defines
the passions in terms of their use, and it is only in terms of this definition
that he is able to establish their taxonomy.

I note that objects which move the senses do not excite different passions
in us in proportion to all of their diversities, but only in proportion to
the different ways they can harm or profit us or, generally, be important
to us, and that the use of all the passions consists in this alone: they dispose the soul to will the things nature tells us are useful and to persist in
this volition, just as the same agitation of spirits that usually causes them
disposes the body to the movements conducive to the execution of those
things. This is why, in order to enumerate them, one needs only to in-
vestigate, in order, in how many different ways that are important to us
our senses can be moved by their objects. I shall effect the enumeration
of all the principal passions here according to the order in which they
may thus be found. (11:372; 1:349)

Typically, the same motions of the gland that cause the passions also
cause the muscles and limbs to move in ways that preserve the integrity,
strength, and health of the body. Thus we may say, however obscurely, that
our passions represent objects or bodily states qua interesting, harmful, or
beneficial to us. Moreover, they generally incline us freely to choose to act
in the manner in which our body is already disposed, that being in a manner beneficial to the body. Descartes's principle of enumeration enables him

to identify six primitive passions: wonder, love, hatred, desire, joy, and sadness. As we shall see, however, these passions can be aroused in us by our judgment of the interest, harm, or benefit of objects, not with respect to our body but to ourselves as embodied souls. Thus, it can happen that we will love something and form an appropriate desire inclining us to act in a manner that, although good for our soul, is harmful to our body. For example, we might risk our life for a friend or endanger our health by dedication to the search for knowledge.[10]

In subsequent articles he explains the use and potential for harm of each of the passions, distinguishing their usefulness for the body from their usefulness for the soul. In general, they are useful when they keep our attention focused on suitable ends and enhance our motivation to promote them. As Descartes puts it, their use "consists only in their strengthening thoughts which it is good that [the soul] preserve and which could otherwise easily be effaced by it, and causing them to endure in the soul" (11:383; 1:354).

The utility of wonder is that it stimulates discovery and retention in memory; those not given to it tend to be ignorant (11:384; 1:354–55). The main varieties of wonder are esteem and scorn, generosity or pride, and humility or servility. "Esteem or Scorn is joined to Wonder according as it is the greatness of an object or its smallness we are wondering at. And we can thus esteem or scorn our own selves, whence come the passions and then the dispositions of Magnanimity or Pride, and Humility or Servility" (11:373–74; 1:350).[11] The other principal passions are enumerated on the basis of their object's usefulness or harmfulness to us. Beginning with love, Descartes observes that an object of love may be represented to us as suit-

10. I mentioned Descartes's originality. All three definitions of the passions are original with him, and so is this particular ordering and enumeration of the principal passions, especially the inclusion of wonder (*l'admiration*). On the other hand, in many respects Descartes's theory of the passions owes much to his predecessors. For an excellent summary account of this, see Rodis-Lewis 1988, 21–32.

11. Themes only hinted at here are more fully set out in articles 149–61 in the third part. In Descartes's moral theory, true generosity is identical with moral virtue. It is notable that in the headnote Descartes uses the term "generosity" and in the text "magnanimity." Descartes discusses his reason for using "generosity" in place of "magnanimity" in article 161. This suggests that the headnote was added to an earlier draft and that Descartes failed to make the corresponding correction in the text. For a full discussion of this matter, see Rodis-Lewis 1987. It is very clear, in any case, that the passion of generosity presupposes a disinterested judgment of worth. In the later articles I have just referred to, Descartes makes the distinction between generosity and pride on the basis of the correctness of the value judgment. One who is proud is simply mistaken about his or her own value. The only true basis of self-esteem, Descartes argues, is the awareness that one is using one's free will well. Well-founded self-esteem is the basis of the passion of generosity; its principal use, moreover, is its inclining the will to cultivate the virtue of generosity.

able or harmful. This language is ambiguous. On the one hand, it naturally suggests that this passion is our response to an intellectual judgment of the value, positive or negative, of some object. This is the most natural reading of articles 56 and 61, as well as of article 79, where he explicitly distinguishes three things—an intellectual judgment, an intellectual emotion of love, and the passion of love—and suggests again that judgment is a causal condition of the passion. This would also fit the account of the passion of love he offers in his famous letter on love to Chanut (February 1, 1647). Nevertheless, his theory requires that love and the other passions can arise independently of any antecedent intellectual judgment of value. And in fact we find him saying in several places, for example, in articles 91–94, that an impression of the brain can represent something as good or bad, as novel, or as one's own. When an impression of the brain represents something to us as suitable, we have only an obscure idea of the value of the object.[12]

Love, according to Descartes's definition, is the passion that incites us to join ourselves in volition (*de volonté*) to objects that appear suitable to us, so as to form a whole of which we are one part. The passion of love is to be distinguished from intellectual love, that is, from judgments inclining the will in the same way, and from intellectual emotions excited by these judgments (11:387; 1:356). Several passions "participate" in love: "the passion an ambitious person has for glory, an avaricious person for money, a drunkard for wine, a brutish man for a woman he wants to violate, a man of honor for his friend or his mistress, and a good father for his children." Only the last is love in a pure form, not mixed with desire for anything from the child nor for any other mode of possession (11:388–89; 1:357). Hatred is the opposite of love; it incites us to separate ourselves in volition from an object represented to us as harmful.

Desire is the passion that disposes us to will for things represented to us as suitable. It is useful so long as it is based on true knowledge, since then it cannot fail to move us in the direction of a true good.[13] The passions that both presuppose and accompany desire are hope and apprehension. We feel hopeful if we believe we are likely to get what we desire, and apprehensive if this is unlikely. Beyond hope lies confidence, when we are certain of getting what we desire; and beyond apprehension, despair, when we

12. For brief discussions of Descartes's definition of love, see Alquié 1989, 3:1013 n. 2 and Voss 1989, 70 n. 30). Voss argues that relating the passion of love to a prior intellectual judgment suffices for the enumeration of the principal passions but that, since this is not a ubiquitous feature of all love it is not sufficient for the definition of love.

13. This point, which will emerge as central to the moral theory of the *Passions*, will be examined in some detail below.

are certain of not getting what we desire.[14] We may feel hope or apprehension concerning things beyond our power, but when they seem within
our power, we may remain apprehensive about the best means or about our
success. Here apprehension may take either the form of irresolution, a passion inclining us not to act but to deliberate,[15] or the form of cowardice,
inclining us not to act at all for fear of failure, even when we have determined the means. Hope, on the other hand, is a passion that inclines us to
believe that what we desire is within reach; it may be seen, therefore, as a
mixture of desire and joy. When we face uncertainties of the sort that inhibit or paralyze those who are apprehensive or cowardly, hope may take
the specific form of courage, inclining us to execute plans of action whose
success we might reasonably doubt.

In articles 177–210, Descartes analyzes passions that either are kinds of
joy or sadness or have joy or sadness as a main component. Of particular
interest are remorse, envy, pity, self-satisfaction, repentance, gratitude and
ingratitude, indignation, anger, vainglory, and shame. Remorse is a species
of sadness and arises from doubt whether something we did was the best
that was in our power. It is useful insofar as it encourages us to do better
in the future, but it would be better were there no occasion for it. It is distinct from repentance, another form of sadness, which presupposes that we
have no doubt but that what we did was bad. Envy, insofar as it is a passion, is sadness mixed with hatred; it arises when we see someone we deem
unworthy receive some benefit. So long as it arises from an offended sense
of justice, this passion is excusable, but that is not its most common form.
Pity, on the other hand, is sadness mixed with love or goodwill; it arises
when we see someone receive some undeserved harm. Those most given
to envy and pity are those who tend to see the distribution of harms and
benefits as a matter of chance, not of providential necessity; those most
susceptible to pity in particular are those who, being apprehensive about
their own good fortune, "represent the misfortune of others to themselves
as possibly happening to them" (11:469; 1:395). In those, on the other
hand, who are not apprehensive about their own future, such sadness over

---

14. About the same object, however, we may feel both hope and despair, since it may happen that the object, viewed one way, seems very likely, but when viewed in another, very unlikely, so that we may vacillate between these two passions.

15. This passion has a use, but it also likely to be harmful. In article 170, Descartes writes:
"Irresolution is also a species of apprehension, which, keeping the soul balanced as it were
among many actions it is able to do, causes it to execute none of them, and thus to have time
for choosing before deciding. In this truly, it has some beneficial use. But when it lasts longer
than necessary and causes the time needed for acting to be spent deliberating, it is extremely
bad" (11:459; 1:390; Voss 1989, 112–13).

the misfortune of others might better be called compassion.[16] The term "self-satisfaction" can refer to a disposition or to a passion. As a disposition, it is tranquillity or repose of conscience. As a passion, it is the feeling that arises when we have done something we believe is good; it is a species of joy, indeed, "the sweetest of all, because its cause depends only on ourselves" (11:471; 1:396).[17] Repentance is the opposite of self-satisfaction, arising from our belief that what we have done is bad; it is the bitterest form of sadness, since it depends entirely on us. Nonetheless, it has a good use, similar to the good use of remorse, since it may encourage us to do better in the future.

Approval, Descartes says, is both a species of love and disinterested. This analysis seems on the face of it inconsistent with his earlier account of love, which was said to be an interested passion, its object being deemed good or suitable. "We are naturally inclined," Descartes writes, "to love those who do things we consider good, even though no good may accrue to us from them." I do not, however, see a deep difficulty here. In the first place, pure love, such as the love of a father for his child, is in one clear sense disinterested, since the father asks nothing from the child that he does not already have; he simply joins himself to the child in volition to form a union. In approval, we can be seen to be inclined in the same way to join ourselves in volition with the other person on account of her good (virtuous) will. In both cases, the disposition to benevolence follows, although the disinterested love and the benevolence are distinct from each other. The passion of gratitude is a mixture of approval of another's goodwill and the desire to reciprocate the benefit we have received. Ingratitude is a vice, but it is not a passion. Indignation is hatred toward those whose action expresses a bad

16. Article 187 continues: "Now there is a difference present here: whereas the common person has compassion for those who lament because he thinks the misfortunes they suffer are extremely grievous, the main object of the pity of the greatest men is the weakness of those they see lamenting, because they consider that no possible accident could be so great a misfortune as the cowardice of those unable to suffer it with steadfastness. And even though they hate vices, they do not on that account hate those they see subject to them; for these they have only pity" (Voss 1989, 121). (Strictly speaking and in accordance with the analysis of compassion given in this article, these occurrences of "pity" should be replaced with "compassion.")

17. The passage continues: "Nevertheless, when this cause is not just, that is, when the actions from which one draws great satisfaction are not of great importance or are even unvirtuous, it is ridiculous and serves only to produce a pride and an impertinent arrogance. This may be observed in particular in those who, believing they are Devout, are merely Bigoted and superstitious—that is, under cover of frequenting the Church, reciting plenty of prayers, wearing their hair short, fasting, and giving alms, think they are entirely perfect, and imagine that they are such friends of God that they can do nothing which would displease him, and that everything their Passion dictates to them is righteous zeal, even though it sometimes dictates to them the greatest crimes man can commit, such as betraying cities, killing Princes, and exterminating whole peoples just because they do not accept their opinions"(Voss 1989, 121–22).

will; it is the opposite of approval and might, like approval, be said to be disinterested. Anger "contains everything indignation does," but it is directed against someone who has intentionally harmed us; it is often mixed with the desire to avenge ourselves" (11:477; 1:399). Vainglory (*la gloire*) is joy founded on love of ourselves, which arises from our hope that others will think us worthy of praise; shame is sadness founded on love of ourselves, which arises from our apprehension that others will find us worthy of blame. Both these passions have the same use; "they incite us to virtue—the one by hope and the other by apprehension" (11:482–83; 1:401). But Descartes adds:

> We need to instruct our judgement concerning what is truly worthy of blame or praise, so that we are not ashamed of acting well and not to be vain about our vices, as happens to others. On the other hand, it is not good to rid ourselves entirely of these passions, in the manner of the Cynics. For although the people [*le peuple*] may judge badly, because we must live among them and because it is important to us to be esteemed by them, we should often follow their opinions rather than our own, at least concerning the external aspect of our actions. (11:483; 1:401)

6. A highly distinctive feature of Descartes's theory, one deriving from his radical separation of mind and body, is that causal connections between psychological and physiological states are all contingent and in many cases alterable, so that, for example, one could change from desiring milk to having a strong aversion to it or, more generally, from having desires for things not entirely in our power to having desires only for those things entirely within our power. The desires in question here are, of course, passions. Suppose I judge (rightly) that your health and freedom from suffering is a true good but only partly in my power. By attending to the truth that the achievement of this good is in some measure dependent on Providence, I can cease to desire this end with excessive passion, although I can will to do whatever is within my power to promote it.[18]

Knowing how to realign these contingent connections between psychological states of the soul and physiological states of the brain (pineal gland) is one thing; knowing what changes to make is another. The former belongs strictly to the applied scientific theory of the passions; the latter belongs to value theory. Descartes says that he writes of the passions as a physicist (*en*

---

18. The Stoics distinguish between ends that are good and valued ends that are indifferent. Descartes draws a distinction that does some of the same work within his theory. He argues that we can (and ought to) limit our desires—our desires as passions—to the desire for virtue; yet we can have other valued ends that we seek to promote, the effort to promote them being part of what virtue consists in.

physicien), by which he would seem to mean he is setting out what passions are and what connection they have to human physiology.[19] But when he tells us what changes we ought to make or what values we should strive to realize, he is in fact writing as a moralist.

Let us begin, then, with Descartes's view that we can take our own passions in hand and to a significant degree shape our own emotional structure—our dispositions to feel and to desire—in the way that we choose.[20] We also start with the idea that having some emotional structure or other is a good thing, indeed, that being passionate is a good thing, so that there is no question *ab initio* of trying to suppress our passions altogether. On Descartes's view, as we have seen, there are six primitive passions: wonder (*l'admiration*),[21] desire, love, hatred, joy, and sadness. Joy,[22] he says, speaking as a moralist, is the only passion that is good as an end, and sadness the only passion that is bad as an end, relative to the soul. Of these, desire is the only passion that leads directly to action.[23] Now if, in general, the passions are useful, not every passion is useful in every circumstance, and, in particular, not every desire is useful; indeed, we may have some desires that are in general harmful. A desire is useful only when it leads us to acquire a

19. Again, his central claim about the passions, which distinguishes his view from all previous ones, is that they are passions precisely because their proximate causes are physical not psychological.

20. In her letter to Descartes of April 25, 1646, Princess Elizabeth comments on Descartes's early draft of the *Passions*: "I find still less difficulty in understanding everything you say about the passions than in practicing the remedies you order against their excesses. For how is one to forsee all the accidents that can happen in life—accidents it is impossible to enumerate? And how can we prevent ourselves from ardently desiring things that necessarily tend to the conservation of man (like health and the means to live), which nevertheless do not depend upon man's decision?" (Blom 1978, 179). Descartes replies with respect to these specific objects of desire: "I do not think that one can sin by excess in desiring things necessary for life; it is only desires for evil or superfluous things that need to be regulated. As for those that tend only to good, it seems to me that the stronger they are, the better. To palliate my own faults I listed a certain irresolution as an excusable passion, but nevertheless I esteem much more highly the diligence of those who are swift and ardent in performing what they conceive to be their duty even when they do not expect much profit from it" (4:411; 3:287).

21. One original feature of Descartes's taxonomy of the passions is the inclusion of *l'admiration*, which he takes to be an essential element of every passion. Wonder includes the element of surprise, perhaps of being in some degree startled by some object, without at the same time having any view about its being beneficial or harmful.

22. Joy is a passion, not a bodily sensation. Typically we have joy when we possess what we take to be good; in these cases our joy presupposes our value judgment. The full contentment that constitutes human happiness arises from our judgment of the value of our own virtue. In general, an action will promise joy as an outcome, then, only if it aims to promote some good other than joy itself, say, the well-being of a friend.

23. This is not to say that if we desire to do *x*, then we directly will to do *x*. It is simply to say that between desire and volition there is no other passion.

true good; otherwise it is harmful. Since, by hypothesis, we can change our desires, the question is, which should we keep and which should we alter?

We can sort desires according to the character of their objects. Some objects of desire are true goods, whereas others are not. Some objects of desire are not in the least in our power to bring about, whereas others are entirely within our power, and still others only partly in our power. If we seek to have only beneficial desires, then we must first rid ourselves of desires for objects that are not true goods and for objects that are not at all in our power, for a desire is useful only if it inclines us to choose in a way that brings a true benefit. Where what we choose to do can in no way effect the bringing about of something good, having a desire for this object cannot be beneficial to us. On the other hand, if we desire a true good and this is entirely within our power, then our desiring it is useful. Indeed, Descartes says that we can hardly desire it with too much passion. What about desires for undisputed goods that are only partly in our power? According to the analysis set out above, we should limit our desires only to that which is entirely in our power and not desire with passion whatever part of the good is in the hands of Providence. It should be remembered throughout that a desire (passion) is a motivational enhancement only; we can will actions for the sake of ends, where we do not have a desire (passion) directed to the end in question.[24] Indeed, not only can we will an end without desiring it and yet desire the means, such willing is the condition of the ideally virtuous person who promotes ends that have value and yet are not entirely within her control. Let us now turn to the Cartesian texts in which this line of argument is set out.

If we consider joy, love, sadness, and hatred only as they relate to the soul (ignoring how they may lead us into actions that are beneficial or harmful to our health), we can say that joy and love are in themselves always good, and sadness and hatred always bad.[25] But as these relate to desire, the matter is more complicated. Descartes begins article 144: "But because these passions cannot lead us to perform any action except by means of the desire they produce, it is this desire which we should take particular care to control; and here lies the chief utility of morality" (11:436; 1:379).

---

24. This is evident from the definition given in article 52. The use of all the passions consists in this: "they dispose the soul to will the things nature tells us are useful and to persist in this volition." Nature indicates benefits to us in two main ways: first, through innate dispositions to love and to hate and, second, through our intellectual powers to make value judgments. The former are confined to bodily homeostasis, the latter range over all other benefits, including that of the good use of our free will.

25. I shall set out a Cartesian theory of value in Part Three, where I take up such value judgments.

The utility of morality with respect to the passions lies in showing us what desires to acquire and what to get rid of. It does this first, as we have just seen, by setting forth the criterion by which we can sort desires into the beneficial and the harmful. The harmful ones are those that promise joy and produce sadness, on the one hand, and preempt our cultivating more useful desires, on the other. And here Descartes repeats his earlier claim.

> As I have just said, desire is always good when it conforms to true knowledge; likewise it cannot fail to be bad when based on some error. *And it seems to me that the error we commit most commonly in respect of desires is failure to distinguish adequately the things which depend wholly on us from those which do not depend on us at all. Regarding those which depend only on us—that is, on our free will—our knowledge of their goodness ensures that we cannot desire them with too much ardour, since the pursuit of virtue consists in doing the good things that depend on us, and it is certain that we cannot have too ardent a desire for virtue.* Moreover, what we desire in this way cannot fail to have a happy outcome for us, since it depends on us alone, and we always receive from it all the satisfaction we expected from it. (11:436–37; 1:379; my italics)

If we cannot desire virtue with too much ardor, we cannot desire external goods not entirely within our power with too little ardor. Indeed, we should endeavor to suppress our desire for such goods. If we fail to do so, we run the risk of disappointment; and if we preoccupy ourselves with them, we run the additional risk of not attending to the good that is within our power. One general remedy for vain desires is generosity (to be discussed later); the other is reflection on Providence. Evidently, if we desire something that we can in no way help to bring about, even if we believe we can do so, our desire is entirely useless, since the whole utility of desire (as a passion) lies in its inclining us to pursue and attain some good, the possessing of which will produce joy.[26]

26. Article 145 continues in part: "we should reflect upon the fact that nothing can possibly happen other than as Providence has determined from all eternity. Providence is, so to speak, a fate or immutable necessity, which we must set against Fortune in order to expose the latter as a chimera which arises solely from an error of our intellect. For we can desire only what we consider in some way to be possible; and things which do not depend on us can be considered possible only in so far as they are thought to depend on Fortune—that is to say, in so far as we judge that they may happen and that similar things have happened at other times. But this opinion is based solely on our not knowing all the causes which contribute to each effect. For when a thing we considered to depend on Fortune does not happen, this indicates that one of the causes necessary for its production was absent, and consequently that it was absolutely impossible and that no similar thing has ever happened, i.e., nothing for the production of which a similar cause was also absent. Had we not been ignorant of this beforehand, we should never have considered it possible and consequently we should never have desired it" (11:438; 1:380).

Suppose I correctly judge that x is good but not in my power. Suppose, nonetheless, I desire x. I can desire x only if I believe that x is possible. In this belief, of course, I may be mistaken. If I knew x to be impossible, I would not reasonably desire it. In this case, a desire for x would be entirely useless. There are two further cases. If my belief that x is possible is false, then again, my desiring x is useless. For if it is not possible, my desire would be harmful both in crowding out other more fruitful preoccupations and in leading to impatience and sadness. If, on the other hand, x is possible, that is, if x occurs, still my desire was harmful in the former respect and I get no additional joy that I would not have received simply from my happily possessing x (in the desired way). Let us agree, then, that desires for outcomes entirely beyond our control are vain and useless and that, therefore, reason counsels us to get rid of them. But does the same hold for desires for outcomes that do, at least in part, appear to be subject to our voluntary control—which embraces most of our desires—as Descartes explicitly remarks in article 146? Here he tells us that "we must take care to pick out just what depends only on us, so as to limit our desire to that alone" (11:439; 1:380).

Again, it is a question only of the *passion* of desire, not of our pursuing ends we judge to be good. So it is not a question of whether we should pursue possible outcomes in some measure within our control, even those we know to depend also on the cooperation of other causal factors of which we are ignorant. The question in this context has to do with the utility of the passion of desire, where we believe that the outcome is only in some degree dependent on what we do. This case, he argues, reduces to the one we have just examined, concerning goods not at all in our power: "although we must consider their outcome to be wholly fated and immutable, so as to prevent our desire from occupying itself with them, yet we must not fail to consider the reasons which make them more or less predictable, so as to use these reasons in governing our actions." Again it is presupposed that we may rationally pursue ends not entirely in our control and that in so doing we ought to take the most likely route to success. The argument is not, then, that we are not to have ends that depend only partly on us, but that to the extent that they do not depend on us, we should not make these ends objects of desire. Descartes gives this illustration.

Thus, for example, suppose we have business in some place to which we might travel by two different routes, one usually much safer than the other. And suppose Providence decrees that if we go by the route we regard as safer we shall not avoid being robbed, whereas we may travel by the other route without any danger. Nevertheless, we should not be in-

different as to which one we choose, or rely upon the immutable fatality
of this decree. Reason insists that we choose the route which is usually
the safer, and our desire in this case must be fulfilled when we have followed this route, whatever evil may befall us; for, since any such evil was
inevitable from our point of view, we had no reason to wish to be exempt
from it: we have reason only to do the best that our intellect was able to
recognize, as I am supposing that we did. And it is certain that when we
apply ourselves to distinguish Fatality from Fortune in this way, we easily acquire the habit of governing our desires so that their fulfillment depends only on us, making it possible for them always to give us complete
satisfaction. (11:439–40; 1:380–81)

Our desire in this case should be limited to willing the means, since the
end is in large measure in the hands of Providence, while our willing the
means, as our reason directs, is entirely in our control. We may will the end
as a condition of willing the means, but we are not to make the end an object of the passion of desire. And over this, Descartes argues, we have voluntary control. To master our desire for ends not entirely in our power, it
will help simply to attend to the truth that such ends are in the hands of
Providence—that is, to reflect that, so far as we are concerned, the intended
result does not occur because it is impossible. Since we do not desire the impossible, this reflection should help us restrict our desires to what is entirely
within our power. Some suppose, mistakenly, that the results of action, so
far as they depend on factors other than our own will, depend on luck and
that therefore they are possible. But there is no such thing as luck. All that
happens that is not entirely dependent on us happens of necessity.[27]

To summarize, Descartes says that we commonly fail to distinguish desires whose objects are entirely in our power and desires whose objects are
not at all in our power, and he argues that the latter desires are all vain and
useless and that we should limit our desires to the former. Now, we might
agree that we cannot *know* of any desire that it is useful unless we can both
know the true value of its object and know that it is within our power to
achieve this object. But we may still ask why we should restrict our desires

---

27. See the previous note. Descartes's example is underdescribed. A fully rational decision
would take into account the value of successfully conducting our business and the disvalue of
being robbed and their respective probabilities. In this example he points out that we must
weigh probabilities. In his letter to Elizabeth of January 1646, he emphasizes the relative
weighting of the values of the possible outcomes.

The question of what contingent ends we either may or ought to pursue—contingent in
the sense of being partly dependent on cooperating agencies—is a question to be dealt with
later, as is the further question of how our commitment to such ends is supposed to fit into
our emotional structure. At this point, we have been told only that this commitment is not
essentially to involve the passion of desire.

to those we know to be useful? After all, we might have a desire based on our belief that its object has a certain value and that if we pursue a certain plan of action we will achieve it, where this belief, although it does not amount to knowledge, is true. A desire so based would be useful, especially if it were also true that we would not have pursued the end in question had we lacked motivation enhanced by hope—that is, had we lacked this desire. If we restrict our desires to those whose objects we know we can realize, we might miss out on possessing true goods that, had we desired them, we would in fact have gained. In the theoretical context Descartes is notoriously averse to risk. But from the *Discourse* onward he urges us to proceed with confidence in the face of inevitable uncertainty, secure in the knowledge that if we have judged as well as we can, any failure to attain our end was not our fault. Indeed, was not this the message of the second maxim, to be decisive and resolute in our actions, where certain knowledge is not to be had?

Certainly, Descartes is not to be seen as revoking the second maxim or counseling us against proceeding with confidence where we cannot be certain of the outcome. He is trying to make a very narrow point about our passions, arguing that we should restrict the passion of desire to goods entirely in our power. All the same, one might object that this passion is often useful. Without it we would be deprived of true goods we might otherwise attain, for example, scientific knowledge and the good health and wellbeing of others, since the persistent effort required to attain them might well depend in some measure on our passionate engagement, or so it would seem. To this objection, I am not certain Descartes has an effective reply. The passion of desire, on his view, enhances motivation, even though it is not necessary for motivation. It could, therefore, make the difference between perseverance and giving up, where only with perseverance would some good outcome be realized.[28] Should it happen that some of these risky desires prompt action that falls short of its goal, then that will be the time for a good dose of reflection on Providential necessity. And it cannot be said—at least Descartes could not say—that if this medication can be successful at all that it would fail to come in the nick of time. Although Des-

---

28. This line of thought is familiar from William James's colorful "Will to Believe," where in a characteristic passage he writes: "How many women's hearts are vanquished by the mere sanguine insistence of some man that they *must* love him! he will not consent to the hypothesis that they cannot. The desire for a certain kind of truth here brings about that special truth's existence; and so it is in innumerable cases of other sorts. Who gains promotions, boons, appointments, but the man in whose life they are seen to play the part of live hypotheses, who discounts them, sacrifices other things for their sake before they have come, and takes risks for them in advance? His faith acts on the powers above him as a claim, and creates its own verification" (James 1949, 104).

cartes has not, then, entirely made his case that we should desire *only* virtue with passion, he has shown in theoretical terms that we should desire virtue with passion, and with a passion proportional both to the value of its object and to the certainty of its being entirely in our power. Accordingly, we might do well to follow Descartes up to the point of agreeing that among desires that are useful to have, the desire for virtue is the most useful. This is the desire to perfect our own will, so that we never fail to act well. In different contexts the object of this desire is given different names: *le bon sens*, *la bonne volonté*, *la sagesse*, virtue, and finally, as we shall see, *générosité*.[29]

---

29. Generosity, as Descartes conceives it, is a virtue, but the term *générosité* also refers to a particular passion, a specific form of admiration or self-esteem. But as an intrinsic good, generosity is virtue itself, not the passionate response to the virtue.

Part 3

VALUE AND GENEROSITY

IF we were to express the moral import of Descartes's theory of the passions in a single maxim, it would read: Desire virtue and virtue only. This injunction applies only to the passion of desire; so far as this particular passion is concerned, we are enjoined to limit it to our acting as well as possible, that is, to our following reason to the limits of our finite intellect, finite knowledge, and available time. The desire for virtue is always good and does not admit of excess. This injunction does not imply that we are to limit our *ends* to this single end, for obviously if we are to act at all, virtuously or otherwise, we require ends other than virtue itself. A full moral theory would have to give an account of such ends. No such account, at least no careful and systematic account, is set out in Descartes's works. In this significant respect, then, his moral theory is incomplete. Although he gives a comparatively complete account of virtue and happiness, he does not spell out the theory of value and appropriate action that this account presupposes. My aim in Part Three is to supply such an account. The exposition will naturally be more speculative than it has been up to this point; this is especially true of the suggestions I make in the final chapter about what a Cartesian account of duty might look like.

Now one might suppose, in view of Descartes's principle concern with virtue, that we should read him simply as a virtue theorist. The idea would be, roughly, that we discover what ends are worth promoting and what sorts of action are most appropriate by studying the paradigm of the virtuous person and reading off from her characteristic attitudes and conduct what ends are worth promoting and what constraints should regulate the pursuit of such ends. Yet we cannot cast Descartes as a virtue theorist for the very reason that has led us to search for a Cartesian first-order morality in the first place. Descartes's analysis of virtue presupposes, and therefore cannot generate on its own, some theory of the right and the good, without which it would be empty. For a related reason, furthermore, we cannot cast Descartes as a precursor of Kantian formalism. On Kant's theory the prior ethical concept is the good, to be sure, but in the special and important sense of the good that is both unconditioned and the condition of the goodness of outcomes of action and of the rightness of actions. It is true that the good will in Kant is the only subject of which this predicate—unconditioned goodness—holds, and it is true that, in Descartes's theory too, the good will is, relative to us, the *bonum supremum*. Nevertheless, while Kant does not define the rational will in terms of goods of the qualified kind, Descartes does define the good or virtuous will in such terms.[1] In constructing a Cartesian first-order morality, therefore, we must start with a theory of the good.

---

1. Descartes does, however, come close to Kant in his account of the attitude characteristic of the virtuous or *généreux* toward others; as he describes it, this is similar to what Kant calls respect, a proper acknowledgment of and reverence for their free will.

CHAPTER EIGHT

A Cartesian Theory of Value

1. ALTHOUGH virtue is the supreme good, it is a second-order good; both its possibility and its achievement are conditional on our believing that our ends are also true goods. Although this belief might in fact be erroneous, it cannot be based on a fiction. There must be ends that are truly worth choosing, even if our beliefs about them are mistaken. For example, our doctor who volunteers to travel abroad to alleviate pain and to cure disease must suppose that his goal merits his time, effort, and sacrifice of other goods. Even if, as a disciple of Descartes, he should hold that virtue is a supreme good and the only good entirely in his control, he must at the same time believe that the well-being of those he is trying to help is a good worth pursuing for its own sake. To be sure, it might cynically be suggested from some perspective external to the doctor's own moral outlook that he could still carry on with his work and retain his thoughts about virtue even if the well-being of his patients had no more value, objectively, than their suffering, so long as he believed otherwise. But whatever someone might make of this suggestion, it is not one that the doctor himself could coherently entertain. If, as a disciple of Descartes, he considers himself virtuous, he also believes he is resolutely trying to judge well, and this is an activity he could not engage in on the supposition that all that matters is that he sincerely reach some determinate decision or other about what goals to pursue.[1]

---

1. What I say here does not run against the grain of the second maxim of the *morale par provision*. For example, although the man lost in the forest might choose which direction to walk in entirely arbitrarily, he does so guided by the thought that his being out of the forest and still alive is a genuine good.

Viewed from the perspective of Descartes's ethical theory, our doctor is not like the archer in Stoic literature. The virtue of the archer is manifest entirely in his trying to hit the target, where hitting the target is held to have no value in itself whatever. There might be doctors modeled on the archer, doctors who seek difficult "targets" in order to exhibit their extraordinary skills. Although these doctors might have the virtue of the craft of medicine, they would not have the *moral* virtue of our doctor. If, therefore, we strive to be virtuous and do what we judge to be good and worthy of our time and effort, we do so only because we believe that our ends have real value. Moreover, we presuppose that there is something—call it a practical fact of the matter—that is the objective standard of our judgment, the standard we are striving to meet. Furthermore, we presuppose that we have a suitable level of cognitive competence, such that when we engage in practical deliberation about what morality demands of us, we are confident that our reflection will tend in the direction of meeting this standard. In this way, then, Descartes's theory of virtue presupposes a theory of value.[2]

Descartes's account of virtue as the supreme good presupposes a theory of value in a further way, for the claim that virtue is the supreme good presupposes some account of the good in general, some account of goodness or (positive) value. There can, of course, be no doubt at all that Descartes has a theory of value in the sense that he has settled views about the range of things that have value and views about what judgments of the form "*x* is good" mean. Following the fashion of moral theory of his time, however, he does not attend expressly to metatheoretical issues such as the meaning of "good," the metaphysics of goodness, or the epistemology of evaluative judgments. My project in this chapter is to indicate what I think his views concerning these matters would have been.

2. In a letter to Chanut (November 1, 1646) Descartes says that were he to write a treatise on moral philosophy, he would among other things undertake "to examine the right value of all the things we can desire or fear" (4:536; 3:299). Among such things he lists health, joy, knowledge, beautiful objects, friends, other human beings,[3] free will,[4] and God.

---

2. The term "theory of value" may be taken in the narrow sense of a theory of the good, desirable, or worthwhile or in a very broad sense as a general theory of all values, not only of goodness but of rightness, beauty, truth, holiness, etc. Here I use the term in the narrow sense. What I have in mind is some account of *(a)* what judgments of the form "*x* is good" mean and *(b)* what grounds or reasons we have for judging of some *x* that it is good, better than *y*, or bad or indifferent.

3. See the relatively early letter to Mersenne, March 18, 1630, in which Descartes refers to his *Compendium Musicae*. Here he tries to explain why sounds please us, and he seems to hold that their pleasing us is what makes music beautiful and gives it value. In this letter, which is brief, he appears to defend an intersubjectivist account of aesthetic value: something is beautiful when it pleases most people (1:132–34; 3:19–20).

4. See especially *Principles*, sec. 37; *Meditations*, III; *Passions*, articles 152, 155–56.

Although this is scarcely an exhaustive list of Cartesian first-order values, it will go some distance toward answering G. E. Moore's question, "What things are good (for their own sakes)?" A full Cartesian theory of value, of course, would contain the complete enumeration of such things. As to Moore's other question, "What does 'good' mean?" Descartes provides no express answer. My conjecture is that he would incline toward Moore's own answer, that the property of being good *simpliciter* is one that cannot yield to further analysis; for he appears to treat such claims as that knowledge is good for its own sake, for example, as synthetic judgments, and he treats the goodness in question as a simple nonempirical property.[5] Thus, placed meta-ethically, in terms of the taxonomy of twentieth-century anglophone moral philosophy, Descartes emerges as a cognitivist and nonnaturalist thinker.

3. My plan is take Descartes's list and set out Cartesian explanations of why they are true goods, explanations designed to show in addition why we should be confident in our belief that they are goods. I begin with the claim that health is a good. The Cartesian defense of this claim, in barest outline, is that health is the outcome projected by the passions, that the passions are in their nature good, having been instituted by a benevolent

---

5. Descartes uses several value terms to refer to things that are desirable or good for their own sake. Thus, virtue is the *souverain bien*. Two terms he frequently uses may be misleading, at least, as they are often translated. These are *bonne à notre égard* and *convenable*. Although these are translated as "good for us" and "useful" or "agreeable," these translations are misleading, since they suggest, not something good for its own sake, but something good as a means. The French word *convenable* comes from the Latin *conveniens*, which was Cicero's translation of the Greek *homologia*. Cicero uses the term specifically in the context of the Stoic's view of man's chief good and what is desirable for its own sake. "So, by the acquisition of knowledge and by reasoning, he reaches the decision that man's chief good, praiseworthy and desirable for its own sake, rests here. Since it does reside in what the Stoics term *homologia* (which, if you like, we shall call 'conformity' [*convenientiam*]), and in this then there is that good which is the standard of reference for everything else" (Cicero 1991, 3.21). For the Stoics, the standard of goodness—the ultimate good-making property—is harmony or agreement with nature. Making allowances for the differences in their respective conceptions of nature, it is not far off the mark to say that this Stoic view is also Descartes's. To strive to use our free will well is to live in harmony with our nature as rational agents.

There is a complication, however, in Descartes's account of value. He distinguishes between what is good in itself or in an absolute sense and what is good for us. God, for example, is good in the first way; virtue and knowledge, for example, are good in the second way. This distinction is not one between two senses of "good"; Descartes predicates the goodness of something in the second way when he considers the thing in question as standing in a certain relation to us, namely, the relation of being in agreement with our nature or as perfecting us in some way. Something is good for us if it is good and if it is something we could in some way possess such that our doing so would be agreeable to our nature. Again, this is not a distinction between types of things. God, for example, is both good absolutely and good for us. God is good for us in this way: God is good absolutely and, owing to our generic similarity to God in some respects, is for this reason a suitable object of our love and, being a suitable object of our love, God is good for us.

deity, and that therefore any outcome they project must itself be considered good.

This line of argument has an important feature that is lacking in the Stoic argument that health is to be preferred. The Stoic learns from nature what act-types are appropriate. Nature first tutors us through our inclinations; we are inclined by our passions to act in health-preserving ways, from which we can infer that nature intends for us to act in these ways, from which in turn we can infer that so acting is appropriate (other things equal). Health, therefore, is to be preferred. For the Stoic, however, it us not truly good. If we are strong and healthy, we are not better than someone who is weak and sickly. Descartes follows the Stoic argument but carries it to the conclusion that health is a true good. From the natural direction of our passions we infer not just that our own health is to be preferred but also that, intended for us by a benevolent God, it is a true good, the achievement of which makes our life better. Yet, again following the Stoics, Descartes does not wish to say that *we* are better for being healthy. *We* are good only as a function of our having free will and using it well. Nonetheless, our being healthy is a true good for us, even if we are not better for being healthy.

In this example, we can see why metaphysics is essential to the theory of value and why Descartes's theory is not subjectivist. Consider the ancient question, Is something good because we prefer it, or do we prefer it because it is good? Descartes chooses the second, although his answer is indirect and mediated by the metaphysical premise that God is benevolent or, more specifically, nondeceiving. It is this that permits the inference from "I prefer *x*" to "*x* is good for me (ceteris paribus)" in an objectivist sense of "good" (*convenable*). The argument is not, it will be noted, that a benevolent God would not have created us to be naturally inclined to act in ways harmful to our health. An argument of this sort would already presuppose what it is designed to show, namely, that health is a true good. A benevolent God wills for us what is good; he wills our health, therefore, if and only if it is a true good. The premise that our inclinations are divinely ordained by a benevolent God serves a strictly epistemic role in the defense of the claim that our health is good.[6] It is not just that God has constituted us to act in health-preserving ways, however. Because our passions represent items that conduce to our health as good for us, God would be deceiving us if these items and the health they project were not true goods. It must be remembered that Cartesian passions have propositional content; they rep-

---

6. To be sure, God's benevolence is involved nonepistemically in providing us with passional incentives to achieve what is good.

resent things as having value or disvalue, where the value in question is to be understood to be objective value. It is owing to the benevolence of God that we can rely on our passion-based judgments of value as being true judgments. Divine benevolence plays the same role with respect to passion-based value judgments as it does with respect to sensory-based judgments about the existence of external objects. Since our passions tend to exaggerate the value of things, however, we need to correct for this distortion in assessing their true value.

About sensible goods in general, by which I mean goods identified through our passions, Descartes's view is this. Some of them we seem naturally drawn to; they are by nature objects of love and of desire. Some we learn to love and to desire through experience. Indeed, through the course of our lives the list of things we spontaneously love or spontaneously hate tends to expand and to change. Nonetheless, according to Descartes, the general tendency of our nature is such as to keep us from forming tastes for items of consumption that are harmful to our health. If one should object that the common addictions to alcohol, tobacco, and drugs are counter-examples, Descartes would reply that we have the means, namely, the good use of our intelligence, to determine that these items are harmful and to avoid them. In the common course of nature, after all, we do not find that animals take to things that are harmful to their health and well-being, and the same is true of us humans at the level of our natural physiology. If we are given to far more experimentation in the things we inhale or ingest, we are also given the means to determine when our experiments fail. The rule for identifying true sensible goods, therefore, at least those of the consumable sort, is to take the representations of our passions as provisionally true — as subject to correction and even to defeat in the light of our experience.

4. So far I have sketched both the argument to support the claim that the health of our bodies is a true good and the procedure we are to use to pick out, among things we are inclined to consume, those that are harmful or beneficial. But many of these goods, in addition to conducing to our health, are conducive to joy. Suppose I am hungry and I see an apple. The desire to eat the apple may arise immediately, owing, no doubt, to a conditioning of the connections between this passion and a constellation of physiological changes effected by my seeing apples when I am hungry. Or the desire may arise more mediately, from my reflecting on my past experience with apples and recalling how nourishing and how delicious they have been. Still, if I am wise I will correct for the distorting effect of my desire for this apple and judge that it would be good to eat, even if not quite so good as my present passion would have me believe. I eat it and thereby conserve my health, which is itself a source of joy. I also enjoy its taste.

While I can distinguish the taste sensation from my enjoying it, however, it cannot be said in this case that my present joy follows on my believing that this taste is good. This is one of those cases, far from rare, in which the joy, as Descartes puts it, is a confused mode of perceiving goodness.

Let us review the role of the passions in this case, that is, the role they play in my judgment that this apple is good. As we have seen, the *effect* of the passions is always to "move and dispose the soul to want the things for which they prepare the body" (11:359; 1:343). The *function* of the passions is that "they dispose our soul to want the things which nature deems useful for us, and to persist in this volition" (11:372; 1:349). Mere knowledge that apples are nourishing and delicious, unaided by the passion of desire, would leave us less likely to will the eating of the apple. So the utility of the passion of desire, in this case, is that it enhances our motivational tendency to take measures to acquire and to eat the apple.[7] The instrumental utility of the passion of desire lies in its motivational force; it leads us to the passion of joy, which is a noninstrumental value with respect to the soul and, since it is at once a sign and a cause of good health, an instrumental value with respect to the body. Joy is not the object of desire but rather the prize for attaining the object of a corrected desire. Joy is a thought, a *pensée*, a state of consciousness, a mode of a thinking substance. When it is not based on false value judgment, joy cannot fail to be good; and in the special case of enjoyment of a particular taste sensation, there is no room for value error and the joy cannot fail to be good.[8]

---

7. In expounding Descartes's account of the role of the passion of desire in normal activity, one repeatedly meets the problem I face here. On the one hand, as we have seen, Descartes argues that we should so condition ourselves so that we desire only virtue (mostly by deeply reflecting both on the role of Providence on determining outcomes not entirely in our power and on our own nature as having free will). On the other hand, he refers to our desires in other contexts as if these too were a good thing, since they tend to keep on the track of true goods, as in the present case. Perhaps what we should say is that desire should be proportionate to the value of the goods in question and that we should condition ourselves further to react stoically to the frustration of desire, as the outcome requires. Descartes's account of motivation, as we have seen, is complex, since he runs a series of strictly intellectual emotions in parallel with the passions. So knowledge that the apple has nourished us and that there are no reasons not to eat it might give rise to the *intellectual* emotion of desire and hence to the volition to eat, without the passion of desire coming into the picture at all. Yet here again, we meet the original problem, since in us, Descartes says, any intellectual emotion tends to give rise to a corresponding passion.

8. The passion of joy can have two causes. One is intellectual, when joy follows the judgment of the goodness of some object and the intellectual judgment of possession. But joy may arise independently of intellectual judgment, as it might in the case of my enjoying the tasting of an apple. In this case, we might say, enjoying this taste just is the passional knowledge that it is good. In article 139 Descartes says, as concerns the soul, love and hatred result from knowledge and precede joy and sadness, "except when the latter stands in place of the knowledge of which they are species." The knowledge that precedes is value knowledge. In the special case of enjoying the taste of the apple, the joy just is the knowledge of its goodness.

5. According to the way I have set out the account, through our passions we come to know that many sensible particulars are good. An apple is typical of that class of sensible particulars of which the suitable possession—consumption—preserves bodily well-being. Suitably possessing other sensible particulars, however, may have no direct effect and little if any indirect effect on bodily well-being, although it may affect well-being more generally. Take the case of seeing a beautiful flower. Here the relevant mode of possessing the valued object may be merely seeing it. Moreover, the joy of seeing it may just be the judgment of its value. On the Cartesian account, we should say that the flower is a good or that it has value, where we mean not instrumental value but value as an end, in this case the value we call beauty. This is again the kind of case in which our enjoyment is a confused idea of the value of the object whose possession (in a suitable way) we enjoy. Just as our natural fear of, say, lions, plays a quasi-cognitive role, according to Descartes's account, so does our enjoyment of a flower. To put the view rather starkly, our natural or corrected enjoyment of beautiful objects gives us epistemic access to the true value of those objects, just as the natural light gives us epistemic access to the true nature of matter. In the case of enjoyment, however, our idea of this value, although clear, is confused.[9]

Is the beauty of the flower an objective value? Well, clearly not, at least not in the same sense as the flower's so-called primary qualities—its shape and size, for example. Is it objective, then, in the same sense as the flower's color? The Cartesian answer to this question seems also to be no. Although Descartes hints at a theory of aesthetic response that remotely foreshadows Kant's, he offers a fairly crude majoritarian analysis of the truth of aesthetic judgments. Consider the following passage from an early letter to Mersenne, in which Descartes refers to his *Compendium Musicae*:

> You ask whether one can discover the essence of beauty. This is the same as your earlier question, why one sound is more pleasant than another, except that the word "beauty" seems to have a special relation to the sense of sight. But in general "beautiful" and "pleasant" signify simply a relation between our judgment and an object; and because the judgments of men differ so much from each other, neither beauty nor pleasantness can be said to have any definite measure. I cannot give any better explanation than the one I gave long ago in my treatise on music; I will quote it word for word, since I have the book before me.
>
> "Among the objects of the senses, those most pleasing to the mind are neither those which are easiest to perceive nor those which are hardest,

---

9. I shall pick up this discussion again below, under the general rubric of the passion of love.

but those which are not so easy to perceive that they fail to satisfy fully
the natural inclination of the senses toward those objects nor yet so hard
to perceive that they tire the senses."

> To explain what I meant by "easy or difficult to perceive by the senses"
> I instanced the divisions of a flower bed. If there are only one or two types
> of shape arranged in the same pattern, they will be taken in more easily
> than if there are ten or twelve arranged in different ways. But this does
> not mean that one design can be called absolutely more beautiful than
> another; to some people's fancy one with three shapes will be the most
> beautiful, to others it will be one with four or five and so on. The one
> that pleases most people can be called the most beautiful without qualifi-
> cation; but which this is cannot be determined. (1:132–33; 3:19–20)

In the special case of beauty, therefore, Descartes begins to lose the distinction he seeks generally to keep in place, between the joy of possessing
a valued object and the value of that object. In this letter, the beauty of the
flower merges with the joy in the eye of the beholder. Nonetheless, here as
elsewhere, the joy itself is a true good.

To sum up to this point, we have identified some of ingredients of the
good life, according to Descartes: health, enjoyment, tasty food, and beautiful objects. What this discussion so far may suggest is the following general thesis: whatever is the object of a corrected passion, of love or desire,
is a true good. I have already argued that Descartes is not a value subjectivist in the standard sense.[10] All the same, we might model his explanation
of the objective value of sensible goods on that of recent informed-desire
views that take the value of some good to depend on a subject's desiring
it. The difference is that in Descartes's case, an agent's passions, corrected
by relevant information, play a cognitive role in identifying values, having
been divinely instituted.[11]

6. I have claimed that our enjoying the possession of some good is a criterion or test of that thing's being a true good. What of enjoyment itself?
Is it also a true good? By enjoyment, I mean the passion joy. This is not the
same thing as the bodily sensation, pleasure (*chatouillement*). Nor is it the
same as intellectual joy, which, although an affection of the soul, is not a

---

10. His account of beauty is perhaps on the borderline.

11. The line of argument found in the sixth of the *Meditations* and developed in the *Passions
of the Soul* is just to this effect, that when we make appropriate corrections in the value representations of our passions, we may then take the representations as veridical. This is not
straightforward value subjectivism, since the values are not constituted entirely from the passions; they are rather lit up or revealed by the passions. Nonetheless, the more sophisticated
subjectivist views can be used as suitable models for this part of the Cartesian theory of value.

passion. Joy (as a passion) can arise in two ways. It can derive from intellectual joy as a resonating passion, in which case it presupposes a judgment by the intellect that I possess some good. But as we have seen, there are important cases in which joy can arise without the mediation of any such thought. Yet in whatever way it arises, it is itself a good. Indeed, "in reality the soul receives no other fruit from all the goods it possesses, and while it is getting no Joy from them it can be said that it does not enjoy them any more than if it did not possess them at all" (11:396–97; 1:360–61). I could conceivably be in a state of good health and accordingly possesses a true good, but if I did not represent my good health as a good, consciously or not, then I would not enjoy it; I would not feel the joy that is the fruit of good health. My being healthy would nonetheless be a good.

Descartes gives the following account of the positive case. "So when one is in sound health and the weather is more serene than usual, one feels a cheerfulness within oneself which does not come from any function of the understanding, but only from impressions which the movement of spirits forms in the brain; and one feels sad in the same way when the body is indisposed, even though one may not know it is" (11:398: 1:361).[12] The question at hand, however, is this: What defense does Descartes offer that the passion of joy, which is the fruit of our representing to ourselves that we possess some other true good, is itself a true good? So far as I can see, he treats this claim as simply self-evident.

If this is right, we should not infer that, for him, health is in the final analysis a mere means. Indeed, given his account of its origin, joy presupposes the possession of some other true good, in the sense of something that is desirable for its own sake. The enjoyment of good health, therefore, presupposes that health is a true good independently of whether or not it is enjoyed.[13] Rather than health's being a mere means to joy, joy is one of nature's signs of good health, which leads to our forming a desire for those things that conduce to maintaining it.[14]

12. Descartes writes in his letter to Chanut of November 1, 1647, that in all likelihood joy was the soul's very first passion, "because it is not credible that the soul was put into the body at a time when the body was not in a good condition; and a good condition of the body naturally gives us joy" (4:605; 3:307).

13. Descartes makes a slight concession to hedonism, however, since he says that, other things equal, joy based on a false opinion about one's possessing some good still has intrinsic value. But other things are not equal, because joy gives rise to a desire to continue possessing the item thought to be good; and since this item is not good, by hypothesis, this desire and the joy that gave rise to it are harmful (11:435; 1:378).

14. "For the soul is immediately informed of things that harm the body only by the sensation it has of pain, which produces in it first the passion of sadness, next hatred of what causes the pain, and in the third place the desire to get rid of it. So also the soul is immediately informed of things useful to the body only by some sort of titillation, which, exciting joy in it,

Two things may be worth remarking in connection with joy (or content-ment). The first is that it is not the sole object, not even the typical object, of the passion of desire. For the most part, the objects of desire or of love are goods other than contentment or joy. To be sure, joy supervenes on our possessing such true goods in some suitable way, even in the cases in which we discover the value of something only by means of our enjoying it, Descartes would seem to hold that the object of love or of desire is this ob-ject itself, not the enjoyment of it. Beauty is a case of this kind.[15]

The second thing worth remarking is that, on Descartes's view, joy or contentment can be measured; it admits of degrees.[16] Its measure is the value of the goods on the possession of which the joy supervenes. Thus the contentment that supervenes on our possessing goods of the body is not so great as that which supervenes on our possessing goods of the soul. For ex-ample, the satisfaction of making an important discovery would be greater than that of eating a fine and nourishing meal (other things equal). The contentment that supervenes on our achieving virtue is supreme in this re-spect. This contentment also has the advantage of being entirely within our power. But here as elsewhere, the contentment presupposes that what is possessed is a true good.

7. Let us now turn to love. According to Stephen Voss, articles 139–42 of the *Passions* make it clear that, for Descartes, love has intrinsic value (Voss 1989, 96 n. 68). I do not think this is correct, although I agree that it is important to bring Descartes's account of love into a discussion of his theory of value. But it is not love itself that has intrinsic value; it is the sev-eral objects of love and the wholes that are constituted by love that have such value. Voss's claim is based on the following passage from article 142:

---

next arouses love of what one believes to be its cause, and finally the desire to acquire what can make one continue having this joy or enjoy one like it later on" (11:430; 1:376).

15. As I have pointed out from time to time, Descartes's official or standard view—found explicitly in the letter on love to Chanut—is that joy supervenes on our belief that we pos-sess in some suitable way an object that is (independently) good. These objects, then, are what love and desire target. Yet as we have also seen, for example, in the long letter in which Des-cartes seeks to reconcile Zeno and Epicurus (see Chapter 4), Descartes seems to flirt with the idea that without the thought of prospective pleasure our motivation to promote the good on which pleasure supervenes would be diminished. His calling virtue the supreme good and contentment the final end does not help to make his position very clear.

16. For example, in his letter to Elizabeth of September 1, 1645, he writes: "According to the rule of reason, each pleasure should be measured by the degree of perfection which pro-duces it; it is thus that we measure those whose causes are clearly known. . . . the true office of reason is to examine the just value of all the goods whose acquisition seems to depend in some way on our conduct in order that we never fail to devote our energies to trying to pro-cure those that are, in fact, the most desirable." We must concede, however, that in the case where it is through joy that we learn of the true value of something we possess, we have no way to determine that value independently of this joy.

it may be doubted whether or not love or joy are good when they are . . . ill founded [that is, founded on some false opinion]; and it seems to me that if one considers in abstraction [*précisément*] only what they are in themselves, with respect to the soul, it can be said that even though joy is less solid and love less advantageous than when they have a better foundation, they remain preferable to sadness and hatred likewise ill founded. So in life's contingencies, in which we cannot avoid the risk of being deceived, we always do much better to incline toward the passions that tend to the good than toward those that concern evil, though this be only to avoid it. (11:435; 1:378)[17]

While it is clear that, on Descartes's view, considered in itself and independently of its instrumental value, joy has intrinsic value even when ill-founded, I fail to see in this passage any reason to interpret Descartes as claiming the same about love. I confess, however, that I do not see clearly why unmerited love, considered in itself, is to be preferred to unmerited hatred, but the reason seems to have to do with its greater utility. Descartes seems to be saying that since we cannot always avoid error in our value judgments, we do better on the whole if we are inclined to see the good in things than if we are inclined to see the evil.[18]

The passion of love Descartes defines as "a movement of the spirits, which impels the soul to join itself willingly to objects that appear agreeable to it (*convenable*)" (11:387; 1:356). This is to be distinguished from judgments that also incline the soul to join itself *de volonté* to objects it judges to be good. Love is also to be distinguished from desire, although love typically gives rise to desire when we love some future state of affairs or condition we regard as possible to achieve through our action.

In principle, human love ranges over all objects that can in any way appear good to one. In article 82 Descartes gives as examples of such objects: glory (of an ambitious man), money (of an avaricious man), wine (of a drunkard), a woman (of a lustful and brutish man), a friend or mistress (of a man of honor), children (of a good father). In the first four examples he notes that what appears good is the possession of the object, not the ob-

---

17. Voss's translation.

18. In his letter on love to Chanut, Descartes writes: "Love, however immoderate, always has the good for its object, and so it seems to me that it cannot corrupt our morals as much as hatred, whose only object is evil. We see by experience that the best people, if they are obliged to hate someone, become malicious by degrees; for even if their hatred is just, they so often call to mind the evils they receive from their enemy, and the evils they wish him, that they become gradually accustomed to malice. By contrast, those who abandon themselves to love, even if their love is immoderate and frivolous, often become more decent and virtuous than they would if they turned their mind to other thoughts" (4:614; 3:312).

ject itself. In each case, the agent in question has "desire mixed with other passions" for the objects themselves. "On the other hand," he continues,

> a good father's love for his children is so pure that he desires to have nothing from them, and wills neither to possess them otherwise than he does nor to be joined to them more closely than he already is; instead, considering them each as another himself, he seeks their good as his own or with even greater solicitude, because, representing to himself that he and they make up a whole of which he is not the best part, he often prefers their interest to his, and is not afraid to lose himself in order to save them. The affection of people of honor have for their friends is of this same nature, though it is rarely so perfect, and that which they have for their mistress participates greatly in it, but also participates a little in the other. (11:389; 1:357)

It is evident from the first four examples that not all the actual objects of human love are worthy of it. That is to say, we often have love for objects that in fact lack the value that they appear to have. Accordingly, the fact that, say, misers love money for its own sake and brutes love sex for its own sake does not show that these objects have even prima facie value as ends, such that in practical deliberation they ought to be given at least some weight.[19]

8. Many common objects of human love, however, do have genuine value, as Descartes explains in article 83. As objects of the form of love he calls affection, he offers flowers, birds, and horses; of the form he calls friendship, other people; and of the form he calls devotion, God, our country, our prince, our city, and even a private person we esteem more highly than we esteem ourselves.

Descartes makes it clear later that the value of flowers is their beauty; he does not comment further on the value of animals, although we might reasonably say that in some cases their value too is aesthetic. The objects of love and hatred, he says, are represented either by the external senses or by what he refers to as the internal senses and our reason. "For we commonly call something 'good' or 'evil' if our internal senses or our reason make us judge it agreeable or contrary to our nature, but we call something 'beautiful' or 'ugly' if it is represented as such by our external senses (chiefly by the sense of sight, of which we take more notice than of all others" (11:391–92; 1:358). Delight and abhorrence, then, are species of love and hatred respectively. In the case of delight, what has value is, say, the visual presentation

---

19. In his letter to Elizabeth of September 15, 1645, he writes that the true object of love is perfection and in that context (the object in question is God) he implies that the standard of love is the objective perfection or value of the object. That is, love presupposes the value of its object; it does not create that value.

of a flower or the auditory presentation of a piece of music. He remarks that these are usually more vigorous than other species of love and hatred but also less inclined to truth, so that "they are the most deceptive of all the passions, and the ones against which we must guard ourselves most carefully" (11:392; 1:358). This liability to being deceived about the true value of the object of delight is dangerous, since delight leads naturally to desire and to action quite contrary to our nature and reason. "Delight," he goes on to say in article 90, "is specially ordained by nature to represent the enjoyment of that which attracts us as the greatest of all the goods belonging to mankind, and so to make us have a burning desire for this enjoyment" (11:395; 1:360). Desires arising from delight vary considerably; "the beauty of flowers . . . only incites us to look at them," but the apparent beauty of a particular member of the opposite sex can make "our soul to feel towards that one alone all the inclination which nature gives it to pursue the good which it represents as the greatest we could possibly possess," a desire that has a fair chance of being excessive.

9. Of particular interest in connection with delight is Descartes's claim (in the passage just cited) that the pleasure or enjoyment supervenient on possessing a beautiful object in some suitable manner can itself be the object of desire. This is as close to hedonism as Descartes gets, but the comment is anomalous; it does not fit Descartes's standard pattern of analysis according to which the object of desire is the valued good, as distinct from the pleasure or joy supervenient on our possessing it. In the standard analysis, the object of love is the same as the object of desire; in this case, love gives rise to a desire to possess the object in some manner other than that of possessing it merely *de volonté*. In the case of pure love (for example, parental love) joy follows immediately, since the relevant mode of possession just is that of love, no more, no less, and here it is as clear as anything could be that the object of love is not the joy itself.

The final and decisive word on the question of whether joy or contentment is the supreme good is to be found in the letter to Princess Elizabeth of October 6, 1645.

> I have sometimes asked myself the following question: Is it better to be cheerful and content, imagining the goods one possesses to be greater and more valuable than they are, and not knowing or caring to consider those one lacks; or is it better to have more consideration and knowledge, so as to know the just value of both, and thus grow sad? If I thought joy the supreme good, I should not doubt that one should try to make oneself joyful at any price, and I should approve the brutishness of those who drown their sorrows in wine, or assuage them with tobacco. But I make a distinction between the supreme good—which consists in the

exercise of virtue, or what comes to the same, the possession of all those goods whose acquisition depends on our free will—and the satisfaction of mind which results from that acquisition. Consequently, seeing that it is a greater perfection to know the truth than to be ignorant of it, even when it is to our disadvantage, I must conclude that it is better to have less cheer and more knowledge. (4:304–5; 3:268)

This letter may be usefully conjoined with Descartes's letter-preface to the French edition of the *Principles*.

No soul, however base, is so strongly attached to the objects of the senses that it does not sometimes turn aside and desire some other, greater good, even though it may often not know what this good consists in. Those who are most favored by fortune and possess health, honor and riches in abundance are no more exempt from this desire than anyone else. On the contrary, I am convinced that it is just such people who long most ardently for another good—a higher good than all those that they already possess. (9B:4: 1:180)

What I have called sensible goods bring joy when suitably possessed, but the joy they bring may be false, since it may flow from a false estimate of their true value. In Descartes's view, this would be so in the case of those who successfully pursue public acclaim and a luxurious style of living as their principal aims in life, to the exclusion of friendship, family, community, not to mention virtue and the love of God.

10. In a number of ways, indeed, God dominates Descartes's theory of value. We have already seen how divine benevolence supports the epistemic reliability of our corrected passions as indicators of value. But this is not the central theme of Descartes's famous letter to Chanut on the love of God. In turning to this letter, we move to a different order of evaluation, a strictly intellectual evaluation. Here Descartes explicitly distinguishes between intellectual or rational love and love as a passion.

The first . . . consists simply in the fact that when our soul perceives some present or absent good, which it judges to be fitting for itself, it joined itself to it willingly [*de volonté*], that is to say, it considers itself and the good in question as forming two parts of a single whole. Then, if on the one hand the good is present—that is, if the soul possesses it, or is possessed by it, or is joined to it not only by its will but also in fact and reality in the appropriate manner—in that case, the movement of the will which accompanies the knowledge that this is good for it is joy; if on the other hand the good is absent, then the movement of the will which accompanies the knowledge that it would be a good thing to acquire it is desire. All these movements of the will which constitute love, joy, sadness and desire, in so far as they are rational thoughts and not passions, could exist in our soul even if it had no body. For instance, if the soul perceived that there are many very fine things to be known about nature, its will would be infallibly impelled to love the knowledge of those things, that is, to consider it as belonging to itself. And if it was aware of having that knowledge, it would have joy; if it observed that it lacked the knowledge, it would have sadness; and if it thought it would be a good thing to acquire it, it would have desire. There is nothing in all these movements of its will which would be obscure to it, or anything of which it could fail to be perfectly aware, provided it reflected on its own thoughts. (4:601–2; 3:306)

Here is one place that Descartes unequivocally asserts that knowledge is a true good, or as he here expresses it, a perfection of the soul, something worth having and worth seeking for its own sake. This view of the value of knowledge, we may recall, was expressed with the same confidence in the *Discourse*; and both there and in this letter to Chanut we have no reason to doubt that he considers the claim that knowledge is good to be a clear, distinct, and certain intuition, involving concepts that are entirely transparent to the thinking and reflecting substance that is our soul. Descartes introduces this example, however, only to illustrate the nature of love. Chanut's second question to Descartes was whether the natural light of our reason instructs us also to love God, as it clearly does to love knowledge. Descartes answers affirmatively:

In my view, the way to reach the love of God is to consider that he is a mind, or a thing that thinks; and that our soul's nature resembles his sufficiently for us to believe that it is an emanation of his supreme intelligence, "breath of divine spirit." Our knowledge seems to be able to grow by degrees to infinity, and since God's knowledge is infinite, it is at the point towards which ours strives; and if we considered nothing more than this, we might arrive at the absurdity of wishing to be gods, and thus make the disastrous mistake of loving divinity instead of loving God. But we must also take account of the infinity of his power, by which he has created so many things of which we are only a tiny part; and of the extent of his providence, which makes him see with a single thought all that has been, all that is, all that will be and all that could be; and of the infallibility of his decrees, which are altogether immutable even though they respect our free will. Finally, we must weight our smallness against the greatness of the created universe, observing how all created things depend on God, and regarding them in a manner proper to his omnipotence instead of enclosing them in a ball as do the people who insist that the world is finite. If a man meditates on these things and understands them properly, he is filled with extreme joy. Far from being so injurious and ungrateful to God as to want to take his place, he thinks that the knowledge with which God has honored him is enough by itself to make his life worth while. Joining himself willingly [*de volonté*] entirely to God, he loves him so perfectly that he desires nothing at all except that his will should be done. Henceforth, because he knows that nothing can befall him which God has not decreed, he no longer fears death, pain or disgrace. He so loves this divine decree, deems it so just and so necessary, and knows that he must be so completely subject to it that even when he expects it to bring death or some other evil, he would not will to change it even if, *per impossible*, he could do so. He does not shun evils and afflictions, because they come to him from divine providence; still less does he eschew the permissible goods or pleasures he may enjoy in this life, since they too come from God. He accepts them with joy, without any fear of evils, and his love makes him perfectly happy. (4:608–9; 3:309–10)

In this letter we meet themes familiar from earlier correspondence with Elizabeth, themes which forcibly indicate the crucial role metaphysics has in the development of Cartesian ethics. It is not that Cartesian, first-order practical morality derives directly from metaphysical premises or that we can somehow deduce moral precepts from our knowledge of God. Rather, it is our knowledge of God that reveals God as a preeminently suitable object of our love. And one direct bearing that the love of God has on Cartesian morality, aside from the joy supervening on this love, is in helping us to adhere to the third rule of morality—to restrict our desires to what is entirely in our power—by getting us to accept what otherwise happens "as expressly sent to us by God," and even to "rejoice in our afflictions," to use the language of the earlier letter to Elizabeth.

11. It may be in order to pause briefly and set out the taxonomy of value on which Descartes is implicitly relying. Let us begin with a basic distinction, one we find, among other places, in the letter Descartes addressed to Queen Christina, who had asked to have his views on the supreme good. A thing, he says, can be judged to be good in two ways: without reference to anything else and in relation to ourselves. God is the supreme good in the former sense "since he is incomparably more perfect than any creature." God is the most perfect being, both *ens perfectissiumum* and *ens realissimum*. When we estimate the value of a thing "without reference to anything else," we are placing it on the great chain of ontological perfection. On this scale of value God is the top, and we, having souls, stand well below God

but well above soulless matter.[20] Descartes often invokes this standard of perfection, for example, when he says to Elizabeth that in our moral deliberations one of the most important truths we are to keep in mind is that our soul is our most noble part and that its perfections, knowledge, and virtue are, accordingly, higher than those of the body, such as health and strength. So deference to our own value and the value of God is not in the least irrelevant to the practical business of deciding how we should best live our lives. Nonetheless, the values that figure more immediately in our practical deliberations are those considered in relation to us. These are goods that in some suitable way we can possess, goods that Descartes otherwise describes as suitable to our nature (*convenable*). These divide into three classes: those we discover through the intellect, those we discover through the external senses, and those we discover through the internal senses.

This basic distinction does not divide the goods themselves, however; God, for example, who is supreme on the ontological scale, also figures among the items on this scale of goods that are *convenable*. As we have just seen, God is a supremely suitable object of our love, and love is the suitable manner in which we possess God, just as love is the suitable manner in which we may possess friends, members of our family, and members of our society. That God is good we know through our intellect. We know also in this way that knowledge is good and that virtue is good; we know furthermore that free will itself is good, even the free will of someone not disposed to judge as well as possible. Beauty is the value we discover through our external sense, and through the internal senses we discover things conducive to our physical well-being. Through the senses we also discover other goods that may have only a marginal effect on our health but contribute importantly to our general sense of well-being. It would be too dismissive to call them harmless pleasures, but they are entirely optional goods. Certain activities fall into this class—for example, tennis or playing the piano. Some amateurs, of course, become very serious about these activities and devote much of their time trying to develop a high level of competence; to the degree that they succeed, they may realize the further good of a sense of accomplishment.[21] And while the choice of one's life's work,

20. Between us and God there might be multitudes of angels, writes Descartes in his letter to Chanut of June 6, 1647. "When Holy Scripture speaks in many places of the innumerable multitude of angels . . . we regard the least of the angels as incomparably more perfect than human beings" (5:56; 3:322).

21. In article 95 of the *Passions* Descartes speaks of the pleasure we take simply in meeting challenges and overcoming obstacles, even if the activity in question may not be profitable, either to oneself or others, in any further way.

where one makes such a choice, may within a certain range also be optional, such activities as constitute one's profession or craft may be goods known both through the internal senses and ends known through the intellect. For reasons I will set out below, health and general well-being of others is a true good, not just relative to them but relative to us.

12. With this general scheme before us, I will try to place the following human goods: friendship, community, and the state. Strictly speaking, friendship, as a form of love, is not good for its own sake. In friendship, what is good for me is my friend and the joy that supervenes on my simply being related *de volonté* with my friend—supervenes, that is, on my making up a whole of which my friend is the other part. What makes only some people friends? What is it about our friends that makes them appropriately different from other persons? We do not, after all, love everyone as we love our friends. Descartes writes to Chanut that we often love someone even before we "know their worth," by which he means their moral character, and without knowing why. Here he must intend passional not intellectual love; passional love is the love we discover through the joy of being related in a single whole with the other, *de volonté*. The explanation for our preference is sometimes rooted in our idiosyncratic physiology.

> when I was a child I loved a little girl of my own age who had a slight squint. The impression made by sight in my brain when I looked at her cross-eyes became so closely connected to the simultaneous impression which aroused in me the passion of love that for a long time afterwards when I saw persons with a squint I felt a special inclination to love them simply because they had that defect. . . . So, when we are inclined to love someone without knowing the reason, we may believe that this is because he has some similarity to something in an earlier object of our love, though we may not be able to identify it. Though it is more often a perfection than a defect that attracts our love, yet since it can sometimes be a defect as in the example I quoted, a wise man will not altogether yield to such a passion without having considered the worth of the person to whom he thus feels drawn. But because we cannot love equally all those in whom we observe equal worth, I think that our only obligation is to esteem them equally; and since the chief good of life is friendship, we are right to prefer those to whom we are joined by secret inclinations, provided we also see worth in them. Moreover, when these secret inclinations are aroused by something in the mind and not by something in the body, I think they should always be followed. (5:57–58; 3:322–23)

This is one explanation of why we prefer our friends to others we equally respect. In general, however, even our deeper personal attachments are nonetheless selective, rooted in the complex contingencies of daily life; and although they are in large part based on shared interests and shared experiences, they nevertheless arise in ways we do not and need not understand. Of course, our friends are human beings with free will and for this reason alone deserve our respect. But what makes them specifically friends—that is, what constitutes their special value for us—is not a value we can determine intellectually; what makes them friends is, although obscure, often discovered through our passions. While respect due to all persons will determine a range of duties to others as well as to ourselves, the special union that is friendship determines further duties.

Descartes describes the bond of friendship in one place as sacred,[22] and in the letter just quoted he says it is the best good in this life. He says this for two reasons. The first is the general reason we have for respecting and therefore valuing persons above other kinds of external goods. I shall return to this topic below. The second—and here I offer only a conjecture— is that the joy that supervenes on friendship (at least on perfect friendship, which is mutual pure love) is directly experienced to be far more satisfying than that which supervenes on the possession of any other external good. Giving as an example of pure love that of a father for his child in article 82 of the *Passions*, Descartes points out that this love is not mixed with a desire to possess the object of love in any other way than by that particular kind of willing that creates a whole of which one is only a part, and often a lesser part at that.[23] When Descartes speaks of friendship, he must be understood to intend a bond of mutual love—at the limit, of mutual pure love. Love itself, of course, does not require love in return. But such reciprocity would seem essential to friendship, and Descartes suggests as much in article 83; there he also sorts the kinds of love according to the esteem we have for their objects. But this manner of sorting presents us with a difficulty we need to deal with before we can get clear about the distinctive value of friendship. The difficulty arises from the two dimensions of value assessment in play, the dimension of love and that of esteem.[24] Our

22. Princess Elizabeth had asked Descartes to give her his opinion of the views of Machiavelli. To some commentators Descartes's comments have seemed disappointingly tolerant of some of Machiavelli's recommendations to the prince; however this may be, Descartes strongly denounces the abuse of friendship between princes, and not only on prudential grounds: "But I rule out one type of deception which is so directly hostile to society that I do not think it is ever permissible to use it, although our author approves it in several places; and that is pretending to be a friend of those one wishes to destroy, in order to take them by surprise. Friendship is too sacred a thing to be abused in this way; and someone who has once feigned love for someone in order to betray him deserves to be disbelieved and hated by those whom he afterwards genuinely wishes to love" (4:488; 3:293).

23. See the passage from this article quoted in section 7 above.

24. This distinction corresponds to the distinction I made earlier between the scale of ontological perfection and the scale of things that are good relative to us.

esteem of objects is disinterested in the same sense in which, by contrast, our love of objects is interested. Esteem places objects on the ontological scale of perfection and does not, in the first instance, relate these objects to us, whereas love places objects on a scale of value in which they do relate to us. How are we to combine these two kinds of assessment into a single coherent scheme?

In his commentary on article 82, Ferdinand Alquié points out that while it is easy to understand how one can love some object in the sense of imagining oneself as a part of a whole of which the object is another part, it is not easy to make sense of the idea that our possessing the object could itself be that other part, as in the·case of the brute who "loves" a woman (Alquié 1989, 3:1015n).[25] If this case presents a problem for Descartes in his attempt to extend his analysis this far, we may put it to one side, since it does not arise in the case of friendship. Here we have to do, at least ideally, with pure love, that is, with love not mixed with desire for possession of the object of love. Alquié's problem is that, on the one hand, we regard our friends as our equals and, on the other hand, as meriting the sacrifice of our own interests to theirs. Such sacrifice, says Descartes, would be absurd in the case of a flower or an animal; it would, on the other hand, be justified in the case of God or an object meriting our devotion. And the argument to this effect is just that we esteem the flower less than we do ourselves and we esteem God more. But how, then, to justify on the basis of value the sacrifice of our interests to those of a friend? Oddly, Descartes does not discuss this case in this article 83; he omits it altogether.

Now, the main point Descartes seeks to make in this article is that through love we can become members of three basic types of unions. The type will depend on the esteem we have for the other member or members

---

25. We might well doubt that this example can be fit into Descartes's definition of love in precisely the manner he suggests. In the case of sheer lust, the other person hardly figures as an object of love, certainly not according to Descartes's own definition; moreover, the object of lust is in the final analysis sexual gratification in the sense of a pleasurable release of pent-up sexual appetite, in which the other figures as a mere means. Here love of the woman drops out of the picture altogether, and we have to do rather more directly with one's desire for one's own pleasure. It would seem, moreover, that we have to do not with joy or contentment but with pleasurable sensation. We need to distinguish joy or contentment from pleasure in the sense of pleasurable sensation; the opposite of the latter is painful sensation, whereas the opposite of the former is sadness or discontent. If the case of lust is to fit in the Cartesian analysis of love, the object of love must be the pleasurable sensation itself, which then becomes the object of desire. Here again, even more directly than in the case of beauty, Descartes would seem to agree that pleasurable experience can be the object of desire, where the means to the satisfaction of desire are then valued as mere means. If we ask what is the value of this satisfaction, the general answer must be given in terms of the joy that supervenes on possessing this pleasurable sensation.

of the union, although it will remain true for any union that, as a natural effect of love, "we feel benevolent towards it—that is, we also join to it willingly the things we believe agreeable to it" (11:388; 1:356). Whether one's interest in the whole will entail sacrificing one's own individual interest when it conflicts with someone else's, however, will depend on one's esteem for the other.

Strictly speaking, as we have seen, esteem is disinterested, whether it be esteem as an intellectual judgment or esteem as a passion (which is a form of wonder). Love, on the other hand, is interested, in the sense that it takes the object to be *convenable*. (Love, to be sure, is a very special kind of interest, since it admits as particular instances the love of God, seen as good, and the love of one's health, seen as good.) Now, the difficulty Alquié finds is that friendship entails equality; we esteem our friends as we esteem ourselves. Esteem, of course, is not love; esteem is one kind of assessment and love is another. Esteem places the loved object on the ontological scale of perfection. But if esteem puts other persons on the same level with us, presumably as beings with a free will, then although benevolence follows, it is not clear why the disposition to sacrifice oneself for another will follow—as Descartes says it will in the ideal case of friendship.

In the letter to Chanut, Descartes writes that our love of God should be "incomparably the greatest and most perfect of all." Alquié complains that Descartes's view is not altogether clear. The problem is this. First, Descartes has defined love in such a way that the love of a bird and the love of God are instances of it. From this it follows that so long as love is based on a correct judgment of value, the love in question will be perfect, and from this love will follow a suitable form of benevolence. "However, within this rationalist conception of love," Alquié points out, "we do not see why I ought necessarily prefer a friend to myself, since the friend cannot be worth more than I (be more estimable than I), and why the love of God would be more perfect, as such, than all other forms of love. These assertions seem indeed to depend on another conception of love, one according to which the measure or perfection of one's love is the degree to which one forgets one's own advantage. But this is a different conception of love" (Alquié 1989, 3:720n).

Alquié makes a good point, but he is not precisely right when he says that Descartes is working with two conceptions of love. Alquié himself does not clearly distinguish love from esteem or appreciate that these are two distinct if overlapping kinds of valuation. Descartes, to be sure, does not explicitly distinguish them either. Nonetheless, there do seem to be in Descartes's theory these two kinds of valuation. Descartes speaks of both love and esteem. Both are responsive to the value of some object, but they assess the value differently. Moreover, esteem itself is represented as responsive to two scales of value. It is responsive to values as fixed on the chain of being and to degrees of moral merit as fixed on the scale of moral virtue. Love, on the other hand, fixes on a much broader range of properties of objects, many obscurely picked out by our passions. Before I address Alquié's objection, I need to point out the second difficulty, one I can formulate in the special case of love of God. Love, as it is defined, is interested, in the sense that the judgment on which love is based, or of which love is the expression, uses the predicate adjective *convenable*. Love as a passion is correspondingly interested. The value to which esteem is responsive, on the other hand, is disinterested.

Once we take note of this distinction between interested and disinterested evaluation, we may be able to answer Alquié's objection. Love is one thing, esteem is another. What makes friends of equal value is esteem, and what is esteemed is their possession of free will and their degree of virtue. But esteem does not distinguish personal friends from other people, at least not from other honorable people. Love, on the other hand, does so. Now, Descartes does not clearly identify these values that we find in our friends and that distinguish them from others. But nor does he say what it is about our children that makes them such eminently suitable candidates for our pure love. He might be observing, however, that such love follows the course of nature and that a child's property of simply being one's child is such a value, picked out by the passion of love; and he might be claiming moreover that since the passion itself has a natural strength and persistence, we may infer that it is a genuine good-making property, one that has the endorsement of God. If this is right, then we might interpret him to be arguing analogously in the case of friendship. When one honorable person finds herself attracted to another on the model of pure love, then, other things being equal and the love being mutual, we should say that the mutual value this expresses is a genuine value and, indeed, one that is proportional to the strength of the mutual benevolence to which the mutual love gives rise. In short, if in the case of such ideal friendship one is prepared to sacrifice one's own interest for the other, we should take this motive to be objectively justified, that is, justified in terms of an objective value, the value one finds in a true friend. The answer to Alquié's problem about friendship, then, would be that although our esteem of all honorable persons is the same as is the esteem we have of ourselves (supposing we are equally honorable), Descartes can easily accommodate the special sacrifices we may make for a friend within his framework without introducing a different kind of love. He can do so because the benevolence we have toward our friends is based on love, not merely on esteem, and because this love in fact tends toward benevolent self-sacrifice. What this solution brings out, however, is that esteem and love are two distinct dimensions or forms of evaluation.

I would quickly summarize Descartes on the value of pure friendship this way: of external goods, our friends are the highest.[26]

13. The fourth truth it is useful to know is that

> though each of us is a person distinct from others, whose interests are accordingly in some way different from those of the rest of the world, we ought still to think that none of us could subsist alone and that each one of us is really one of the many parts of the universe, and more particularly a part of the earth, the state, the society and the family to which we belong by our domicile, our oath of allegiance and our birth. And the interests of the whole, of which each of us is a part, must always be preferred to those of our own particular person—with measure, of course, and discretion, because it would be wrong to expose ourselves to a great evil in order to procure only a slight benefit to our kinsfolk or our country. (Indeed if someone were worth more, by himself, than all his fellow citizens, he would have no reason to destroy himself to save his city.) But if someone saw everything in relation to himself, he would not hesitate to injure others greatly when he thought he could draw some slight advantage; and he would have no true friendship, no fidelity, no virtue at all. (4:293; 3:266)

Here, in a letter to Princess Elizabeth written on September 15, 1645, Descartes expresses the view that our state, our society, and our family are objects that merit our love and that they are parts of the union formed by love that warrant our sacrifice, when that should be called for. These views are more crisply and forcibly expressed in the letter on love to Chanut more than a year later. Referring to the degrees of esteem that the objects of our love merit, he says that even the perfect love of a flower or a building could not justify our sacrificing our lives for it; this would be as preposterous as our sacrificing our whole body for the preservation of our hair. "But when two human beings love each other, charity requires that each of the two should value his friend above himself. . . . Similarly, when an individual is joined willingly to his prince or his country, if his love is perfect he should regard himself as only a tiny part of the whole which he and they constitute. He should be no more afraid to go to certain death for their service

---

26. In a letter of consolation written in 1637 to Constantijn Huygens, whose wife had recently died, Descartes observes: "Although we cannot submit ourselves to God's law without some pain, I value love so highly that I think that whatever we go through for the sake of it is pleasant—so much so that even those who are ready to die for the good of those they love seem to me to be happy to their last breath" (1:632–33; 3:54).

than one is afraid to draw a little blood from one's arm to improve the health of the rest of the body" (4:612; 3:311).

Even if we agree with Descartes about both the value and the possible demands of friendship, we might well find these claims about the value and demands of society and the state both problematic and obscure. We can perhaps think of a small society made up of family and friends as a special case of friendship, in which the other members are bound by the same love to each other as we are to them. We can then make some sense of the value Descartes finds in society and of the demands that membership in it makes on us, for in this conception of society we meet no elements that were not present in simple friendship. To the extent that the enjoyment of community is phenomenologically comparable to that of intimate friendship, the value of community would be confirmed. But I do not think we can plausibly extend the concept of friendship beyond a small community to a larger society, much less to a nation state. And even if (following Aristotle) we speak of civic friendship, this is not the utopian conception of all the members of a community being tied by reciprocal bonds of pure friendship of the sort that tie two intimate friends.

In the letter on love to Chanut, however, Descartes does talk as if there were a hierarchy of estimable goods, beginning with individuals and moving through community, the state, and the prince to God as the most estimable; and he goes on to suggest, implausibly, that the model of personal friendship can be used to interpret our membership in these different unions. But except for the final union with God, at the one extreme, and possibly also one's membership in a small community, this model is inapt. Although it is undeniable that— as individuals, families, and small communities—we are dependent on society and the state, as Descartes says in this letter to Elizabeth, still our dependence cannot plausibly be understood on the model of personal friendship. Our relationship to society or the state, as well as to the individuals that constitute it, needs an altogether different and no doubt far more complex analysis. This would be the stuff of moral political theory. The seeds of such a theory—of an egalitarian form of such a theory—are visible in Descartes's important notion of *générosité*. Yet, reluctant as he was to write on moral topics, Descartes was evidently even more reluctant to develop the moral political implications of this focal concept in his theory of virtue.[27] In any case, beyond the bare histori-

27. There is much that could be said on this topic, but the following remark by Nannerl O. Keohane sums up the matter well: "Descartes humbly noted that politics is the business of sovereigns, not private individuals; his sense of priorities for philosophy relegated politics to a derivative status, in any case. Yet his ethics and his epistemology suggest the possibility of a wonderful new community for human-kind, made up of rational individuals devoting their energies to useful activities for the progress of the species, united willingly in love and

cal fact that some people in Descartes's day came to love their society and devote themselves to their prince in the way Descartes's letter to Chanut suggests, there is no good argument that one's society or one's prince is more than an instrumental good, not a true good for its own sake. However, in a sequence of letters following his letter of September 1645 to Elizabeth, where he first suggested extending the model of friendship to the community and state, Descartes backs away from this model and moves tentatively and implicitly in the direction of Hobbes.

14. In a 1643 letter whose recipient is not known, Descartes makes the following comment on Hobbes as a moral theorist:

> All I can say about the book *De Cive* is that I believe its author to be the person who wrote the Third Objections against my *Meditations*, and that I find him much more astute in moral philosophy than in metaphysics or physics. Not that I could approve in any way his principles or his maxims. They are extremely bad and quite dangerous in that he supposes all persons to be wicked, or gives them cause to be so. His whole aim is to write in favor of the monarchy; but one could do this more effectively and soundly by adopting maxims which are more virtuous and solid. (4:67; 3:230–31)

In letter to Princess Elizabeth a couple of years later, Descartes says that it is difficult to determine how far reason demands that we devote ourselves to the community and that we must rely on our conscience. He goes on to say, however, that even if we related everything outside us to ourselves—convinced that God has so established the order of things—then even if we lacked charity we would find it in our interest to work for others as much as we could, "and especially if [we] lived in an age in which morals were not corrupted." Here we may detect a hint of Hobbes, although it is not evident that Descartes conceived the special character of social cooperation as conventional in the way Hobbes did, where my duty to cooperate is conditional on *(a)* my cooperation not going uncompensated and *(b)* my reasonable belief that others are doing their part. But this may be the point of Descartes's adding, "if we lived in an age in which morals were not corrupted." It does seem significant that Descartes had read *De Cive* and saw in it that its author was a good moral philosopher.

But if Descartes had a glimmer of the distinction that Hobbes, Hume, and others made between benevolence and justice, in this letter he is cer-

---

service to one another. It is impossible to be sure how much Descartes himself was aware of these possibilities. His own scattered statements on politics are consistently conservative, and he wanted to protect society against confusion or disorder from the premature or ill-conceived application of his radically new methods" (Keohane 1980, 203).

tainly not keeping the two clearly distinct. It is nobler and more glorious, he says, to do good to others than to oneself, and it is the noblest souls that are so inclined. "Only weak and base souls value themselves more than they ought, and are like small vessels that a few drops of water can fill. . . . Base souls cannot be persuaded to take trouble for others unless you can show them that they will reap some profit for themselves" (4:317; 3:273). This is his response to Elizabeth, who was in turn responding to an earlier letter of Descartes's in which he had emphasized our duty to the larger wholes on which we depend. She writes:

> The consideration that we are part of a whole of which we ought to seek the advantage is indeed the source of all generous actions; but I find many difficulties concerning the conditions you prescribe for such actions. How measure the pains one takes in serving the public against the good that comes from them, without these evils seeming greater in proportion as their idea is the more distinct? [La considération que nous sommes une partie du tout, dont nous devons chercher l'avantage, est bien la source de toutes les actions généreuses; mais je trouve beaucoup de difficultés aux conditions que vous leur prescrivez. Comment mesurer les maux qu'on se donne pour le public, contre le bien que en arrivera, sans qu'ils nous paraissent plus grands, d'autant que leur idée est plus distincte?] And what rule shall we have to compare things not equally known, such as our individual worth and the worth of those with whom we live? One who is naturally arrogant will always tip the balance in his own favor; and one who is modest will esteem himself less than his worth. (Blom 1978, 155)

The exchange between Descartes and Elizabeth would have profited from their clearly distinguishing wider duties of benevolence from stricter duties defined, at least in part, in terms of customary rules of some social practice. With respect to the former, Descartes's reply, "Only weak and base souls value themselves more than they ought," is, although brief almost to the point of rudeness, on the right track. On the other hand, if it is a matter of duty to do one's part in a social practice with rules that are more or less agreed upon, then the question might already be answered in terms of these rules.[28] Moreover, in the case of such a practice, the worth of the other participants does not really come into view in practical deliberation, unless it figures in the practice itself. (It is not clear, of course, what specific kind of worth is in question here.)

Nonetheless, all the social wholes of which Descartes speaks in his earlier letter, as I have noted, seem to be modeled in his analysis of friendship. This

---

28. Descartes does get around to this point in a later letter. See below.

is what allows him to speak of our being the lesser part of the whole and yet—as a consequence of our duty (or at least our right) of self-sacrifice for the sake of the other—the better part. Whatever one thinks of this account—Alquié raises a good point against it—it does not apply to wholes conceived along Hobbesian lines, where these are mutually advantageous cooperative schemes that do not at all depend on the virtue of charity. The confusion that permeates this exchange between Descartes and Elizabeth arises from neither being clear about the kind of duty to others that is in question. Descartes's modeling of the larger community and even the state in terms of personal friendship encourages this confusion. If, as seems to be the case, Elizabeth is asking what are the burdens of social cooperation, Descartes is missing the point when he replies that so long as we satisfy the demands of our conscience, charity requires no more.

In *De Cive* Hobbes does not speak of charity or generosity, but he does say (the ninth law of nature) that we are not to be useless (that is, troublesome); we are not to ask more than is necessary but instead accommodate ourselves to the needs of others. The law of nature is that each render himself useful to others. Since, in Hobbes's view, all these laws oblige *in foro interno*, each of us is enjoined to become an accommodating person. This is far from being Cartesian love in the form of friendship. But it is a move in the direction of benevolence and distinct from strict justice. Justice requires only that one be trustworthy, on the condition that others may reasonably be presumed to act in a trustworthy manner. One can be just without being accommodating. Although Descartes says he respects Hobbes as a moral theorist, he does not appear to have learned much from him, since he could well have brought some of the important distinctions set out in *De Cive* to bear in his replies to Princess Elizabeth.

Moreover, distinctions may be made among types of friendships. At one extreme lie justice and social convention; at the other, pure charity. In between are, in Aristotle's taxonomy, character friendships, advantage friendships, and pleasure friendships. Descartes's answer to Elizabeth hardly discriminates among the various contexts in which her question, How far should we trouble ourselves in order to benefit others? might arise.

Not surprisingly, Elizabeth was not satisfied with Descartes's answer. On October 28, 1645, she writes:

> You do not believe one has need of an exact knowledge about the extent to which reason orders us to interest ourselves in behalf of the public; for you think that, although each person related everything to himself, he would still also work for others were he to use prudence. And this prudence is the end-all of which I ask from you but a part. For in possessing

it one would not fail to do justice to others as to oneself, and want of such prudence is the cause why a sincere mind sometimes loses the means of serving his fatherland by abandoning himself too lightly for its interests, and similarly, why a timid person perishes along with it instead of hazarding his well being and fortune for its conservation. (Blom 1978, 167)

Here she makes it clear that her question has to do with one's duty, not to friends but to the larger public. In fact, she is following Descartes's lead from his earlier letter in which he shifted from couching the issue in terms of friendship to phrasing it in more Hobbesian terms of self-interest. Descartes replies:

If prudence were the mistress of events, I have no doubt that your Highness would accomplish everything she wished to undertake; however, that would require all men to be perfectly wise, so that, knowing what they ought to do, one could be assured what they would do. Or else it would be required that one know in particular the humor of everyone with whom one has some dealings; and even that would not suffice since, beyond their humor, they also have their free decision, whose movements are known only to God. And because one ordinarily judges concerning what others will do by reference to what one would wish to do were one in their place, it often happens that ordinary and mediocre minds, being similar to those with whom they deal, better penetrate their designs and are more easily successful in what they undertake than are more elevated souls, who in dealing only with those very much inferior in knowledge and prudence, judge very differently of things than do they. (Blom 1978, 170–71)

Descartes here clearly has the idea of a social convention, where what one has reason to do is conditional upon what one reasonably believes others will do, and where the question is whether others will in fact do their part in a practice that defines what their part is.

Elizabeth responds: "As regards prudence, as far as human society is concerned, I do not await an infallible rule; but I should be very pleased to see those rules you would give to one who, in living only for himself, in whatever profession he has, would nevertheless not fail to work for others—that I should wish to see were I to dare ask of you more light after having so badly employed that which you have already given to" (Blom 1978, 172–73). In his reply, which foreshadows much of the following century's moral theory, Descartes points out the considerable advantages of a deservedly good reputation.

One ordinarily sees it occur that those who are deemed obliging and prompt to please also receive a quantity of good deeds from others, even from people who have never been obliged to them; and these things they would not receive did people believe them of another humor; and the pains they take to please other people are not so great as the conveniences that the friendship of those who know them proves to be. For others expect of us only those deeds we can render conveniently, nor do we expect more of them; but it often happens that deeds that cost others little profit us very much, and can even save our life. It is true that occasionally one wastes his toil in doing good and that, on the other hand, occasionally one gains in doing evil; but that cannot change the rule of prudence that relates only to things that happen most often. As for me, the maxim I have most often observed in all the conduct of my life has been to follow only the grand path, and to believe that the principle shrewdness is not to wish at all to use shrewdness. The common laws of society, which all tend to do each other mutual good, or at least not evil, are, it seems to be, so well established that whoever follows them frankly, without any dissimulation or artifice, leads a life very much more assured than those who seek their utility by other ways. It is true these other ways occasionally succeed for those who follow them, because of the ignorance of other men and the favor of fortune; but it happens much more often that such people go wrong and, thinking they are establishing themselves, they ruin themselves. (Blom 1978, 176–77)[29]

Under repeated questioning from Elizabeth, Descartes appears to have backed off from his earlier analysis of the larger social union in terms of friendship and moved in the direction of some sort of social convention or compact account of our duties to others. Within such an account, one might make room for civic friendship, where virtue would consist in one's being not only trustworthy but accommodating. But this virtue is a far cry from the ideal of pure friendship and the virtue of charity.

What emerges from this discussion is that pure friendship is the highest of all external goods. If Descartes suggests in one letter that our community and our state are even higher goods (although modeled on personal friendship), not only does he not defend this view, he backs down from it. This is not the place to explore Descartes's political theory or, rather, his reasons for not wishing to explore the political implications of his moral theory, particularly his view that all persons merit respect, since my present purpose is to set our his theory of value. Here I conclude that one's community and one's state, aside from their considerable instrumental value, are not such objects of love and joy as to be greater goods than one's friends.[30]

29. This is from Descartes's letter to Elizabeth of January 1646. This part of the letter is not included in the Cambridge University Press edition of Descartes's correspondence (Descartes 1991).

30. As I read him, Descartes would have endorsed Montaigne's view of friendship: "There is nothing to which Nature seems so much to have inclined us as to society. And Aristotle says

15. The objective external goods that contribute to a happy life are health and strength of the body, the experience of beautiful objects, satisfying activities and occupations, knowledge, and above all intimate friends. Other goods that typically figure importantly in a happy life are primarily instrumental goods such as wealth, security, and social stability. Depending on the kind of community one lives in and on the kind of membership in the larger political community, these wholes may also figure not only as instrumental values but also as external goods for their own sake, that is, as suitable objects of love.

To round out this chapter, we are obliged to talk about God as an external good. In the long passage cited above from Descartes's letter to Chanut on love, we saw that if we meditate properly on the nature of God—his omnipotence, omniscience, the infallibility of his decrees—and "weigh our smallness against the greatness of the created universe, observing how all created things depend on God," and understand these things perfectly, we shall be filled with extreme joy. The thought is that through perfect understanding of the nature of God, we will join ourselves *de volonté* to God and love God so perfectly that we will desire "nothing at all except that his will should be done." We will neither "shun evils and afflictions" nor "eschew permissible goods or pleasures" but accept afflictions without fear and greet pleasures with joy, and our love of God will make us perfectly happy (4:609; 3:310). It is obvious, he continues, "that our love for God should be, beyond all comparison, the greatest and most perfect of all our loves." He admits that meditation and understanding of the requisite kind is not easy, since it demands that we detach ourselves from "the traffic of the senses"; such detachment, Descartes confesses, can be tiring and hard to sustain (4:612–13; 3:311).

That our love of God should be incomparably the greatest of our loves calls for comment in the light of what I have already said about the value of friends. What I said was that among external goods our friends are the greatest goods we can have. How is this to be reconciled with that claim that, at least for those who properly understand the nature of God, the greatest love is the love of God? Can God be our friend? The difficulty with this suggestion is that God is not our equal, and friendship, Descartes has said, is a bond only among those who merit the same degree of esteem. First, it must be said, God is a very special case. Certainly, God is a proper object

---

that good law-givers had more respect to friendship than to justice. Now the supreme point of its perfection is this. For, speaking generally, all those amities that are created and nourished by pleasure or profit, public or private needs, are so much the less noble and beautiful, and so much the less friendships, as they introduce some other cause and design and fruit into friendship, than itself" (Montaigne 1927, 184).

of veneration, devotion, and respect, as are, says Descartes, our prince and our state. Yet while we can be said to love our prince and our state, we would not call either of these our friends. Moreover, Descartes adds, it would be contrary to good manners to express our love to a prince or princess. Why? "I think that the reason for this is that friendship between human beings makes those in whom it is reciprocated in some way equal to each other, and so if, while trying to make oneself loved by some great person, one said that one loved him, he might think that one was treating him as an equal and so doing him wrong" (4:610: 3:310). There is no impropriety, however, in expressing our love of God and no remote suggestion in our so doing that we should be wronging God. Would it not still be presumptuous to suppose that the reciprocal love that is the essence of true friendship could obtain between us and God? While I would not insist that the answer to this question is clear, I think there is something in the thought that we may infer from the nature of God, just as from mutual friendship, that we may be assured of the full measure of the other's beneficence and goodwill that our own love and esteem deserve. So it could remain true that among external goods our friends are the best we can have in this life, and Descartes might be seen as allowing, as a very special case, that God is not an exception but rather an exceptional friend.[31]

31. In his letter on love to Chanut, while not exactly taking back his distinction between friendship and devotion, he does appear to say that we can regard those to whom we are devoted as a special kind of friend.

CHAPTER NINE

Morality as Generosity

1. SINCE Descartes's theory of the good is pluralistic, we are left with the
task of ordering goods effectively within an account of practical deliberation. We might approach this task from the perspective of the virtuous
moral agent, one who is disposed to judge as well as possible and to adhere
firmly and decisively to his best practical judgment. What we can say in a
very general way is that, so far as I am virtuous, I always aim at what I reasonably take to be good. This follows from Descartes's (traditional) understanding of the object of the rational will, namely, the good.[1] And we may

---

1. What we will is always chosen *sub ratione boni*. Descartes says that our will is free, but
there is some controversy about what his conception of free will precisely is. In a letter taken
by some to have been written to Mesland in February 1645, Descartes writes that when an evident reason inclines us exclusively to one of two contrary actions—one that, morally speaking, we cannot but choose—we can, absolutely speaking, nevertheless choose the opposite
(contrary to evident reason). Impressed by this letter, Alquié writes: "It is therefore possible,
according to Descartes (and contrary to the opinion of almost all the commentators) to reject evidence in the presence of this very evidence, to turn away from the good even under
the spell of its attractiveness. To the liberty adapted to the good and to being is opposed the
free man, and, if the degree of our liberty is determined, in the case of fully enlightened liberty, by the ease of our choice, it is determined, in the case of pure liberty, by putting into play
the positive power which is ours to follow the worse although we know the better" (Alquié
1987, 289). While Alquié's view merits serious consideration, I am inclined to agree with Anthony Kenny's arguments against it. Moreover, for purposes of grounding his claims about
the value of our free will, it is not necessary for Descartes to hold that our will is free in the
sense of having the positive power to will the worse while fully recognizing that it is the worse;
what is necessary, rather, is that our choice of the good not be mechanistically determined in
the way in which the animal's actions are determined. Thus it may be that we cannot but
chose some good that is clearly and evidently the best, just as we cannot but assent to some

also say that where I have several goods in view which are not jointly realizable, I will choose the best of these. Up to this point, however, we have been given a list of goods, and although these have been presented in a rough hierarchy, it is by no means evident how in particular circumstances I am to determine what is best, all things considered. If we may say, in a general way and abstracting from the context of practical deliberation, that some goods are better than others—that knowledge, for example, being a perfection of the soul, is better than health, which is a perfection of the body— we cannot infer that whenever I have a choice between pursuing knowledge and pursuing health I should always choose knowledge, even to the detriment of my health. Of course, in this case, so far as good health is an aid to the successful pursuit of knowledge, I might find some reasonable plan of action that will give adequate attention both to my bodily needs and to my search for knowledge. But what of the other goods—beauty, enjoyable activities, friends—how are these to be integrated or balanced? Moreover, some goods that I might seek are not mine but yours—your health or your knowledge, for example. Goods, we need to recall, are objective goods. Accordingly, while the value of my health gives me a reason to promote it, so does the value of your health give me a reason to promote that as well. How do I weigh these reasons in my practical deliberation? We have already seen that in Descartes's view the answer to this question will depend in part on whether you are my friend, a member of my community, a member of my state, or simply a fellow human being. It will also depend on whether my contribution is crucial to your achieving the good in question. Perhaps someone else will provide it for you, someone better able than I. Perhaps, moreover, it is a good that I can promote only on the condition that others cooperate, in which case what is appropriate for me to do will depend on how trustworthy these others are. When Elizabeth asked Descartes just how far she ought to go in taking care of the needs and interests of others, she raised a question requiring a more complex answer than the response she actually received—namely, that she should do enough to satisfy her conscience—which, although true enough, is singularly unhelpful.

To summarize: Descartes asserts that virtue is the supreme good for us,[2] that there are other goods, and that these, either as positive or as negative

---

clear and evident proposition; yet we can in both cases choose freely. Indeed, this would be the highest form or degree of freedom, since it would be the fullest or most perfect expression of our rational nature. See Kenny 1972; also Rodis-Lewis 1987.

2. Descartes's most succinct expression of his argument to this effect is given in his letter to Queen Christina (November 20, 1647): "the supreme good of each individual . . . consists only in a firm will to do well and the contentment which this produces. My reason for saying this is that I can discover no other good which seems so great or so entirely within each man's

ends, are the values we seek to promote through our actions.[3] In some circumstances, of course, it may be clear what the best thing to do is, say, when my health requires that I take daily medication. Perhaps other cases also will be fairly clear cut. For example, other things equal, we are not to do or threaten bodily harm to others or to pursue goods through fraud or deceit. These are not, of course, controversial claims, but to fill out Descartes's first-order morality we need to set out where they fit and how they are secured. The best way to do this, I think, as well as to begin to develop a more general account of appropriate action and a more specific account of duty, is to start with the culminating point of Descartes's developed theory in the *Passions*, his conception of *générosité*.

2. What is *générosité*?[4] In one place Descartes says it is the justified good opinion we have of ourselves (11:451; 1:386). In another he writes that generosity is the self-esteem that results from "the volition we feel within ourselves always to make good use of our free will" (11:449; 1:386). Elsewhere he says true generosity has two components, a feeling of a "firm and constant resolution to use [our free will] well" and two items of knowledge,

---

power. For the goods of the body and of fortune do not depend absolutely upon us; and those of the soul can all be reduced to two heads, the one being to know, and the other to will, what is good. But knowledge is often beyond our powers; and so there remains only our will, which is absolutely within our disposal. And I do not see that it is possible to dispose it better than by a firm and constant resolution to carry out to the letter all the things which one judges to be best, and to employ all the powers of one's mind in finding out what these are. This by itself constitutes all the virtues; this alone really deserves praise and glory; this alone, finally, produces the greatest and most solid contentment in life. So I conclude that it is this which constitutes the supreme good" (5:82–83; 3:324–25).

3. One might refer to these as the material ends of action, distinguishing them from the single, formal end, which is virtue. In this sense, even God could be a material end.

4. In his note to article 153, Ferdinand Alquié comments that the term *générosité* was much in vogue as expressing a certain moral ideal current at the time and was celebrated by the contemporary dramatist Corneille. "Indeed, it is because he finds a notion quite commonly used in his time, of which he wishes nonetheless to change the sense, that he speaks of *true generosity* [*vraie générosité*]. But true generosity rests above all on true judgment. It differs therefore from the glorious generosity of the Corneillian hero [*la générosité glorieuse de héros cornélien*]. The text has the look of a kind of lesson in morality suited to the customs of the period" (Alquié 1989, 3:1067n). Descartes first introduces the term "generosity" in the title of article 54 of the *Passions* (11:373; 1:350), but in the text he uses the term "magnanimity" to refer to the same passion. The latter term suggests a virtue of the nobility, a virtue inaccessible to the common man. But Descartes's conception of generosity is far more democratic or egalitarian, as we see in article 161, where he says that by reflecting on our own free will and on the many advantages that we may expect from a firm resolution to make good use of it, we may acquire, first, the passion, and then the virtue of generosity. Geneviève Rodis-Lewis suggests in a recent article that this more egalitarian conception of the *passion* that Descartes calls "generosity" in article 161 differs from the "magnanimity" of article 54; she suggests, furthermore, that Descartes's analysis of generosity, both as a virtue and as a passion, in articles 153–206 was probably not present in the first, unpublished version, which Descartes submitted to Princess Elizabeth for comment in the spring of 1646. See Rodis-Lewis 1987, 43–54.

namely, that only our freedom to dispose our volitions belongs to us and that we are rightly praised or blamed only for how we use our freedom. As I shall interpret Descartes, the term "generosity," taken narrowly, refers to the firm and constant resolution to use our free will well, that is, "never to lack the will to undertake and carry out what [we] judge to be best" (11:446; 1:384).

Taken in this narrow sense, generosity is a volitional disposition. It is a necessary but not sufficient condition for legitimate self-esteem. Self-esteem is an emotion or feeling arising from a judgment of value of one's worth, and the necessary condition for an assessment of one's worth is freedom of the will. Descartes assumes that if I am firmly and sincerely committed always to choose in accordance with my best practical judgment and that, moreover, I know that I merit praise only when this commitment itself is an expression or product of my own freedom, then I shall have the emotion of self-satisfaction.[5] This is in accord with his general claim that a suitable emotion of self-approbation must follow on our awareness of having some perfection. Self-approbation or self-esteem is, here, an internal emotion of the soul, an "emotion produced in the soul by the soul itself" (11:440; 1:381). In article 160 Descartes says that we could also use *générosité* to refer to a passion, although he points out that, strictly as a passion, generosity would arise from the same "movement of the spirits" and involve the same mix of wonder, joy, and self-love as the passion he calls vanity. The only difference, although it is crucial, between the passion of generosity and the passion of vanity is that the former is justified and the latter not. But the so-called passion of generosity is the passion that resonates with justified self-approbation.[6] In any event, it must be clear that generosity as a virtue is a volitional disposition, an activity of free will; it is not and could not be a passion of the soul.

Properly grounded self-esteem and the associated passion of generosity will be manifest in a range of more specific conative and affective dispositions, notably in our dealing with and attitude toward others. First, concerning their characteristic attitude toward others Descartes says that the

5. This satisfaction, as an internal emotion of the soul itself, he also calls tranquillity and peace of mind (in articles 148 and 190). It is distinct from self-satisfaction as a passion that arises when we perform an action we think good (article 190).

6. The usefulness of this passion lies in its concentrating our attention on the development of generosity as a virtue. "If one frequently occupies oneself in considering what free will is and how great the advantages are that come from a firm resolution to use it well and also, on the other hand, how vain and useless all the cares are that trouble the ambitious, one may excite in oneself the passion and then acquire the virtue of generosity. And since this is, as it were, the key to all the other virtues, and a general remedy for all the disorders of the passions, it seems to me that this consideration is well worth noting" (11:454; 3:388; Voss 1989, 109).

généreux never have contempt for anyone, not even for those who exhibit
some vice or who do wrong (11:446; 1:384). Why is this? He does not expressly spell out his answer, but it would clearly be along the following
lines. First, in the special case of a *généreux* not only not having contempt
but having esteem for a fellow *généreux*, what legitimizes self-esteem must
also legitimize esteem for others who have free will and exhibit a firm and
constant resolution to use it well. Judgments of moral worth can, after all,
be universalized. The case of those who are characteristically unjust, cruel,
brutal, greedy, arrogant, deceitful, ungrateful, bigoted, and boorish, on the
other hand, would seem to be quite different. Since esteem is the proper
response only to a virtuous will, these certainly do not merit our esteem.
But why do they not merit our contempt? Descartes's answer, I believe, is
that they do not merit contempt because, vicious as they may be, they have
free will and are therefore capable of becoming *généreux* themselves.
Clearly, for this answer to stand, we must agree that simply in the fact that
we have free will we possess a good. As I noted in the previous chapter, the
kind of valuation that Descartes calls esteem is one that fixes, first, on ontological perfection and, second, on something of a certain ontological kind
developing its own perfection appropriate to it. Because they possess intelligence and will, others merit our esteem as beings of a certain kind, beings
having the potential for a specific kind of development, both intellectual
and moral. The suggested line of argument is that since free will is not only
a necessary condition but also the only condition that anyone requires to
achieve the supreme good, we cannot hold anyone in contempt so long as
he has this power. By "contempt," here, Descartes must have in mind view-
ing others as we might view, say, animals. Even those who use their freedom badly do not lose their potential for becoming virtuous. And freedom,
as the potential for the supreme good, Descartes seems to be arguing, always deserves a minimum of respect, even if it does not merit the esteem of
virtue achieved.[7]

   3. What, then, is the characteristic attitude of the *généreux* toward other
persons? Although Descartes does not use the term in this way, I think we
should call this attitude that of respect.[8] Respect looks to the value of others as rational agents with free will, and it is this freedom that establishes a
benchmark of equality among all human beings; it serves, therefore, as the

---

   7. We find one particularly striking passage in Descartes's letter to Queen Christina of November 20, 1647, where he writes that "freewill is in itself the noblest thing we have because it
makes us in a certain manner equal to God and exempts us from being his subjects" (5:85;
3:326). And the heading article 37 of the *Principles* reads: "The supreme perfection of man is
that he acts freely or voluntarily, and it is this which makes him deserve praise or blame"
(8A:18; 1:205).
   8. Descartes uses "respect" as a synonym for "veneration." See article 162 of the *Passions*.

valuational ground not only for not harming others but for seeking to promote their true good. I shall return to these topics below.

Descartes next argues that in the *généreux* a minimal respect for others is combined with true (i.e., virtuous) humility. And the reason is that although we must, as *généreux*, be sincerely committed to judging and acting well, we cannot fail to be aware of "the infirmity of our nature," and the "wrongs we may previously have done or are capable of doing," so that "we do not prefer ourselves to anyone else and we think that since others have free will just as much as we do, they may use it just as well as we use ours" (11:447; 1:385).

To these attitudes of humility and respect is added a strong disposition to general beneficence combined with weak self-love. The *généreux*, he says, are "naturally led to do great deeds" and "esteem nothing more highly than doing good to others" (11:447–48; 1:385). At a minimum, then, they are "courteous, gracious and obliging to everyone." Moreover, since they have mastery over their passions, they are not generally given to excessive or misdirected jealousy, envy, or hatred, and their anger tends to be short lived, so that the impulses that often lead others to wrongdoing are characteristically lacking.[9] To see what the appropriate limit on these passions is, we need to look at several articles in which they are taken up. Jealousy he describes as a kind of anxiety about losing some possession we value, its strength being a function of the value we set on this possession; it is necessarily accompanied by the belief, more or less robust, that we shall not lose it. Jealousy is justified if our valuation is correct, and it is useful in stimulating us to take appropriate care. Envy—that is, the passion of envy, which is quite different from the vice of envy—Descartes describes as "a kind of sadness mingled with hatred, which results from our seeing good coming to those we think unworthy of it" (11:466; 1:394). Envy is justified only in the case of goods of fortune (not gifts of nature) and only when the recipients of the goods are not worthy of them. Descartes sees justified envy as

9. In article 156 Descartes says that the *généreux* are not given to excessive anger because "they have esteem for everyone." Now, not having contempt is not the same as having esteem. In article 154, Descartes argues that the *généreux* has no contempt for others. But the logic of his argument would not lead to the stronger conclusion that he would have esteem for others. Indeed, so far as esteem is legitimate only if it is based on the virtuous will of the person esteemed, it would not be legitimate in the case of someone with a vicious disposition. What Descartes needs—and, indeed, as I have argued above, what articles 154–56 imply—is a distinction between minimum respect for persons, on the one hand, and esteem, on the other.

Descartes also lists fear as a passion to which the *généreux* is not liable. In his later discussion of timidity and fear (or terror) he finds little use for the first and none for the second; the *généreux* is, by contrast, given to the passions of courage and boldness. He also has the virtue (as distinct from the passion) of courage, which is essentially the confidence and determination to do whatever he judges to be best.

arising from a natural love of justice; indeed, the justified passion Descartes calls envy might for this reason also be described as hatred of injustice.

As we have seen in the previous chapter, the *généreux* are effectively beyond the power of fortune (11:470; 1:395). But they do not for that reason lack compassion, for, since they have goodwill toward everyone, and pity itself is sadness mixed with goodwill, they are made sad by seeing another suffer undeserved deprivation of some good. The *généreux*'s chief object of pity, however, "is the weakness of those whom they see complaining." "For they think that no misfortune could be so great an evil as the timidity of those who cannot endure it with forbearance. And although they hate vices, they do not on that account hate those whom they see prone to them: they merely pity them." [10]

Next, we come to some special forms of love and hatred characteristic of the *généreux*: favor and gratitude, on the one hand, and indignation and anger, on the other. Favor is the special feeling of love or approbation of another aroused in us by his performing some good deed or, indeed, having a sincere intention to do so. The same feeling takes the form of gratitude when we are the beneficiary. Favor, being a form of love, gives rise to the desire that some good come to the doer of good deeds and in the case of gratitude, to the desire to reciprocate. Indignation is a special form of hatred or aversion, directed to those who do benefit or harm others who do not merit it. For the *généreux*, however, although they cannot fail to disapprove wrongdoing and vice, the passion of indignation is comparatively moderate; only in the case of "the most extraordinary vices" do they "become incensed" (11:477; 1:398). Anger, the form this hatred takes when we are the victim of wrongdoing, gives rise to the desire for vengeance, which, says Descartes, "is the most compelling of all desires" (11:477; 1:399). The *généreux*, who, owing to their characteristic goodwill, will always expect the best of others, are therefore surprised by wrongdoing. The anger they feel when, for example, they are the victim of theft, is accordingly mixed with astonishment. As their surprise diminishes and they reflect on the low esteem they have for such goods as may have been taken from them, and on the satisfaction they take in the control they have over their desires, their anger soon turns to "contempt, or at the most indignation." [11]

The passions of repentance, pride, and shame remain to be considered. Liability to the passions of pride and shame I have not taken the to be part

---

10. A similar point is made in connection with indignation; the specific object of the passion of indignation is some vice or wrongdoing, not the person who performs it. Thus we can consistently censure wrongdoing and vice and at the same time neither hate nor condemn the agent.

11. Here, I think we should take the term "contempt" to refer to the moral judgment that the action is bad or wrong, not to the passion of contempt.

of the moral sensibility of the perfectly *généreux*. Nor have I mentioned repentance. Were virtue perfected, these passions would be absent. Repentance, Descartes writes, is a kind of sadness, the most bitter kind, which "results from our believing that we have done some evil deed" (11:472; 1:396). Since such evil deeds would be prompted typically by envy or anger, the perfectly *généreux* would lack any motive for the kind of wrongdoing that would occasion repentance. Occasions for pride and shame would be similarly few. Descartes describes pride as joy deriving from the expectation of the praise of others and shame as the sadness deriving from the expectation of blame; their function is to "move us to virtue, the one through hope and the other through anxiety." He adds, however—and the remark would presumably apply to the *généreux*—that it is not entirely desirable to rid ourselves of these passions, "for although the common people are very bad judges, yet because we cannot live without them and it is important for us to be an object of their esteem, we should often follow their opinions rather than our own regarding the outward appearance of our actions" (11:483; 1:401). We should not read this remark as a mere counsel of prudence or as an invitation to hypocrisy. In the first place, we must remember that in the context in which it applies, namely, our deciding what to do in particular circumstances, we seldom if ever will have knowledge even approximating clear and distinct perception of what is right and what wrong. In the second place, since, as *généreux*, we have virtuous humility, we will be disposed to have genuine respect for the moral views of others. To be sure, we cannot be uncritical, but it is sometimes a narrow line between following others' moral advice uncritically and not giving it the hearing it merits, which is the point Descartes makes in his letter to Elizabeth of September 15, 1645: "One must . . . examine minutely all the customs of one's place of abode to see how far they should be followed. There we cannot have certain proofs of everything, still we must take sides, and in matters of custom embrace the opinions that seem the most probable, so that we may never be irresolute when we need to act" (4:295; 3:267).

We can say in summary, then, that although the *généreux* are generally benevolent and respectful in addition to their being philosophically enlightened,[12] their beneficence is sensitive to justice or merit; while they are

---

12. They know the several useful things to know, which Descartes lists in his letter to Elizabeth of September 15, 1645: that God is good, that the soul is immortal, and that the universe is immense. They also know how to achieve self-mastery, and they know the theory of the passions on which their knowledge of this technique is based. The knowledge of God, of immortality, of matter, of free will, and of human nature is all knowledge at the fifth degree of wisdom. Since knowledge at this level is philosophical knowledge, according to Descartes's conception of philosophy, knowing how to live well—to walk with assurance in this life— and, therefore, knowing how to attain *béatitude*, presupposes philosophy. Thus, we should understand the following passage from the French preface to the *Principles*: "Living without

compassionate and readily moved by indignation, they are never vengeful, and owing to their predisposition of goodwill they are given rather to excuse than to blame others for wrongdoing.

4. Beyond being supremely content, the *généreux* is characteristically respectful, forgiving, and charitable attitude toward others. If, then, the dominant attitude toward others of the *généreux* is due respect for persons on account of their freedom and rationality, we might reasonably try to base a Cartesian first-order morality on the value of human freedom. We could adopt as the ground for such a morality that *freedom of persons establishes a benchmark of equality among all human beings and provides at once a moral barrier to their being ill-treated, on the one hand, and moral reasons for seeking their true good, on the other.*[13] It is important to keep in mind that this principle is, in one sense, overdetermined, since the moral barrier to the ill-treatment of others is a function both of the goods that, through our actions, others might be led to possess and of the respect or esteem that is owed to them simply as rational beings with a free will. The general or imperfect duty to promote the well-being of others is similarly overdetermined.

This talk of respect for free and equal moral persons calls to mind Kant's second formulation of the categorical imperative or, perhaps, some more recent contractualist theory of justice or, more generally, of the right. I do not intend to follow up the idea that Cartesian first-order morality could be developed along contractualist lines, although I believe this would be a natural way to proceed, once we follow Descartes and take the *généreux*'s conception of other persons as correct. "Cartesian contractualism" would be morally motivated, however, not—as in Hobbes's contractualism—prudentially motivated. Although Descartes says that many well-established conventions that more or less effectively control social conduct could no doubt be explained as a kind of unconscious resolution of the problem presented by the Hobbesian state of nature, principles seen only in this way could not, for Descartes, be construed as specifically moral principles, for

---

philosophizing is exactly like having one's eyes closed without ever trying to open them; and the pleasure of seeing everything which our sight reveals is in no way comparable to the satisfaction accorded by knowledge of the things which philosophy enables us to discover. Lastly, the study of philosophy is more necessary for the regulation of our morals and our conduct in this life than is the use of our eyes to guide our steps" (9B:3–4; 1:180).

13. In article 83 Descartes speaks of a universal friendship we are to have for all other human beings. Speaking of others, he writes, "they are so truly the objects of this passion [love in the form of friendship, as distinct from either mere affection or devotion] that there is no person so imperfect that we could not have for him a very perfect friendship [*une amitié très parfaite*], given that we believe ourselves loved by him and that we have a truly noble and generous soul" (11:390; 1:357).

they flow not from fundamental love and respect but from interest, fear, and suspicion. A Cartesian morality of *amitié*—of mutual love and respect—could use the notion of a contract or ideal agreement as a device to help clarify what is impermissible, permissible, or required among persons who are (we may suppose) already morally motivated. Indeed, I believe that Descartes might have found the idea of a contract or ideal agreement as a canon for moral judgment congenial, although as a moral realist he could not accept the contemporary contractualist idea that we are to define moral truth in terms of such an agreement.

In any case, what we know clearly and distinctly, in Descartes's view, is that persons have value as being free and rational. They are therefore proper objects of our esteem, and we are to treat them accordingly. But what, precisely, treating them accordingly amounts to in specific cases we cannot always know for certain. As a first approximation, however, we may say that to treat them accordingly is, on the one hand, not to harm them and, on the other, to bestow some benefits on them. But what constitutes the true good of another, relative to which we define harm and benefit? And is the injunction to promote the good of others to be understood collectively or distributively? To answer the first question, we can refer back to Descartes's theory of the good. The supreme good of each person, of course, is virtue. What might be called the complete good of each person is virtue completed by gifts of nature and gifts of fortune. Gifts of fortune include economic, social, and political power, opportunity to develop native talents and to acquire useful skills, and the conditions for conserving health and strength of the body. Up to a point, these goods are necessary for human development and for a distinctively human mode of life. Among gifts of nature are those that concern the body: a strong constitution, latent physical skills, and talents; and those that concern the mind: beside *le bon sens* itself, intelligence, good memory, and a creative imagination. Since the use and development of gifts of nature, including *le bon sens*, must depend in large part on education, even our attaining the supreme good must inevitably owe something to good fortune. To be sure, as we have seen in the previous chapter, Descartes argues that our attaining virtue—the supreme good—is entirely within our power. And although this is true, in the sense that, with proper understanding of our nature and our place in it, we can come to see what the supreme good for us is and how we may achieve it through the proper use of our freedom, it is nonetheless a matter of good fortune that we come to have the requisite understanding. Descartes was understandably grateful to his tutors at La Flèche and no doubt for the other ways in which fortune paved the way for his own intellectual and moral development. If this is not a point Descartes himself dwells on, he touches on

it in a different ways—when, for example, he concedes to Princess Elizabeth that bad health can effectively deprive us of the free use of our reason, or when he extols the value of philosophy. Since the value of gifts of
nature is thus dependent in some measure on fortune, we may simplify our
account of human well-being by saying it is partly a matter of our gifts and
partly a matter of our will. Our achieving the supreme good is essentially
dependent on us, but, as I have just pointed out, our attainment of virtue
is not *entirely* independent of what is given to us; indeed, in many obvious
ways, it is dependent on physical and social conditions. So we might put
the matter this way. Although virtue is a matter of self-mastery and is therefore a good that we can acquire only through the proper use of our own
will, the conditions and opportunity for self-mastery are in part a matter of
fortune and, in particular, a matter of what others do for us.

   5. Descartes's older contemporary, Hugo Grotius, it has been said, was
the first to systematize commonsense morality,[14] but more thoroughly systematic still was the natural law theory of Samuel Pufendorf, whose taxonomy Kant used (in slightly modified form) to organize his discussion of
duty in the *Grundlegung zur Metaphysik der Sitten*.[15] I plan to use Pufendorf's taxonomy here. The two main distinctions are between duties to self
and duties to others, on the one hand, and between perfect and imperfect
duties, on the other. A duty is perfect when it is the duty to perform or re-
frain from a specific action; it is true of some perfect duties that they can be
externally enforced and of some also that they are correlated with rights of
others.[16] A duty is imperfect just when it is a duty to have a certain purpose

----

   14. "In 1788 Thomas Reid praised the 'immortal Hugo Grotius' as the author of the first
noteworthy attempt to systematize the commonsense morality of the human race with the
aid of the civil law's technical apparatus" (Schneewind 1990, 1:88).
   15. Kant departed from this simple scheme in his later *Metaphysik der Sitten*. Pufendorf
writes: "Of the duties incumbent upon man in accordance with natural law the most convenient division seems to be according to the objects in regard to which they are to be practiced. From this standpoint they are classified under three main heads: the first of which instructs us how, according to the dictate of sound reason alone, a man should conduct himself
toward God, the second, how toward himself, the third, how toward other men" (Schneewind
1990, 1:164). Concerning duties to self, Pufendorf writes: "But duties of man to himself
spring from religion and sociability conjointly. For the reason why he cannot determine certain acts concerning himself in accordance with his own free will, is partly that he may be a fit
worshiper of the Deity, and partly that he may be a good and useful member of human society" (1:164–65). As to absolute duties to others—duties that do not presuppose human in-
stitution—Pufendorf gives the following three in this order: the duty not to injure another;
the duty to esteem and treat every other as a natural equal; the duty to promote the advantage of another so far as one conveniently can.
   16. Kant later called these duties "juridical" and argued not only that they can but that
they ought to be enforced through state power, fairly and impartially administered.

or end; such duties cannot be externally enforced, and they do not typi-cally translate into a specific requirement to perform a particular action.[17]

We may begin with perfect duties to oneself. As we have seen, for such duties, there will be, in general, a twofold rationale, one grounded in the value of what perfects us and the other in the esteem we owe ourselves as free and rational yet human beings. Since the supreme good is virtue, we may be said to have a duty—a duty to ourselves—to cultivate virtue, but on the face of it this duty would not seem to be a perfect one, since it is a duty to have a certain end without at the same time requiring the perfor-mance of specific actions. On the other hand, it would be inconsistent with our having that end if we acted in ways that made its attainment impossible or even less likely. Accordingly, other things equal, it is morally impermis-sible voluntarily to take our own life or in other ways permanently to cor-rupt our own intellect and will. Let us call suicide the act of voluntarily killing oneself where that is the primary intention, thereby distinguishing suicide from taking one's own life in order to protect the rights or promote the well-being of others, or to escape defilement or the loss of one's rea-son and humanity. In the case of suicide, so understood, it would seem that the values in play would always be decisive against it, since no value to be realized through suicide could trump the value of virtue itself.

Now, we know from the *Discourse* that Descartes took a very dim view of the Stoic doctrine that suicide was, at least for the sage, morally per-missible. And we learn from his correspondence with Princess Elizabeth some years later, when she pressed him on the matter, that in his view, so long as our condition is not such as to deprive us of the use of our own reason, the goods and joy available to us by choosing to live always outweigh the evils and sorrow we would escape by ending our life. Since, however, this argument would appear to fall short of a defense of the perfect duty never to commit suicide, we are left with the question of whether a Carte-sian first-order morality should include a categorical prohibition of suicide.

Before meeting this question head on, let us consider some passages from Descartes's correspondence that bear on this question, even if they do not address it directly. The first comes from his letter to Elizabeth of Septem-ber 1, 1645. After summarizing a remark of Elizabeth's—"You observe very truly that there are diseases which take away the power of reasoning and with it the power of enjoying the satisfaction proper to a rational mind. . . . We cannot altogether answer for ourselves except when we are in our own

---

17. The duty to promote the well-being of others is imperfect, but in special circumstances it may demand that one render aid to this person here and now, for example, when one can without great effort or cost save the life of another.

power. It is better to lose one's life than to lose the use of reason" (4:281–82; 3:262)—he continues:

> There other indispositions which do no harm to one's reason but which merely alter the humours, and make a man unusually inclined to sadness, or anger, or some other passion. These certainly cause distress, but they can be overcome; and the harder they are to conquer, the more satisfaction the soul can take in doing so. The same is true of all exterior handicaps, such as the splendour of high birth, the flatteries of courts, the adversities of fortune, and also great prosperity, which commonly does more than misfortune to hamper the would-be philosopher. When everything goes according to our wishes we forget to think of ourselves; when fortune changes we are the more surprised the more we trusted it. Altogether, we can say, nothing can completely take away our power of making ourselves happy provided that it does not trouble our reason. (4:283; 3:263)

In his later letter of October 6, 1645, speaking of those who claim to be "tired of this life" and who would leave it, he writes that "true philosophy, on the contrary, teaches that even amid the saddest disasters and most bitter pains a man can always be content, provided that he knows how to use his reason" (4:315; 3:272). And in January, 1646, he enlarges upon this idea:

> there are always more good things than evil in this life; and I said this because I think we should make little account of all things outside us that do not depend on our free will in comparison with those that do depend on it. Provided we know how to use our will well, we can make everything which depends on it good and thus prevent the evils that come from elsewhere, however great they may be, from penetrating any further into our souls than the sadness which actors arouse when they enact before us some tragic history. But I agree that to reach such a point a man has to be very philosophical indeed. Nevertheless, I think that even those who most give rein to their passions, really judge deep down, even if they do not themselves perceive it, that there is more good than evil in this life. Sometimes they may call death to help them when they feel great pain, but it is only to help them bear their burden, as in the fable, and for all that they do not want to lose their life. And if there are some who do want to lose it, and who kill themselves, it is due to an intellectual error and not to a well-reasoned judgement, nor to an opinion imprinted on them by nature, like the one which makes a man prefer the goods of this life to its evils. (4:355–56; 3:283)

In summary, so long as they have no acknowledged prospects of losing their reason, those who deliberately commit suicide must be seen as having judged badly, sacrificing a lessor for a greater good entirely in their power. The texts do not readily suggest the Kantian argument that suicide entails treating oneself as a means and must therefore be categorically proscribed, although we might conjecture that Descartes, in view of the distinction between two kinds of ends that we can ascribe to him, would have approved of an argument of this kind. Nevertheless, the prohibition against suicide, in Descartes's expressed view, derives from the imperfect duty of self-perfection, which is to cultivate virtue, that is, to strive to achieve the ideal of *générosité* described in the early articles of part 3 of the *Passions of the Soul*.[18] So long as we have our rational powers, virtue and the full contentment that supervenes on it are within our power, and these are goods that must always outweigh the loss of other external goods, even the loss of our cherished friends.

Cultivating virtue, as we have seen, is the certain route to happiness. It involves adhering strictly to the three rules of morality and duly attending to certain truths of metaphysics. More specifically, it involves disciplining the passions, thereby effecting courage in the pursuit of our chosen ends and temperance in our choice of ends; acknowledging Providence and one's place in and dependence on one's family and one's society; and choosing a mode of life, profession, or craft that is appropriate to our natural talents and predilections and is of use to the larger wholes on which one depends. Particularly useful for the cultivation of virtue is the passion of *générosité*.

> if we occupy ourselves frequently in considering the nature of free will and the many advantages which proceed from a firm resolution to make good use of it—while also considering, on the other hand, the many vain and useless cares which trouble ambitious people—we may arouse the passion of generosity in ourselves and then acquire the virtue. Since this virtue is, as it were, the key to all the other virtues and a general remedy for every disorder of the passions, it seems to me that this consideration deserves serious attention. (11:454; 1:388)

Two other duties are also to be included under the heading of imperfect duties to ourselves: the duty to develop our cognitive powers, since these

---

18. When Pierre Charron, in *On Wisdom*, speaks of the duty to self, he clearly views it as a Kantian imperfect duty; it is, in sum, the duty to take charge of one's life as a whole and to see to it that one is not a simple reactor to present desire and circumstance; it is, in short, to live life seriously. When, later, Samuel Pufendorf speaks of man's duty to himself, he says that it is a mixture of man's duty to God and man's sociability, that is, his duty to others: "The duties of man to himself spring from religion and sociability conjointly. For the reason why he cannot determine certain acts concerning himself in accordance with his own free will, is partly that he may be a fit worshiper of the Deity, and partly that he may be a good and useful member of human society" (Schneewind 1990, 1:164–65). Neither has the conception of a perfect duty to self that Kant has.

are the necessary means for the acquisition of knowledge and the perfection of the self, and the duty to maintain our physical well-being, both as a perfection of our animal nature and as a condition for the effective pursuit of other eligible ends, most especially, virtue itself.

6. The duties to others may be divided between the perfect duties of justice and the imperfect duties of charity or benevolence.[19] One way of interpreting the former—which would place Cartesian ethics squarely in the tradition in which he was educated at La Flèche—would be to follow a tradition beginning with Aristotle and divide duties of justice into those of distributive justice and those of commutative justice. In general, justice has to do with the distribution of goods, that is, of such goods as admit of distribution by human agents and their institutions. Some distributions are just and others unjust. Commutative justice has to do with the exchanges among individuals in their private capacity, as in, paradigmatically, buying and selling. Aristotle and, following him, Aquinas distinguish between voluntary and involuntary transactions; the latter are those in which consent is only unilateral, not mutual. Closely following Aristotle, Thomas Aquinas lists the following types of involuntary transaction as unjust: fraud, violence, theft, robbery, murder, assault, maiming, bearing false witness, calumny (Thomas Aquinas 1988, 169). Commutative justice is also known as rectificatory justice. In these cases, the nonconsenting party suffers a loss while the consenting party profits unjustly. Justice is the condition in which each party's equal loss is "rectified" by each party's equal gain. Many involuntary transactions, however, effectively preclude meaningful rectification, since they leave one party in no condition to receive suitable compensation. Thus, it would be a clear violation of commutative justice to kill a person "involuntarily" in order to save the lives of five others. In the case of voluntary transactions, where there is no force or fraud, the presumption is that the exchange of goods leaves the parties equally well off after the exchange as they were before. Injustice occurs when one party fails to pay her voluntarily incurred debt to the other. The prescriptions and proscriptions of commutative justice are grounded for a Cartesian first-order morality in the moral equality of each person as such, an equality grounded in their rationality and free will. The ideal for all transactions among pri-

---

19. Descartes's occasional references to justice do not suggest that he had anything very specific or controversial in mind. Oddly enough, perhaps the majority of his references to justice are made in connection with God; but even here, starting from the claim that God is perfectly just, Descartes confines himself principally to two substantive inferences, that God would not deceive us and that all is ordered for the best. As to the human virtue of justice, Descartes mostly leaves it to us to work out what we might expect of those who possess this virtue. Nonetheless, we can fill in some of the demands of justice with reasonable confidence, since these are both commonplace and well-grounded in his theory of the value of persons as such.

vate individuals is for all parties to act toward other parties only in a manner that permits their informed and uncoerced consent. The moral proscriptions against deceit and violence are, of course, moral commonplaces. The point to be made here is just that they are well grounded in the Cartesian conception of persons, which entails that the reason and will of each person is owed respect, one person having no more intrinsic value than any other.

But to say that such acts as constitute theft, fraud, violence, etc., are unjust does not imply immediately that all such acts must be morally condemned. If in an emergency I steal critically needed drugs to save my wife's life, I act contrary to justice, but it is not so clear that what I do is wrong in the circumstances and given my intention. Of course, in such a case, it may be possible to restore the balance by compensating the pharmacist for her loss, so that the injustice is adequately rectified. The case of killing one innocent to save five others, however, does not admit of this sort of "rectification." And for this very reason, a Cartesian moralist might well argue that unrectifiable unjust acts cannot be morally justified, no matter how desirable the ends that they alone can attain might be.[20] So too, by the same argument, would it be morally impermissible to kill one innocent person in order to prevent someone else from murdering five innocent persons. On the other hand, it would be permissible to kill someone if this were the only reasonable way to prevent him from murdering others. It would be allowable for something like Kant's justification of coercion: it sometimes is needed to prevent unjustified coercion; the former cancels out or "rectifies" the latter.[21]

7. Let us now turn to distributive justice, which concerns the distribution of goods by some authority to members of some group according to their merit.[22] The group may be a family or some voluntary association. Of

20. Thus do Eleonore Stump and Norman Kretzman interpret Aquinas. The doctor's action of taking the life of Smith, whose organs he uses to save the lives of five others, is morally bad, since it is unrectifiably unjust to Smith (Stump and Kretzman 1991, 120).

21. "Any opposition that counteracts the hindrance of an effect promotes that effect and is consistent with it. Now, everything that is unjust is a hindrance to freedom according to universal laws. Coercion, however, is a hindrance or opposition to freedom. Consequently, if a certain use of freedom is itself a hindrance to freedom according to universal laws (that is, unjust), then the use of coercion to counteract it, inasmuch as it is the prevention of a hindrance to freedom, is consistent with freedom according to universal laws; in other words, this use of coercion is just" (Kant 1965, 35–36).

22. Aristotle distinguishes between commutative and distributive justice in terms of two kinds of proportional equality, arithmetic and geometric. In the case of commutative justice, each party to a transaction is taken as equal, with the moral consequence that a fair share in any exchange among equals is an equal share. In the case of distributive justice, it is assumed that the persons to whom shares are distributed are in a relevant sense unequal (for example, one person may be of greater value to the community and hence deserving of a larger share); their comparative value (to the community, in this example) will stand in a certain ratio, and this ratio will be equal to the ratio of the value of their shares.

particular interest here is distributive justice at the level of the state. And here we may distinguish between ideal distributive justice and de facto distributive justice. By the latter I mean the legally authorized set of practices that in fact determine the distribution of goods in a given civic society. By ideal distributive justice I mean the distribution of goods that would be effected by legally authorized practices in a morally ideal civic society (as determined by some moral conception of society and of persons that make it up). When Descartes remarked, as he occasionally did, that he did not wish to write about morality, what he had especially in mind is that he did not wish to write about ideal distributive justice, that is, about moral politics. He did not wish to challenge the established social and political hierarchies or the practice of distributing the benefits and burdens of such social cooperation as existed in his time—however unjust he may have found them. In the *Discourse* he expresses a view on this issue he often repeated. Acknowledging the difficulties attendant on his private intellectual reform, he notes that they

> could not be compared with those encountered in the reform of even minor matters affecting public institutions. These large bodies are too difficult to raise up once overthrown, or even to hold up once they begin to totter, and their fall cannot but be a hard one. Moreover, any imperfections they may possess—and their very diversity suffices to ensure that many do possess them—have doubtless been much smoothed over by custom; and custom has even prevented or imperceptibly correct many imperfections that prudence could not so well provide against. . . . That is why I cannot by any means approve of those meddlesome and restless characters who, called neither by birth nor by fortune to the management of public affairs, are yet forever thinking up some new reform. And if I thought this book contained the slightest ground for suspecting me of such folly, I would be very reluctant to permit its publication. (6:14; 1:117–18)

Elsewhere he observes that "as regards conduct, everyone is so full of his own wisdom that we might find as many reformers as heads if permission to institute change in these matters were granted to anyone other than those whom God has set up as sovereigns over his people or those on whom he has bestowed sufficient grace and zeal to be prophets" (6:61; 1:142).[23] To

23. Descartes was scarcely alone in holding such conservative views. We find in Montaigne, for example: "Not in theory only, but in truth, the best and most excellent form of government for every nation is that under which it has maintained itself. For its form and essential suitability it is dependent on custom. . . . Nothing presses so hard upon a state as innovation; mere change gives scope to injustice and tyranny. When some part becomes loosened, it may be propped; we may guard against the alteration and corruption natural to all things carrying us too far from our beginnings and principles. But to undertake to put so great a mass back into the melting-pot, to renew the foundations of so great an edifice, is to efface a picture in

have the virtue of justice, in sum, is to be disposed to respect the principle of commutative justice and, so far as this is judged to permit it, to adhere to the positive laws and customs of one's state and community.

8. But suppose one is born to rule or in some other way assumes political power. Are there reasons of state that take precedence over the rules of commutative justice? Can princes lie, dissemble, use preemptive violence? Obliged by his respect for Princess Elizabeth, Descartes reluctantly turns to such questions. He considers first a prince who is unjust and who has come to power through unjust means. He concedes that Machiavelli's rules for such a prince's remaining in power are correct. But this is scarcely an endorsement of such practices, much less a concession that, in the case of such a prince, the rules of justice may have to be suspended. What of the just prince? Here again, Descartes makes no concessions to dirty hands. He considers only the case in which the just prince must deal with his enemies. Speaking of such a prince, he writes: "A distinction must be made between subjects, friends or allies, and enemies. With regard to these last, one has a virtual license to do anything, provided that some advantage to oneself or one's subjects ensues; and I do not think it wrong in such a case to join the fox with the lion and use artifice as well as force" (4:488; 3:293).[24] Here the underlying rationale is that once another threatens violence or may be suspected of deceit, the prince may defend the state by the use of means that would, in normal contexts, be unjust, such as violence and deceit, if such devices seem to be required.[25]

9. This brings us finally to the imperfect duty of beneficence and to the end of our study. About the duty of beneficence little remains to be said. Descartes says of the *généreux*, who manifest beneficence in its ideal form, that "they esteem nothing more highly than doing good to others and dis-

---

the cleaning, to reform particular defects by a general confusion, to cure a disease by killing the patient, *to be not so much for changing as for overturning everything* (Cicero)" (Montaigne 1927, 2:422–23).

24. Even in dealing with enemies, domestic or foreign, Descartes draws the line at abusing friendship. "But I rule out one kind of deception which is so directly hostile to society that I do not think it is ever permissible to use it, although our author [Machiavelli] approves it in several places; and that is pretending to be a friend of those one wishes to destroy, in order to take them by surprise. Friendship is too sacred a thing to be abused in this way; and someone who has once feigned love for someone in order to betray him deserves to be disbelieved and hated by those whom he afterwards genuinely wishes to love" (4:488; 3:293).

25. It is not my purpose here to settle this controversial issue of the degree to which Descartes makes concessions to Machiavelli's views. In the letter just quoted he also writes that "justice between sovereigns does not have the same bounds as justice between individuals. It seems to me that in this instance God gives the right to those to whom he gives power. But of course the most just actions become unjust when those who do them think them so." I interpret this to say that a sovereign who believes he is just, who has not unjustly usurped power, and who faces an enemy threatening the stability and common good of the state may then use the forces at his disposal, or even deceit, to reduce the enemy's threat.

regarding their own self-interest" and that they are accordingly "perfectly courteous, gracious and obliging to everyone" (11:448; 1:385). They encounter only two limitations (aside from duties of justice) on their promotion of others' well-being: first, their benevolence should not threaten their own use of reason, which would be contrary to an imperfect duty to self; second, they should not undertake beneficent projects they do not believe they are adequate to carry out. If, by the standards of ordinary morality, the activities of the perfectly *généreux* would often seem supererogatory, it must be remembered that the perfectly *généreux* are also perfectly content.

Works Cited

Alquié, Ferdinand. 1987. *La découverte métaphysique de l'homme chez Descartes*. Paris: Presses universitaires de France.

———. 1988. *Oeuvres philosophiques de Descartes*. Vol. 1 (1618–1637). Classiques Garnier. Paris: Bordas.

———. 1989. *Oeuvres philosophiques de Descartes*. Vol. 3 (1643–1650). Classiques Garnier. Paris: Bordas.

Annas, Julia. 1993. *The Morality of Happiness*. New York: Oxford University Press.

Annas, Julia, and Jonathan Barnes. 1985. *The Modes of Scepticism*. Cambridge: Cambridge University Press.

Ariew, Roger, and Daniel Garber, ed. and trans. 1989. *G. W. Leibniz: Philosophical Essays*. Indianapolis: Hackett.

Blom, John J. 1978. *Descartes: His Moral Philosophy and Psychology*. New York: New York University Press.

Cicero. 1990. *De officiis*. Trans. Walter Miller. Loeb Classical Library. Cambridge: Harvard University Press.

———. 1991. *On Stoic Good and Evil. De finibus bonorum et malorum*. Book 3. Trans. and commentary M. R. Wright. Warminster: Aris & Phillips.

Cottingham, John, trans. and commentary. 1976. *Descartes' Conversation with Burman*. Oxford: Clarendon Press,

Cumming, Robert. 1955. "Descartes' Provisional Morality." *Review of Metaphysics* 9:207–35.

Curley, Edwin. 1993. "Certainty: Psychological, Moral and Metaphysical." In *Essays on the Philosophy and Science of René Descartes*, ed. Stephen Voss. New York: Oxford University Press.

D'Angers, Julien Eymard. 1954. "Sénèque, Épictète et le Stoïcisme dans l'oeuvre de René Descartes." *Revue de Théologie et de Philosophie* 3:169–96.

———. 1976. *Recherches sur le Stoïcisme aux XVIE et XVIIE siècles*. Ed. L. Antoine. *Studien und Materialien Zur Geschichte der Philosophie*. New York: Georg Olms Verlag.

Descartes, René. 1911. *The Philosophical Works of Descartes*. Vol. 1. Trans. Elizabeth S. Haldane and G. R. T. Ross. Cambridge: Cambridge University Press.

———. 1958. *Descartes Philosophical Writings*. Trans. Norman Kemp Smith. New York: Random House.

———. 1964–76. *Oeuvres de Descartes*. Edited by Ch. Adam and P. Tannery. Rev. ed. Paris: J. Vrin/C.N.R.S.

———. 1985. *The Philosophical Writings of Descartes*. Vols. 1 and 2. Trans. John Cottingham, Robert Stoothoff, and Dugald Murdoch. Cambridge: Cambridge University Press.

———. 1991. *The Philosophical Writings of Descartes*. Vol. 3, *The Correspondence*. Trans. John Cottingham, Robert Stoothoff, and Dugald Murdoch. Cambridge: Cambridge University Press.

Du Vair, Guillaume. 1951. *The Moral Philosophie of the Stoicks*. Ed. Rudolf Kirk. Trans. Thomas James. 1598. Reprint, New Brunswick, N.J.: Rutgers University Press.

Elster, Jon. 1984. *Ulysses and the Sirens*. Cambridge: Cambridge University Press.

Epictetus. 1983. *The Handbook of Epictetus*. Trans. Nicholas P. White. Indianapolis: Hackett.

Espinas, Alfred. 1925. *Descartes et la morale*. Paris: Bossard.

Garber, Daniel. 1987. "Descartes et la méthode en 1637." In *Le discours et sa méthode*. Ed. N. Grimaldi. Paris: Presses Universitaires de France.

Gaukroger, Stephen. 1995. *Descartes: An Intellectual Biography*. Oxford: Clarendon Press.

Gilson, Étienne. 1947. *Discours de la méthode: texte et commentaire*. Paris: J. Vrin.

Gouhier, Henri. 1924. *La pensée religieuse de Descartes*. Paris: J. Vrin.

Gueroult, Martial. 1985. *Descartes' Philosophy Interpreted according to the Order of Reasons*. Trans. Roger Ariew. 2 vols. Minneapolis: University of Minnesota Press. Originally published as *Descartes selon l'ordre des raisons* (Paris: Aubier-Montaigne, 1968).

Hamelin, O. 1921. *Le système de Descartes*. Paris.

James, William. 1949. *Essays in Pragmatism*. Ed. Alburey Castel. New York: Hafner.

Kant, Immanuel. 1965. *The Metaphysical Elements of Justice*. Trans. John Ladd. New York: Bobbs-Merrill.

Kenny, Anthony. 1972. "Descartes on the Will." In *Cartesian Studies*, ed. R. J. Butler. Oxford: Basil Blackwell.

Keohane, Nannerl O. 1980. *Philosophy and the State in France*. Princeton: Princeton University Press.

Le Doeuff, Michèle. 1989. *The Philosophical Imaginary*. Trans. Colin Gordon. London: Athlone.

Leibniz, G. W. 1989. *Philosophical Essays*. Trans. Roger Ariew and Daniel Garber. Indianapolis: Hackett.

Levi, Anthony, S.J. 1964. *French Moralists*. Oxford: Clarendon Press.

Mesnard, Pierre. 1936. *Essai sur la morale de Descartes*. Paris: Boivin.

Montaigne, Michel de. 1927. *The Essays of Montaigne*. 2 vols. Trans. E. J. Trechmann. London: Oxford University Press.

Rodis-Lewis, Geneviève. 1970. *La morale de Descartes*. Paris: Presses Universitaires de France.

———. 1987 "Le dernier fruit de la métaphysique Cartésienne: La générosité." *Les études Philosophiques* 1 (Jan–Mar):43–54.

———. 1988. Introduction and notes to *Descartes: Les passions de l'âme*. Paris: J. Vrin.

———. 1995. *Descartes: Biographie*. Paris: Calmann-Lévy.

Rorty, Amélie Oksenberg. 1986. "Cartesian Passions and the Union of Mind and Body." In *Essays on Descartes's Meditations*, ed. Amélie Oksenberg Rorty. Berkeley: University of California Press.

Russell, Bertrand. 1945. *A History of Western Philosophy*. New York: Simon and Shuster.

Schneewind, Jerome B. 1990. *Moral Philosophy from Montaigne to Kant*. Vol. 1. Cambridge: Cambridge University Press.

Seneca. 1965. "On the Happy Life." In *Moral Essays*, trans. John W. Basore. Loeb Classical Library. Cambridge: Harvard University Press.

Sidgwick, Henry. 1954. *Outlines of the History of Ethics*. New York: St. Martin's.

Sirven, J. 1928. *Les années d'apprentissage de Descartes (1596–1628)*. Albi: Imprimerie Coopérative du Sud-Ouest.

Stump, Eleonore, and Norman Kretzman. 1991. "Being and Goodness." In *Being and Goodness*, ed. Scott MacDonald. Ithaca: Cornell University Press.

Thomas Aquinas, Saint. 1988. *On Law, Morality, and Politics*. Ed. William P. Baumgarth and Richard J. Regan. Indianapolis: Hackett.

Tuck, Richard. 1988. "Optics and Sceptics." In *Conscience and Casuistry in Early Modern Europe*, ed. Edmund Leites. Cambridge: Cambridge University Press.

Voss, Stephen H., ed. and trans. 1989. *The Passions of the Soul*, by René Descartes. Introduction by G. Rodis-Lewis. Indianapolis: Hackett.

Vuillemin, J. 1988. "L'intuitionnisme moral de Descartes et le traité *Des passions de l'âme*." *Kantstudien* 79:17–32.

Index

**SAUK VALLEY COMMUNITY COLLEGE
LIBRARY
DIXON, IL 61021**

GAYLORD MG